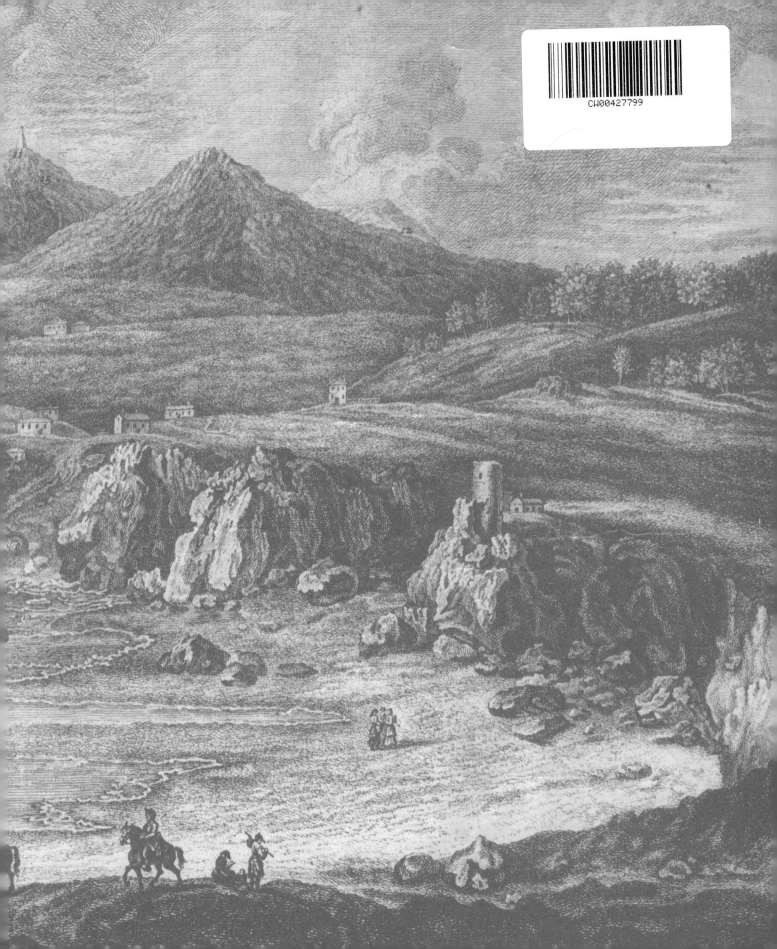

THE
GRANITE
COAST

DEDICATION

In memory of Michael O'Brien and for all those who have fallen under the spell of Dún Laoghaire's granite coast.

AUTHOR'S NOTES

The anglicised name Dunleary is employed when discussing the town's pre-1821 history, while Kingstown refers to the period 1821–1920.

Old Dunleary refers to the location of the original village, and now consists of only a few houses at the Purty Kitchen near Salthill.

Trying to convert historical monetary values into present-day equivalents is a fraught – and subjective – business. I have done so only occasionally in the text, to provide the reader with one possible interpretation. For this, I have used the marvellous tool provided by the National Archives at nationalarchives.gov.uk/currency-converter. This not only tells you that in 1860 £1 is today worth Stg£59.13 (€70 approx.), but that in 1860 it was five days' wages for a skilled tradesman, which is a far more meaningful gauge.

THE GRANITE COAST

DÚN LAOGHAIRE · SANDYCOVE · DALKEY

PETER PEARSON

THE O'BRIEN PRESS

DUBLIN

First published 2022 by
The O'Brien Press Ltd,
12 Terenure Road East, Rathgar,
Dublin 6, D06 HD27, Ireland.
Tel: +353 1 4923333; Fax: +353 1 4922777
E-mail: books@obrien.ie
Website: obrien.ie
The O'Brien Press is a member of Publishing Ireland

ISBN: 978-1-78849-354-3

1 3 5 7 8 6 4 2
22 24 26 25 23

Printed by EDELVIVES, Spain.
The paper in this book is produced using pulp from managed forests.

All photographs are from the author's own collection unless otherwise credited.
Maps by Cathal Cudden of Bright Idea Graphic Design, County Kerry.
Index compiled by Lisa Scholey.
Book and cover design by Emma Byrne.

Jacket photographs
Front: East Pier lighthouse, Dún Laoghaire, courtesy Shutterstock. *Back*: A lobster fisherman in Dalkey
Sound as a steamship arrives (main), courtesy Hamilton collection/DLR archives; (l–r) Sandycove Martello
tower; Dún Laoghaire Baths; George's Street Upper, early 1920s, courtesy DLR postcard collection. *Front
flap*: (top, l–r) Lexicon Library and Mariners' Church; Davy Stephens, Kingstown newspaper vendor, early
1900s, courtesy Lawrence collection/NLI; (bottom) Victorian fanlight, George's Street. *Back flap*: (top)
author photograph courtesy Phil Stewart; (bottom) an 1850 painting view of Dalkey village from Dalkey
Quarry, courtesy Gillman collection.

Published in
DUBLIN
UNESCO
City of Literature

Enjoying life with
O'BRIEN
obrien.ie

Co-funded
by
dlr
Comhairle Contae County Council

ACKNOWLEDGEMENTS

I wish to thank all those who have generously assisted me over the years in all my researches into the history of this district, including those now passed away, such as Daniel Gillman and John de Courcy Ireland, who contributed much to my first book, *Dun Laoghaire: Kingstown*, which was published in 1981 by Michael O'Brien, who sadly died suddenly in August 2022. Michael loved visual books and was passionate about the campaigning and recording nature of my work, going on to publish another three books for me as well as many revised editions. To him and all at The O'Brien Press, I express my gratitude.

As regards this book, I am grateful to all those who helped with queries and photographs, and those who supported the publication in other ways, in particular the staff at the Lexicon Library in Dún Laoghaire, including the heritage officer Deirdre Black, Patricia Corish, David Gunning, Carmel Kelly and Marian Keyes. I would also like to thank Peter Barrow, Edith Byrne, Seamus Cannon, harbour master Simon Coate, Tom Conlon, Mary Conway, Michael Craig, Carol Cullen, Jason Ellis, Brian Fitzelle, Rob Goodbody, Peter Harding, James Howley, Cormac Louth, Justin Merrigan, Francis D. Murnaghan, Charles Pearson, Michael Rowan, Shaffrey Associates, Colin and Anna Scudds, Brian Smith, Robert Vance, Geoffrey Willis, and members of the Dún Laoghaire Historical Society.

My thanks also to the National Gallery of Ireland, the National Library of Ireland, the National Portrait Gallery of Scotland, the Ordnance Survey of Ireland, the Royal Irish Academy and the Royal St George Yacht Club for permission to use photographs.

PHOTOGRAPH CREDITS

Derek Pearson: pp 2, 51 (left), 64 (top, and bottom left), and 107 (left); Dún Laoghaire Harbour Archives: pp 5 (top right, photo by Peter Barrow), 27, 31 (bottom left), 34, 49 (top, photo by Peter Barrow), 51 (right), 60 (right); Lett collection: pp 6, 13 (top right), 40, 44, 60 (left), 63 (left), 96, 101, 104 (top), 105 (both), 106 (left), 108 (top), 130 (right), 212 (bottom), 217, 223; Murnaghan family collection: p. 7 (top); National Gallery of Ireland: p. 11 (bottom); Collection of the late Daniel Gillman: pp 12, 24, 38 (top right), 56, 58 (left), 62, 67, 76, 78, 84 (left), 85 (right), 90 (bottom right), 95 (both), 99, 110, 124, 125 (right), 140, 147 (bottom), 155, 165, 168 (left), 175 (right), 183 (both), 192, 213, 214 (right), 215 (right), 224 (right), 239; Dún Laoghaire–Rathdown Lexicon Library: (*Hamilton collection*) pp 13 (bottom), 39 (left), 131 (left), 133, 135, 144 (right), 147 (top left and top right), (*general collection*) pp 65, 86, 87 (left), 88 (top), 112 (bottom), 119 (right), 128 (top), 149, 150, 159, 170, 215 (left), 218 (left), 220, 221; *Journal of the Royal Society of Antiquaries* (1932): p. 15; National Library of Ireland: (*Longfield collection*) p. 18 (top), (*Brocas collection*) p. 20, (*Lawrence collection*) pp 78, 179, 199 (top), 201, 214 (left), 219; Dennis Horgan: pp 23, 143, 157; Brian Fitzelle: p. 26; Royal St George Yacht Club: pp 30, 31 (top left), 61, 97, 104 (bottom); National Galleries of Scotland: p. 32; the late Matt Byrne: p. 39 (right); Justin Merrigan: p. 63 (right); Colin Scudds: pp 72, 84 (right); 102, 182; Brian Smith: pp 74, 212 (top); The O'Brien Press (photographer Peter Harding): pp 122, 218 (right); Robert Vance: pp 141, 145 (right); Royal Irish Academy: p. 142 (top right); Phil Stewart: pp 154, 233; Manning Robertson: p. 195 (left); Archive of An Post: p. 200; Sean Kennedy: pp 208, 231 (right), 237, 238; Geoffrey Willis: p. 225 (left).

TABLE *of* CONTENTS

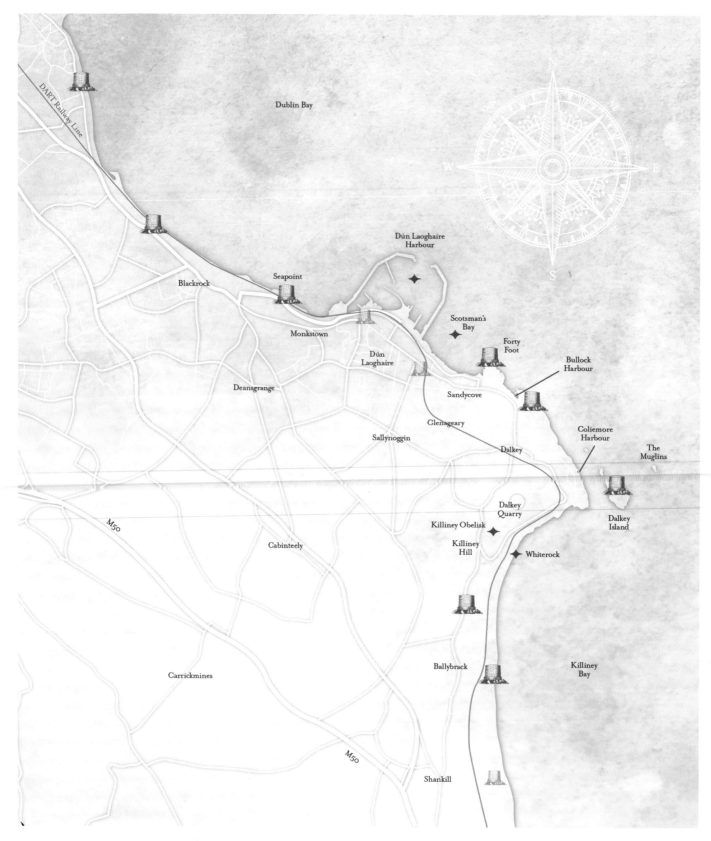

Dublin Bay

Dún Laoghaire
Harbour

DART Railway Line

Blackrock

Seapoint

Monkstown

Dún
Laoghaire

Scotsman's
Bay

Forty
Foot

Bullock
Harbour

Deansgrange

Sandycove

Glenageary

Coliemore
Harbour

The
Muglins

Sallynoggin

Dalkey

Dalkey
Island

M50

Cabinteely

Dalkey
Quarry

Killiney Obelisk

Killiney
Hill

Whiterock

Killiney
Bay

Carrickmines

Ballybrack

M50

Shankill

DÚN LAOGHAIRE DISTRICT

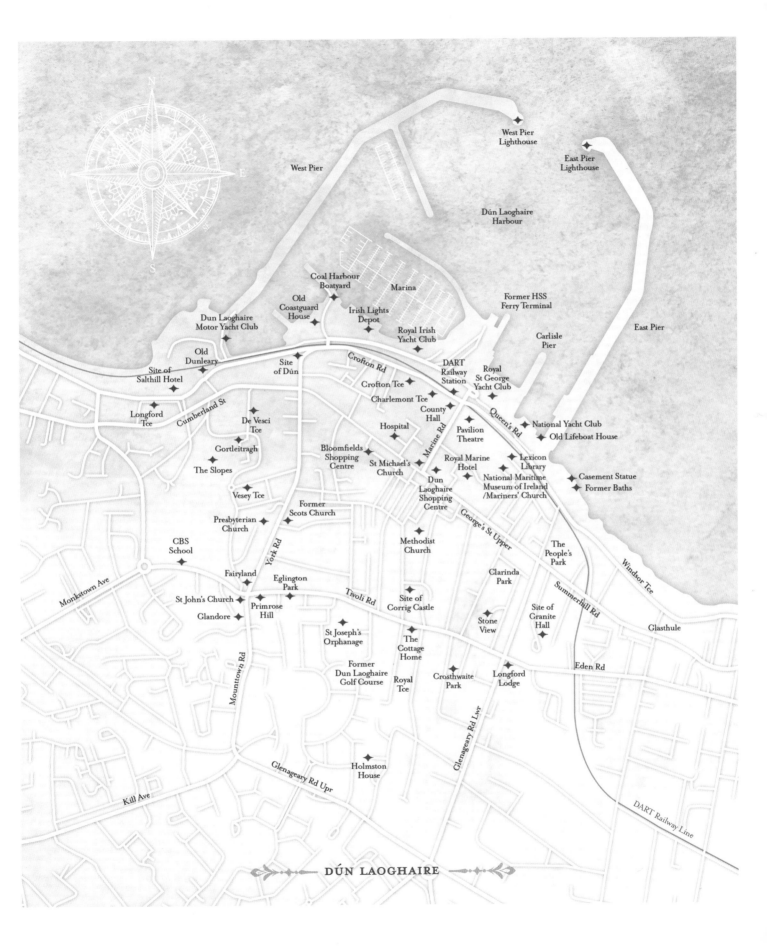

DÚN LAOGHAIRE

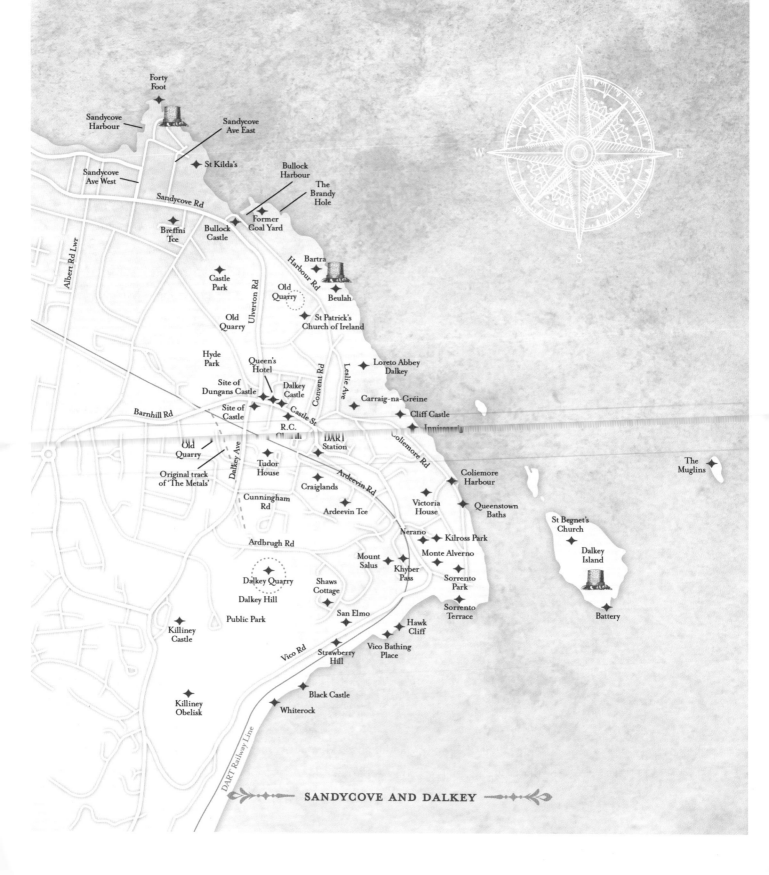

Forty
Foot

Sandycove
Harbour

Sandycove
Ave East

Sandycove
Ave West

✦ St Kilda's

Bullock
Harbour

The
Brandy
Hole

Sandycove Rd

✦ Breffni
Tce

Bullock
Castle

Former
Coal Yard

Harbour Rd

✦ Bartra

Castle
Park

Old
Quarry

✦ Beulah

Old
Quarry

Ulverton Rd

✦ St Patrick's
Church of Ireland

Hyde
Park

Queen's
Hotel

Convent Rd

Leslie Ave

✦ Loreto Abbey
Dalkey

Site of
Dungans Castle

✦ Dalkey
Castle

✦ Carraig-na-Gréine

Barnhill Rd

Site of
Castle

Castle St

✦ Cliff Castle

R.C.

✦ Inniscrone

Coliemore Rd

Old
Quarry

Dalkey Ave

DART
Station

Original track
of 'The Metals'

✦ Tudor
House

Ardeevin Rd

✦ Craiglands

✦ Coliemore
Harbour

The
Muglins

Cunningham
Rd

✦ Ardeevin Tce

✦ Victoria
House

✦ Queenstown
Baths

Ardbrugh Rd

Nerano

✦ Kilross Park

St Begnet's
Church

Dalkey Quarry

Mount
Salus

✦ Monte Alverno

Dalkey
Island

Dalkey Hill

Shaws
Cottage

Khyber
Pass

✦ Sorrento
Park

Public Park

✦ San Elmo

✦ Sorrento
Terrace

Battery

✦ Killiney
Castle

Vico Rd

✦ Hawk
Cliff

Strawberry
Hill

Vico Bathing
Place

✦ Killiney
Obelisk

✦ Black Castle

✦ Whiterock

DART Railway Line

SANDYCOVE AND DALKEY

INTRODUCTION

Dún Laoghaire's claim to attention lies not only in the remarkable history of its harbour but also in the rapidity of the town's growth, a direct result of the development of steamships and the coming of the railway. It is one of the few towns in Ireland to have started from nothing and reached maturity all within seventy-five years of the nineteenth century. For this reason it is particularly Victorian in character and atmosphere. There are only a handful of buildings that can claim to be of earlier date. In parallel, the development of the coastline from Blackrock to Dalkey also took place mostly in the nineteenth century.

As a child born and bred in Dún Laoghaire, I was much drawn to the environs of the harbour. The turquoise waters lapping on the granite steps, the colourful old trawlers in the Coal Harbour, their greens and reds reflected in the dark waters by the stone pier, and the boatyard with its old wrecks and smell of fresh paint in springtime held enchantment for me. Pale blue dredgers with exotic names appeared in the harbour from time to time to deepen the mailboat channel. At the back of the West Pier lay a dump containing old timber and ironwork, pieces of marble, smooth granite setts, ancient bottles, all buried in rubble and discarded builders' waste: abandoned treasures for a young boy.

When I was ten I witnessed the fire that destroyed St Michael's Church, a Victorian Gothic landmark in the centre of Dún Laoghaire, and the following year the deliberate destruction of Nelson's Pillar in Dublin. I found it shocking that these landmarks of the past, such seemingly permanent monuments of stone, could so easily be lost and swept away, that inheritance and memory could count for so little. I began to notice the dozens of old houses and shops, details of street furniture like railings or milestones, not just in Dún Laoghaire, but in Dublin and beyond, that were regarded just as rubbish and discarded.

In the 1970s the spoil from the demolition of Gresham Terrace, bulldozed to make way for the new shopping centre, was dumped in the harbour as infill, an act that seemed to

Dredgers moored in the Coal Harbour had evocative names such as Saxifrage, Sisyphus *and* Fag-an-Balach.

go against the grain in so many ways: the destruction of the whole centre of the Victorian town and the filling-in of the beautiful harbour. In the rubble I found a decorative iron railing spike, a fleur-de-lis, made for the houses of Gresham Terrace back in the 1830s. A keen sense of loss and waste prompted me to become involved during the 1980s in the process of describing and listing for protection the more interesting buildings in the town and county. In 1981 my first book, *Dun Laoghaire: Kingstown*, was published, a record of the fragile treasures of Dún Laoghaire's past.

More than forty years have passed since then and in that time many changes have taken place in Dún Laoghaire and its environs. There have been significant physical changes, such as the completion of the DART railway system, the construction of the yachting marina in the harbour and many new buildings, both private and public. New public buildings include the Irish Lights headquarters, the now-redundant ferry terminal, the Dún Laoghaire–Rathdown office extension to the town hall, the Pavilion Theatre and the Lexicon Library. Many new and quite large apartment blocks have appeared. There have also been major social changes too, such as the disappearance of schools and hospitals and the closure in 2015 of the 200-year-old ferry link between Dún Laoghaire and Holyhead. Other dramatic changes in terms of planning and development have occurred, such as the sale and development of the once very extensive Dun Laoghaire Golf Club lands at the back of the town. Property prices in Dún Laoghaire have remained consistently strong and are even stronger in Sandycove and Dalkey, and this has meant that younger buyers are often priced out of the area.

The HSS Dún Laoghaire–Holyhead ferry, once a familiar sight, was the last serving vessel on this route.

Changes in public attitudes and revised planning legislation have brought about a new awareness of the architectural heritage and cultural identity, which was the prime focus of my 1981 book. At that time, much was threatened with demolition. Buildings and shopfronts that featured in the book, accompanied by adverse commentary, have long since been improved or rebuilt.

Much of Dún Laoghaire's Victorian architecture is now a great deal more secure and better looked after than it was in the 1980s. Dún Laoghaire and its wider area now has a large number of listed buildings, which means, at least in theory, that they cannot be altered or demolished without planning permission. In fact, the local authority has probably one of the highest number of listed buildings in the country. Over the years An Taisce – the National Trust for Ireland – has played a significant role in highlighting conservation problems but now most county councils have their own staff to deal with such issues. In the 1990s we began to see new buildings constructed in a manner that respected the architectural tradition of the area. The new lifeboat office, for instance, is a small but sensitive addition to the harbour. The redevelopment of the shelter at the People's Park as a restaurant thoughtfully blends past and present. Various residential developments, such as the apartments at Salthill, also reflect a search for a sympathetic modern style. On the other hand, there have been some new houses and extensions that are positively brutalist in style and clash stridently with the prevailing Victorian character of the district. The dogma of forcing new structures of concrete, glass and steel into older environments on the grounds of architectural honesty is not always convincing. There have also been a number of bland large-scale developments, such as the apartments and offices at the Adelphi, the Bloomfields Shopping Centre, and the garda station and courthouse on Corrig Avenue.

County Dublin's stock of old houses, mostly nineteenth century in the case of Dún Laoghaire and the surrounding residential areas, are better cared for than ever before, many having been lovingly restored with all their historical details such as fanlights, windows and decorative ironwork intact. This is a far cry from the situation in the latter half of the twentieth century when whole terraces of houses were demolished. The county council now offers small grants to incentivise such repairs.

While it cannot be claimed that Dún Laoghaire's buildings all comprise first-rate historic architecture, the town as a whole in its harbour setting, in its relationship to the capital and in the variety of its Victorian townscape, deserves to be kept intact and safeguarded from unsympathetic new developments, whether roads, car parks or buildings. It was right, for example, that there should have been a great deal of public debate over marina proposals and other developments for the harbour, such as the berth for cruise ships or the floating swimming pool, because the harbour is a unique monument as well as a resource. The safeguarding of the built heritage of Dún Laoghaire and its harbour, of Bullock, Sandycove and Dalkey, can be best achieved by first understanding the area's history and then appreciating its unique character, a character that could so easily be replaced with anonymous new structures. In the case of the harbour, the Dún Laoghaire Harbour Company, which took over control from the Office of Public Works (OPW) in 1997, carried out many exemplary projects to preserve and enhance it. This body was eventually disbanded and its considerable responsibilities were handed over to the county council in 2018.

Dún Laoghaire's streetscapes remained unchanged until the 1970s, after which many fine Victorian houses were swept away, such as this one on Crosthwaite Park South.

One of my objectives in this book is to trace Dún Laoghaire's growth from a small fishing village to a grand Victorian 'watering place' and to examine the characteristics of the adjoining coastline and older buildings as far as Dalkey, including parts of Monkstown and Glasthule, with particular attention to Bullock and Sandycove.

The comparative affluence of Kingstown is reflected in the buildings and construction of the town – the magnificent stone harbour, the elegant railway station, the impressive yacht clubs, the shops and houses, and later an excellent tram system. Due to its proximity to the capital and pleasant location in Dublin Bay, the town has always been predominantly residential. There was never any serious industry to speak of.

In Kingstown, there existed a lifestyle that was not generally typical of Irish towns. The Dublin professional classes, merchants, bankers, retired army and navy officers, and other well-to-do people flocked to live in its handsome terraces and squares. The arrival of the railway made possible a way of life whereby one worked in Dublin but resided in the

Above left: The East Pier bandstand, restored by the Harbour Company and pictured here after the resurfacing of the pier in 2005.

Above right: An aerial view of Dún Laoghaire Harbour, viewed from above Old Dunleary, c. 2006, showing the extent of the new marina. This intervention with the new breakwaters represents the greatest change to the harbour since the nineteenth century.

more salubrious climate of coastal Kingstown. The slums and back alleys of Kingstown housed an army of domestics and labourers who tended the houses of the better-off, built the harbour, manned the ships and hauled the coal. Living conditions for those families were extremely poor and often unsanitary, until the new artisans' dwellings or council houses were built at the turn of the twentieth century.

Since *Dun Laoghaire: Kingstown* was published in 1981 many previously unknown photos and records have come to light and a substantial number of excellent publications have appeared which deal with different aspects of the town, the harbour, the county and its varied heritage. These are listed in the bibliography.

The Dún Laoghaire of today, including its adjoining coastline, is a special place, displaying a rich and diverse architectural heritage, situated in an attractive natural maritime environment of rocky foreshore and hill. It is a place much sought after, where houses are very expensive, but it is also much frequented by the general public who enjoy the sea air and residential calm, walk the piers and hills, swim in the various bathing places and dine in the numerous restaurants and hostelries.

While Kingstown became the key port of arrival and departure by the mid-nineteenth century and was associated with the carrying of mail across the Irish Sea, it was for many their last glimpse of home as they emigrated to England and beyond. Carlisle Pier today is largely unused and cleared of its old structures.

Chapter 1

DUBLIN BAY'S GRANITE COAST

The visitor to modern Dún Laoghaire might be surprised to learn that some 250 years ago there was only a small village here and the landscape was one of wild scrub and protruding granite bedrock. Granite is one of the hardest rocks to be found in Ireland and was formed by volcanic activity aeons ago when molten rock solidified beneath the earth's crust. Millions of years later, in a geological event known as the Caledonian Upheaval, the granite was folded and forced upwards through other shaley rocks to form the land mass of granite that is now the Wicklow mountains, extending from Dalkey down into south Leinster. This granite was then subjected to a process of persistent erosion and smoothing during the last ice age, leaving us with hills and rocks of rounded profile. The rounded, fissured granite bedrock that is seen in the Dalkey and Killiney hills was once named 'roches moutonées' by geologists, owing to its fleece-like furrowed humps or resemblance to eighteenth-century wigs, which were smoothed down with mutton fat.

The granite in the Dún Laoghaire and Dalkey area has a lovely quality – a coarse, hard grain and a bright colour, sometimes tinged with ochre or pink, flecked with sparkling mica – and it is no wonder that it has proved such an attractive building material. It is harder than Wicklow granite and can supply very large blocks. All of the railway stations and coastguard stations in the environs of Dún Laoghaire were built of it. It was used in the construction of most of the houses of the district, and for the facings of Kylemore Abbey in Connemara. It was also used in the building of Butt Bridge and Essex Bridge on the Liffey and for the Thames Embankment in London in the 1870s.

Apart from the natural occurrence of granite along the coast and in the bedrock of

the area, it is a joy to see it in the many stone walls of gardens and other boundaries. These random rubble granite walls, which were carefully coursed (i.e. laid according to the shape and grain of the stone), can be seen everywhere from Blackrock through to Shankill and, as well as being a tribute to the skill of the nineteenth-century builders, also represent a finite aspect of the built heritage in that it is not possible to easily replicate the character of time-worn stones. Granite was universally employed for footpaths, window sills, steps, copings, kerbstones and trackways and was frequently cut and shaped for handsome entrance piers and gateways. There is so much cut granite in evidence that many people take it for granted. The fact that the harbours of Dún Laoghaire, Sandycove, Bullock and Coliemore were all constructed with this beautiful stone has helped to confirm their status as monuments in their own right.

Up until the early nineteenth century, the coast from Blackrock to Dalkey remained as nature left it – rocky granite outcrops along the coast and in the sea with land rising at times to low cliffs and many submerged rocks and reefs just offshore. Various eighteenth-century maps (e.g. Rocque's 1760 map, see p. 16), charts, prints and paintings confirm this picture of the coastal landscape and show that there was nowhere for ships to shelter in the event of adverse winds or tides.

Many sketches and prints of Dublin Bay depict a rocky and generally steeper foreshore than exists today. While this might be put down to artistic licence, there was certainly a

Above left: The circular granite paving around the West Pier lighthouse is a work of art.

Above right: Harbour master Simon Coate stands behind one of the substantial granite bollards of the East Pier.

This painting by James Arthur O'Connor, dated 1820, of bathers at Salthill shows steep cliffs (which were subsequently levelled off when the railway was constructed in the 1830s). In the background three ships lie at Dunleary Pier, below the Martello tower.

An eighteenth-century print, 'A View of the Black Rocks', by William Jones. This view, drawn in about 1740, shows the unquarried hill of Dalkey, Killiney Hill without its obelisk (built 1747) and Roche's Hill.

View *of the* BLACK ROCKS, New Town Bourn, Bray Head, &c. *in* IRELAND.

good deal of actual levelling of the coast by quarrying, the construction of the railway and subsequent natural silting-up of the bay. A highly exaggerated print of the shore, dating from about 1740 by William Jones, hints at a wilder and steeper coastline. Various views of the coffee house at Dunleary, such as a sepia print by Francis Wheatley of 1785, show it to have been perched on high ground overlooking the sea. Images of Seapoint's Martello tower before the construction of the railway in the 1830s show a much steeper and more threatening shoreline. Seapoint, with its prominent tower and rocky foreshore, was to witness Dublin Bay's most tragic shipwrecks with an estimated 380 people drowned there in a freak storm in November 1807. Place names such as Corrig or Carrig reflect the local topography, and also Blackrock, where an outcrop of black rocks may still be seen just seaward of the old baths.

Interesting names for some of the more dangerous rocks remain while others are long forgotten. The Sunk Rock or *Leac Buide*, lying between Maiden Rock at Dalkey Island and the Muglins, has only recently been buoyed and was previously treacherous to the unwary sailor. The Muglins, whose evocative name has never been explained, is a large rocky outcrop lying to the northeast of Dalkey Island and is a dramatic feature at the southern entrance to Dublin Bay. It is crowned by an iconic 9-metre red-and-white cone and has a light, powered by the sun since 1997, which is visible up to 18 kilometres off. The Codling Rock has been largely covered by the East Pier while Court Lough Rock and Full Tide Rock in Scotsman's Bay and Ducking Point (the site of the traders' wharf) are only recalled on early charts. The Ducking Point was most likely a suitable swimming place close to the Martello tower where one could dive or duck into the sea. An interesting feature on Rennie's chart of 1817 is the Glummach (meaning Lobster) Rock, which was covered by the Victoria Wharf in the 1830s, later called St Michael's Wharf and now lost beneath the former car ferry terminal. Indeed, the pre-1815 coastline from here to Sandycove was very rocky and it is evident from the low blasted rock remains that much stone was quarried from the foreshore. It would appear that similar quarrying was carried on between Sandycove Point and Bullock Harbour, where there is much evidence of boreholes and blasting.

Scotsman's Bay appears as early as Rocque's map of 1760, as does the Chickens, sometimes referred to as Hen and Chickens, which was an outcrop of rocks in the sea just off Dunleary village. (These are shown on early harbour plans of 1817 – see p. 19 – but were eventually covered by the construction of the West Pier.) Further west lies Seal Rock, a popular destination for swimmers and not far from Seapoint tower. The Churl Rocks stood on what used to be Moran Park and became the site of a granite quarry shortly after 1815, eventually leaving a deep pond or reservoir which disappeared only a

few years ago when the Lexicon Library and car park were built there. The jagged quarried edge of the workings was visible in the deep pond and at the eastern edge the old park. One remaining outcrop of the Three Churls, as they were also known, forms the base of the George IV obelisk. In the Forty Foot there are a number of very prominent rocks, one of which is the Peak Rock, once the location of the diving board.

A well-known aquatint of the Dunleary Coffee House by Francis Wheatley shows precipitous rocks above a sandy beach not far from the place now occupied by the Clearwater Cove apartments, just below Cumberland Street. Another small print by John Martyn (*c.*1800) shows a similar view with prominent rocks and cliffs of boulder clay in the foreground.

Top left: Dramatic outcrops of fissured granite at the back of Bullock Harbour, at the Brandy Hole, give us an idea of what some of the coast was like before quarrying began.

Left: This 1785 engraving by Thomas Malton (1726–1801) of an aquatint by Francis Wheatley (1747–1801), entitled Dublin Bay, Coffee House, Dun Laoghaire, *shows the beach and rocks at Old Dunleary with the coffee house perched on high ground above the sea. The drinking of coffee was made fashionable in the Georgian period, but travellers could also stay here to await the arrival of their ship.*

(Photo © National Gallery of Ireland.)

The port of Dublin had a long-standing reputation in centuries past for its dangerous approaches, with the shallow sands of the North and South Bulls on either side of the entrance to the Liffey, the sand bank or bar at the mouth of the river, not to mention the rocky shoreline on the south and north sides of the bay. Many a sailing ship trying to reach Dublin foundered on this stretch of coast in northeasterly gales and such tragedies led to the call for a protective pier or asylum harbour in Dublin Bay. With the exception of a cove and short pier at Dunleary, which effectively dried out at low water, and the fishing inlet at Bullock, there was nowhere to shelter or come safely ashore. Ships awaiting favourable winds and tides had to anchor in the bay and hope for the best.

The completion of the South Bull Wall in the middle of the eighteenth century, and later the North Bull Wall, improved matters slightly by deepening the channel of the River Liffey.

The hard and enduring quality of south Dublin granite was exploited by the Ballast Board, who opened several small quarries at Sandycove and Bullock in the eighteenth

This eighteenth-century map of Dublin Bay shows the dangers posed by 'Dublin Barr' and the massive sandy shallows known as the North and South Bulls. The approaches to Dublin with its prevailing west winds could be treacherous for sailing ships as they could easily run aground.

Throughout the nineteenth century and well into the early twentieth century almost all trading ships were sail powered, which meant they were at the mercy of the elements. Many had poor equipment such as anchors, chains and rigging, and shipwrecks were commonplace.

Top left: *A terrible easterly storm of 1861 wrecked numerous ships along the east coast. Here an artist from the* Illustrated London News *depicts the final minutes of the coal ship* Neptune, *as it was smashed up on the back of the East Pier.*

Top right: *The wreck of the* Hampton, *a coal boat frequently seen in Kingstown in the 1890s (see p. 223), was much photographed as it lay stranded on the railway embankment at Salthill.*

Above: *An unidentified wreck, probably also a coal boat, on Killiney beach, late nineteenth century.*

century and which, to this day, manages Bullock Harbour. Long finger-shaped slabs of stone were shipped across the bay to complete the building of the South Bull Wall and the sturdy Poolbeg lighthouse. More stone was quarried there for the building of Howth Harbour in the early 1800s – a costly project which proved to be of very little use at the time. A small quarry, which is marked on an early nineteenth-century plan of the Martello tower defences, stood below the cliffs at Sandycove. The evidence of a very substantial quarry at Bullock remains today in the form of an unusual and beautiful garden which has been created around an old quarry pond, situated just to the north of St Patrick's Church. Another substantial quarry stood between the church and Ulverton Road and there were three smaller ones around the area of Castlepark and Bullock. All of these granite quarries appear on the very detailed large-scale Ordnance Survey map of 1867, but most of them were filled in when quarrying ceased.

Close inspection of the rocky shore beneath the cliffs at the Forty Foot reveals marks of drilling and chiselling where borers and masons worked the stone which was to be shipped in barges across the bay.

FROM DÚN TO DUNLEARY

Dún Laoghaire is a place of ancient origin, as the Irish name suggests. It means 'Laoghaire's fort', and it is generally assumed that a dún or fort once stood here. This fort belonged to Laoghaire, almost certainly King Laoghaire of the fifth century, whose principal abode was at Tara, about 60 kilometres north of Dublin. A circular fort is hinted at on John Rocque's map of 1760 but a circular structure like that of an early earth-banked fort is clearly marked on an estate map of 1790.

The fort was located where the railway bridge now gives access to the Inner and Outer Coal Harbours, almost exactly on the line of the present DART railway track. A Martello tower, erected on this site shortly after 1800, was reputedly built within the ring of the old fort. However, in 1836 the railway from Dublin was extended from Salthill to its present terminus in Dún Laoghaire. Its route bisected the old Dunleary harbour (known later as the Inner Coal Harbour) and necessitated the demolition of the Martello tower and dún beneath. The rubble from the dún and tower was apparently dumped on the back of the West Pier and used to fill in the old harbour – the site of the former coal yards, gasworks and Albright & Wilson chemical factory, and now occupied by apartments at Clearwater.

It is also possible that much of the rubble was required to create the three ramped roadways on the harbour side of the railway. The reconfiguration of road and rail levels have so changed the topography here that it is very hard to imagine the archaeological site of the dún or Martello tower.

It is curious that the subject of the dún has been largely ignored by archaeologists except for a detailed 1932 article by Father Myles Ronan in the *Journal of the Royal Society of Antiquaries of Ireland*, but it is perfectly reasonable to ask why the name Dún Laoghaire would be adopted for the place unless there was good reason to believe that such a fort once existed. And if it existed, is it not possible that some stones or other relics have survived?

In the early 1930s two inscribed stones were discovered by workmen laying an edge to a flowerbed. The history of these stones, their discovery, their peculiarly small size and the presence of both Bronze Age decoration and ogham inscription made in identical cutting led to a suspicion of forgery or recent manufacture! Experts differ as to whether the stones might be genuine or not but new methods of testing might give us the answer.

It is perhaps odd that both stones should have been found at the one time in the 1930s, while during the clearance of the fort in 1836 nothing is known to have been found. On the other hand, a thirty-year-old Martello tower and some ancient earthworks might not have aroused much interest at that time. In 1930 the Borough of Dún Laoghaire was officially established: the name Kingstown, which was bitter to many, had been banished since 1920. It is therefore possible, but I think unlikely, that in about 1930 a 'Dún Laoghaire' enthusiast organised the making and finding of the stones. I would prefer to believe that the stones are authentic, but further evidence will have to be provided before this is certain.

Drawings of two inscribed stones found in 1932 and attributed to the site of the dún by the antiquarian Father Myles Ronan.

The stones were loaned by the National Museum of Ireland for a local history exhibition in the National Maritime Museum in 1978 and they were subsequently transferred to the town hall for safekeeping, but have not been seen since the 1990s, and so the mystery continues.

A stone seat standing in the De Vesci Gardens may constitute another relic of the dún. The seat, which is just wide enough for two, was unearthed in the 1930s when the gardens were cut back for the widening of Cumberland Street, again not very far from the site of the dún.

Besides these few traces of an ancient dún, we know little of Dún Laoghaire's early history. Eighteenth-century maps of Dublin Bay, such as that of Thomas Burgh (1728) depict Dunleary or 'Dunlary' as a small village of fishermen's houses, grouped around an inlet at the mouth of a tiny stream flowing from Monkstown Castle (built in the thirteenth century, along with another at Bullock, by the Cistercian monks to protect their farm and fishery). The coastal lands where the town would eventually be developed was largely scrub and rock with grazing for sheep while the better parts inland were farmed, as Rocque's 1760 map (below) shows. The name Glenageary – *Gleann na Caorach* (glen of the sheep) – reflects the wild state of the landscape.

Since the days of King Laoghaire's fort, the village had remained insignificant. It served occasionally as a point of arrival or departure to England, but throughout the Middle Ages down to the sixteenth century, Dalkey, rather than Dunleary, was considered to be the principal port south of Dublin.

John Rocque's map of the coast of Dublin Bay, c. 1760, showing Old Dunleary village and harbour, with a quarry marked on the rocky seaward shore. Blackrock village and Monkstown Castle are also prominent features.

By the eighteenth century, however, Dunleary had begun to acquire importance. As we have seen, the inner half of Dublin Bay had become so badly silted up that the approach to the port was extremely hazardous. The bar at the mouth of the Liffey was a serious obstacle. Many ships had to await favourable tides and winds in the safe anchoring 'roads' off Dunleary. Passengers from these vessels put in to Dunleary by pinnace (a small boat acting as ferry) and then proceeded by road to Dublin. This passenger traffic through Dunleary led to the establishment of a coffee house, sited on an eminence overlooking Dunleary Creek and Dublin Bay. (It was, like the dún and Martello tower, demolished in 1836 to make way for the railway; its location was probably on the site of the present West Pier filling station.) As a contemporary print shows (see p. 11), it was a large two-storey gabled premises and must have done a brisk business with travellers, tourists, and day trippers from Dublin. Coffee was a newly popular drink in the eighteenth century and much business was transacted in the many coffee houses of Dublin city.

Sea bathing was favoured at Dunleary as early as 1710 and, as can be seen in an early nineteenth-century painting of Salthill by J.A. O'Connor, people bathed in the nude; swimming attire became de rigueur in Victorian times. When the railway was extended across Salthill and old Dunleary in 1834 there was an outcry over the cutting-off of public access to the sea for bathing. With a lack of any piped water supply to houses, sea bathing was for many an important means of keeping clean and healthy. Charles Haliday of Monkstown Park, a noted philanthropist, successfully campaigned in 1847 to have bridges, baths and steps provided by the railway company for public use. There were separate men's and women's bathing pools at the back of the West Pier, but these disappeared under the town's sewage works, which were built in 1877. The women's pool was oval in shape and filled up with fresh seawater at every high tide. There were three small shelters built against the rear wall.

Strengthened Anglo-Irish links in the eighteenth century brought about the need for more efficient communication between Dublin and London. It was partly in light of this that the Irish House of Commons in 1755 granted a substantial sum of money for the erection of a new pier at Dunleary. It became known as the 'Dry Pier', for it rapidly silted up. It is shown, along with an older curved pier, on the Longford and de Vesci estate map of 1790 (see p. 18) with a rounded pier head, a detail which is matched in a coloured engraving of 1799 by Jukes Howland. This later engraving also depicts a parapet wall that was demolished, together with the rounded pier head, in the 1890s, leaving Dún Laoghaire's earliest surviving pier in its present form. Today it is the Inner Coal Harbour pier and affords enough depth for only the odd motorboat and cruiser.

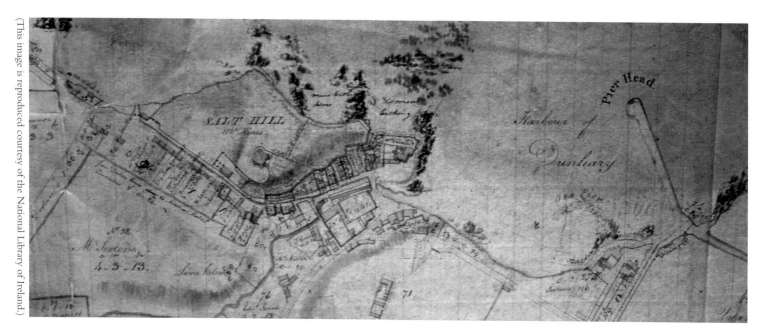

Above: The Longford and de Vesci estate map of the 1790s shows a compact village of over seventy dwellings and cottages, and a mill and millrace — all swept away, by various developments including the building of the Top Hat Ballroom and the new apartments which are there now. Old Dunleary village extended back towards Salthill where there was, until 1840, a narrow street of old houses called Tully's Row. This row stood on what is now the main road between Salthill and Longford Terrace.

Of the original village of Dunleary, now only fifteen houses remain, including the present Purty Kitchen ('Purty' means 'pretty'), and these would seem to have been largely rebuilt, or at least refronted, in the nineteenth century or later.

Right: These street signs are among the last references to the old village of Dunleary.

MARTELLO TOWERS AND THE NAPOLEONIC THREAT

The history of Martello towers is well known and much has been written about them. The uprisings of 1798 and 1803 were fresh in people's memory and the Act of Union in 1800 cemented the idea in the minds of the British administration of keeping a firm hand on Ireland. The story of how the British Navy adopted the design from Corsica in the 1790s, that they were built in Ireland in the early 1800s and never saw military action is well rehearsed. The defensive towers and adjoining forts, or batteries as they were called, were constructed around the Irish coastline. Of the twenty-six or so that were built in County Dublin, twenty still stand. A few of the towers continue to be lived in or have adjacent modern extensions but most remain standing as well-loved landmarks. The most famous – Joyce's Tower in Sandycove (officially known as tower no. 11) – serves as

a small museum to James Joyce. The towers are difficult to adapt to other uses because of their circular shape, lack of windows, narrow winding stone stairs and solid stone construction. In effect, they have only two floors and most of the original entrances were high off the ground.

The comprehensive study *The Martello Towers of Dublin*, published by Fingal and Dún Laoghaire–Rathdown county councils, tells us that the south Dublin towers were built very speedily and were completed almost within the space of the year 1804–05. The authors also remind us that most of the coastline at that time was largely uninhabited and certainly not yet developed with fine villas and gardens. As already noted, there were small clusters of fishermen's cottages at Bray, Bullock, Sandycove and Dunleary, and some fine houses in Blackrock like Frescati or Temple Hill, but otherwise the coastal landscape was undeveloped – given over to grazing sheep or goats. An engraving by Petrie of Sandycove, made in 1820, is evocative and shows only the Martello towers and Bullock Castle.

Above: The Martello tower at Sandycove stands on a high rocky outcrop above the sea. Narrow internal stone stairs give access to the roof where a large gun was once mounted. The tower is today regarded as a shrine to the memory and writings of James Joyce.

Right: The 1817 design for an Asylum Harbour at Dunleary by John Rennie. The plan also shows how George's Street was formed on the line of the old Military Road linking the now-vanished Martello towers of Dún Laoghaire.

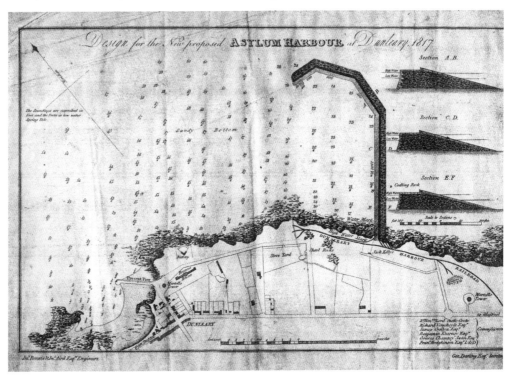

The Martello towers of this region are distinguished by the beautiful sparkling granite of which they are built and they are generally in such good condition that it is hard to believe they are over 200 years old. Most of the towers are sited dramatically on rocky outcrops overlooking the sea. Those at Seapoint, Sandycove and Dalkey Island stand out as among the most conspicuous. Although the towers appear to be almost identical, in fact they vary in size and style. The tower on Dalkey Island is larger and is called a double tower because it has space for two roof-mounted swivel guns. It is also unusual in that it originally had no door and access was by way of a long ladder to the roof.

By 1827, the minutes of the Harbour Commissioners note that the contractors supplying stone for the harbour were storing gunpowder in the disused Glasthule tower (no. 12). It was demolished in the 1890s to fill a dangerous quarry hole and clear the site for what would become the People's Park. The battery, which faced east and had three guns, was later covered by the roadway and the public baths.

A sketch of Seapoint Martello tower after the 1809 shipwreck of the Prince of Wales *and the* Rochdale. (This image is reproduced courtesy of the National Library of Ireland [PD 2064 TX 40].)

In 1820 Thomas Cromwell illustrated a small engraving of the Dunleary Pier in which the Martello tower is just visible, and remarked approvingly, 'the white Martello Towers which line the whole Southern sweep of the bay are not unpleasing objects in the general view'. The fact that they were built of the finest local granite added much to their visual appeal.

An important result of the erection of the towers was the construction of new roads on which the military could move easily and quickly. The long straight road joining the Dunleary and Glasthule towers later became George's Street, Upper and Lower. The existence of the towers also drew people to the village and encouraged the building of new houses.

Part of a large block called the Revenue Houses was incorporated into the present-day Crofton Terrace. One house there still has important features such as large granite fireplaces, as would be found in a barracks, in the basement kitchens and a handsome classical entrance door in the rear garden, which was once the front entrance to the Revenue block. The presence of a Revenue base at Dunleary suggests that the port was dealing more and more with the traffic of incoming ships and with matters of customs and excise, not to mention smuggling. The former boat harbour or depot – now approximately the site of the marina offices – once had a small customs building, and is shown on an early admiralty chart of 1838.

Dún Laoghaire is unfortunate to have lost both its Martello towers, though a fine engraved image of the one that stood on the People's Park site was published as a cartouche on Duncan's map of County Dublin in 1821. It is shown, complete with machicolations over the entrance, flagpole and gun on the roof, with a view of the sea beyond.

The tower at Killiney has been spectacularly restored by a private owner, Niall O'Donoghue, and a working replica gun has been mounted on the original gun platform on the roof. A similar gun was placed on the roof of Seapoint tower. The presence of these guns and furnaces for heating cannonballs (heating them maximised damage to enemy ships by causing fire) remind us of the serious military purpose for which theses defences were built and that the political climate of the time was tense, with the 1798 rebellion just over and the ever-increasing spread of Napoleon's power in Europe. The British fear of a back-door invasion of Ireland was very real at that time. The merchants of Dublin later showed their appreciation of the defeat of the French and consequently of making safe the worldwide shipping routes by erecting

Plan dated 1843, showing Glasthule Martello tower and battery, along with the rocky foreshore and shoals of Scotsman's Bay.

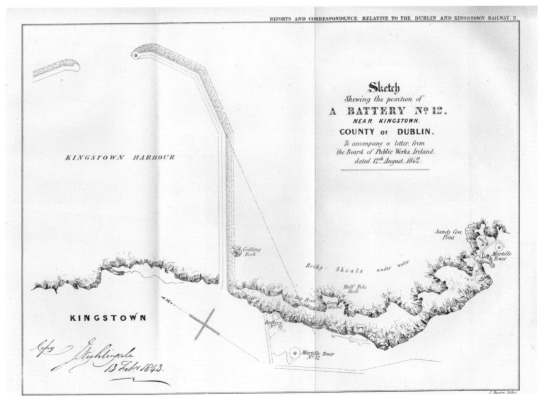

Nelson's Pillar in the city. A French publication of the 1790s, entitled *Description des Côtes d'Irlande*, by P. Leveque shows how much the French knew and gives very detailed information about depths and access to Irish ports, large and small. Of Dunleary (today's Inner Coal Harbour) he wrote: '*Endedans de la jetée, il y a 12 pieds d'eau, de haute mer dans les grandes marées*' and '*en entrant dans ce port, il faut se tenir a une demi encablure dans la partie la plus avancée de la jetée, afin d'eviter un banc, et une petit roche*' and a lot more navigational detail besides. (In other words, he noted that within the jetty, there was 12 foot (3.6 metres) of water, high water at high tides and that when entering the port, half a cable's clearance of the outmost part of the pier was advised, to avoid a bank and a small rock.)

It would be interesting to know if Monsieur Leveque came in person to Ireland as a 'spy' or if he had knowledgeable researchers on the ground. The book was republished in 1804, at the height of the Martello tower building.

Below left: *A view of the entrance to the Forty Foot from the walls of Sandycove battery, showing the sloping granite masonry.*

Below right: *Sandycove battery: a flight of steps leads from the soldiers' quarters and guardroom to the battery storehouse.*

Many of the towers were attached to forts or batteries as these were equipped with more guns and accommodation and stores for soldiers. The surviving battery at Sandycove is probably in the best condition of any, having been altered very little since the time it was built. The buildings incorporate the guardroom, the master gunner's store, a vaulted gunpowder room, the soldier's quarters, water cisterns and privies. A spring well in the grounds of the Martello tower provided fresh drinking water. Below the sloping or 'battered' walls of the Sandycove fort is the famous Forty Foot bathing place, with its various steps and platforms leading into the fresh and bracing waters of Dublin Bay. Part of the battery was converted into a private dwelling in 1955, following its sale by the OPW. This tower and battery were built in 1804 by John Murray, a busy contractor who was also responsible for the erection of the two Dún Laoghaire towers and Seapoint tower.

The survival of most of the early nineteenth-century Martello towers is very fortunate, both for aesthetic and historic reasons. As we have seen, they were designed as a defensive chain to protect Ireland, and Dublin in particular, from invasion; even though they never saw action, they served as an effective deterrent. For several decades after the Napoleonic Wars ended, they continued to be garrisoned.

The striking location of the Martello tower and battery at Sandycove harbour is seen to good effect in this aerial photograph.

Chapter 2

THE VICTORIAN HARBOUR –
A MASTERPIECE IN STONE

FROM DUNLEARY TO KINGSTOWN

By the turn of the nineteenth century, Dunleary was the scene of growing maritime activity based on fishing, the movement of packet ships and the importation of coal. Records show that in 1764 two British men-o'-war, the *Wasp* and the *Ranger*, took

Dunleary pier in 1799, showing a brig, a sailing vessel that carried mail and passengers to Holyhead. The structure, minus its parapet wall and curved end, survives today as the Inner Coal Harbour quay.

shelter and were repaired in the old harbour. Granite had been quarried near Dunleary and Bullock since the eighteenth century and in 1772, John Rutty, in his *Natural History of County Dublin*, noted, 'they are building their piers at Dunlary with it'. However, the harbour was steadily deteriorating and becoming incapable of accommodating the shipping, which had nowhere else to seek shelter in Dublin Bay under bad conditions.

An Act of Parliament was passed in 1786 that had significant implications for Dunleary. The Act aimed to promote 'the trade of Dublin, by rendering its port and harbour more commodious'. New regulations replaced earlier laws, which had been found 'ineffectual' (for example, ships frequently dumped ballast into the River Liffey and damaged the old stone quays of the city). The Act established 'The Corporation for Preserving and Improving the Port of Dublin' – a body which had the powers to govern all aspects of shipping in the port and the bay beyond, levy charges, control pilots, supply ballast from their own gabbards and lighters and impose fines on deviant shipowners and masters. A scale of charges was also laid down. For instance, ships laden with coal had to pay 4d per ton, while other ships belonging to the king's subjects had to pay 6d per ton. Foreign ships had to pay 1s per ton.

The Act also reveals that old Dunleary pier and the rest of the bay fell under the control of Dublin Port. It stated that 'the harbour of Dunleary is a landing place within the Port of Dublin, and of singular use to the trade thereof …' and that the Corporation was empowered to raise ballast (or dredge sand) from Dunleary Harbour, as it had become much silted up. In order to 'cleanse, deepen, and improve the said harbour and pier' every master or commander of every ship taking ballast in Dunleary was subject to the same charges as in Dublin Port, to be administered by an officer stationed in Dunleary. The Act extended their powers all the way to Dalkey and noted 'it may be found expedient to fix buoys in the channel between Dalkey and the Main, so as to render lying in that road more safe and commodious, whereby vessels may at all times of the tide find shelter'.

In 1800 Thomas Archer reported that there were eleven yawls at Dunleary and that salmon fishing was carried on in Dublin Bay. He described Dunleary as 'a handsome and well inhabited seaport town, resorted to by Packets at low water'. In the same year, Captain W.M. Bligh (who had survived the ordeal of being mutinied against in 1787 when he was the commanding lieutenant of HMS *Bounty*) recorded that the pier at Dunleary was 163 yards (140 metres) long and offered 14 feet (4.3 metres) of high water at the full moon. However, he also noted that 'the harbour has nothing to recommend it, being ill-adapted for its purpose'.

A print of the South Bull Wall lighthouse, from a piece of sheet music, c. 1840.

We are so used to the coastal landscape of Dublin Bay with Dún Laoghaire Harbour lying in its present form that it is hard to visualise an alternative configuration. Yet before John Rennie's ultimately successful plan was even provisionally adopted, a multitude of other proposals had been made. In the eighteenth century, improvements concentrated on the Liffey and its approaches. The South Bull Wall was constructed to prevent silt from accumulating, but it was not fully effective until the North Bull Wall was finally added in the 1820s. During the first fifteen years of the nineteenth century a number of pamphlets and petitions appeared proposing a variety of harbour schemes.

Captain Bligh's careful and accurate survey of Dublin Bay in 1800 was accompanied by descriptions and proposals for a harbour and improvements made by his colleague, a royal engineer named Thomas Hyde-Page. The latter's often highly imaginative schemes were addressed to the Directors of the Board of Inland Navigation since all proposed the idea of a canal link between Sandycove or Dunleary and the Grand Canal in Dublin. Captain Bligh, however, was critical of plans for a canal to Dublin, believing it would drain the financial resources that were needed to channel and deepen the Liffey. His view was supported by general professional opinion, which by 1802 placed priority on improving the approaches to the Liffey. It was perhaps fortunate that no canal was built, for its estimated cost was about half a million pounds and it would have become obsolete with the arrival of the railway in the 1830s.

By the early 1800s it was recognised that a large harbour in Dublin Bay was necessary. It was essential that such a harbour remain deep at all states of the tide and be accessible and safe under all weather conditions. One of Hyde-Page's more fanciful schemes involved the construction of a 1½-mile (2.4-km) breakwater off Bullock, which would have sheltered a vast acreage of water towards Dunleary. He also designed a harbour and lock at Dunleary. The harbour would have accommodated 'forty sail' waiting to enter the canal to Dublin. Still another scheme proposed converting Dalkey Sound into a deep-water port by partly closing off Sorrento Point with a breakwater of sunken rocks and 'pierre-perdue' (blocks of stone heaped loosely in the sea). Captain Huddart and engineer John Rennie added their voices to the discussion: Rennie opposed the Dalkey Harbour proposal because it lacked sufficient sea room for manoeuvring.

Despite all the discussion and the recognised need for a harbour in Dublin Bay, the Ballast Office in Dublin began building at Howth in 1807.

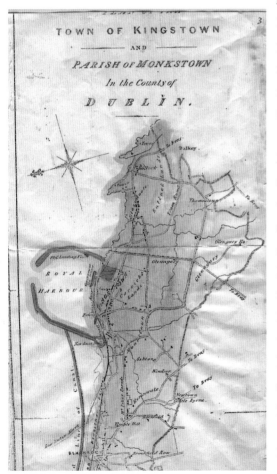

An 1830s sketch of one of the proposals for a canal link between Dunleary and Dublin.

When completed, over £300,000 of public money had been spent on a harbour that was not only outside Dublin Bay but was also difficult to approach (especially for sailing vessels in adverse conditions) because of the position of Ireland's Eye and its neighbouring rocks on the north and the closeness of the shallows to the west. Furthermore, Howth Harbour was sixty per cent dry at low water.

In the same year that Howth Harbour was begun, an appalling tragedy took place that underlined the urgency of building a harbour in Dublin Bay. In 1807 a November gale wrecked two ships on the south coast of Dublin Bay. Some of the 380 people who lost their lives are remembered by a tombstone in Dalkey churchyard, others by a plaque in Monkstown graveyard and a tombstone in Booterstown graveyard. The HMS *Prince of Wales* and a crowded transport ship, *Rochdale*, were driven ashore at Seapoint and Blackrock respectively. Their wreckage was strewn along the shoreline from Ringsend to Dalkey amidst parted limbs and shattered bodies. The horror of this incident provoked the drawing up of a petition signed in 1808 in Monkstown Church by the nobility and gentry of Rathdown calling for the provision of an asylum harbour in Dublin Bay.

The following year, the Rev. W. Dawson published plans for new harbours at Holyhead and Dunleary. His chief concern was for the safety and improved efficiency of the mail packet boats. He condemned the harbour then being built at Howth and recommended that a new pier be erected at Dunleary. He drew a plan for a small breakwater near the site of the present East Pier in Dun Laoghaire, advising that a gap be left between the pier and the mainland so that sand and silt could not accumulate. His ideas were characterised by a common-sense approach and simplicity, rather than the technical knowledge of contemporary engineers.

In 1811 a pamphlet, entitled *Considerations on the Necessity and Importance of an Asylum Port in the Bay of Dublin* and anonymously signed by 'A. Seaman', appeared, favouring a harbour at Dunleary. The pamphlet was very critical of Howth Harbour and maintained, perhaps rightly, that the whole scheme was perpetrated by individuals, both private and official, to enhance the value of their own land in the Howth area. Three years later, an intense, personal campaign was begun, which eventually led to the building of Dunleary Harbour. In 1814 Captain Richard Toutcher, who had personally leased part of Dalkey Common, asked for and succeeded in obtaining from all those who had rights of commonage on the Hill of Dalkey the free right to extract stone for the building of a harbour. He also appealed to the owners of land on Killiney Hill, concluding a letter to a Mr Henry with the words, 'the immense waste of life and property annually occuring [*sic*] in the Bay of Dublin, from the want of an Asylum Harbour for Mariners in distress has repeatedly called forth the cry of

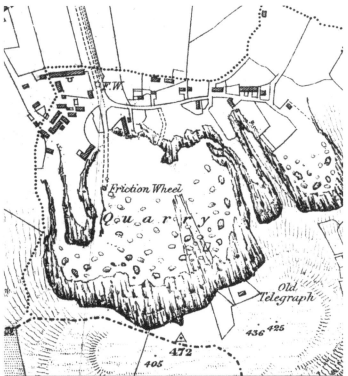

Top: *Dalkey Quarry today is a haven for rock climbers.*
Below: *The 1843 Ordnance Survey map of Dalkey showing the extent of the quarry.*

necessity, and a place eastward of Dunleary, is, by Scientific and Nautical men, marked as the most proper for the erection of a pier to meet those sorrowful exigencies.'

It seems almost certain that Captain Toutcher and 'A. Seaman' are one and the same person. In a manuscript written in 1823 and addressed to the Harbour Commissioners, Toutcher reiterates the same theories and points made in the Seaman pamphlet. Both totally condemned the Howth project, noting that no nautical people, including Dublin skippers and seamen, had ever been consulted about its utility. Both proposed a larger Dunleary Harbour with an east pier of 2,500 feet (760 metres), rather than one of 1,500 feet (460 metres) as proposed in the official plan then in the Dublin Custom House. Both displayed detailed knowledge of all background facts: the economics of the project, the preferences of seamen, the devious expenditures to date and the disinterest of officialdom. Both also called for the erection of a lighthouse on the Dunleary pier, favoured the construction of the North Bull Wall, and questioned the way in which public appointments, such as those in the Ballast Office, had been made.

In his letters and petition (the manuscript of which survives in the National Library), Toutcher eloquently pleaded the case for Dunleary Harbour. The Seaman pamphlet states that while the removal of the Liffey sandbar 'is an object of magnitude to Commerce', 'erecting an asylum port [at Dunleary] is the grand concern of humanity'. Toutcher obtained the support of most of the Dublin merchants, shipowners and shipmasters. But perhaps his greatest achievement was in obtaining all the stone for the harbour, free, from Dalkey Common. It would seem largely due to Toutcher that the foundation stone of Dunleary Asylum Harbour was laid as early as 1817 by the Lord Lieutenant of Ireland, Earl Whitworth.

Eight Harbour Commissioners were appointed to control and regulate construction of the harbour. All were members of the well-to-do aristocracy. Some, like James Crofton, had property interests in Dunleary, although most lived elsewhere. At first it seems strange that Toutcher was not appointed to the Harbour Commissioners. However, when it is known that he was a Norwegian by birth (b. 1757), and that he was a captain of a merchant ship rather than a captain in the Royal Navy, one begins to suspect that he was the object of some social discrimination, either on account of his foreign origins or some difference of social class. Although Toutcher was not appointed to the Harbour Commissioners and received no public thanks or prestige for his dedication to Dunleary Harbour, he was, financially speaking, treated reasonably well. He was appointed storekeeper to the harbour works for which he received £200 yearly.

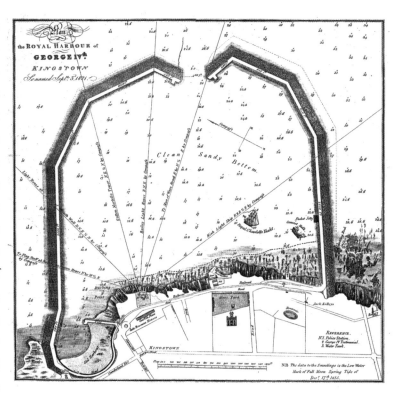

He held his job from about 1816, and when it was later expanded to include the duties of pay clerk and water master, he was earning £400 per annum. In 1833 he was pensioned off with a gift of £400. Earlier he had claimed compensation for £1,031, which he had spent in the interest of the harbour and was refunded £583 by the Harbour Commissioners. Toutcher claimed that he lost about £100 of his own income each year through leasing ten acres of Dalkey Common, which became the quarry for the harbour.

Today the George IV Obelisk on the Dún Laoghaire seafront commemorates the officials associated with the construction of the harbour. Recorded on it are the names of the Harbour Commissioners and engineers, but not Toutcher. An outside observer, Samuel Lewis, writing in 1837, states categorically that it was Toutcher who selected the site for the harbour, and we know of his earlier efforts. It must have been embittering for him in later life to see all the credit for his efforts attributed to the various grandees who sat on the Board of Commissioners and to the Lord Lieutenants Richmond and Whitworth, and even to King George IV, who simply embarked from Dunleary and so graciously gave his name to the harbour. When Toutcher died in 1841 *The Freeman's Journal* lamented that he had been treated so badly.

The plan of the Royal Harbour of George IV, Kingstown was published in 1821 and shows many interesting features, such as the old pier and Martello tower, the late revenue offices, the Harbour Commissioners' house and the reservoir, now covered by the Lexicon Library car park. The Boat Harbour (the Depot), the Royal Charlotte and the convict hulk are also noteworthy.

Top: *An 1821 plan showing the administrative offices of the Harbour Commissioners and Harbour Master.*

Above: *The leather-bound Proceedings of the Harbour Commissioners from 1815 are held in the Public Records Office and shed much light on the design and costs as well as the living and working conditions during the construction of Dún Laoghaire Harbour.*

Right: *A c. 1840 print by George Petrie of the obelisk erected to commemorate the visit of George IV to Dunleary in 1821, which also shows a small pump house in the background.*

MEMORIAL OF THE KING'S VISIT TO IRELAND,

In 1815 yet another petition was sent to parliament to plead the case for an Asylum Harbour at Dunleary. This time £5,000 was granted so that a survey might be made. The Harbour Commissioners and the engineer John Rennie were appointed and in the same year, Lords Longford and de Vesci, the ground landlords, gave their permission for stone to be quarried at Dunleary. On 20 June 1816 an Act authorising the construction of a pier at Dunleary was passed. Such news no doubt greatly pleased Toutcher, who had once confidently stated that most merchants and seamen would willingly bear the burden of various port levies to help fund the harbour. Yet that same year, a Dublin agent for a businessman named Colvill complained sorely about increased port duties, writing 'Dunleary Harbour has been forced down the throats of the traders.' Colvill had been a warm supporter of the Howth Harbour scheme and was almost certainly one of 'the Howth harbour gentry' involved in 'jobbing speculation' described in the Seaman pamphlet.

An official plan for the pier was published and like Taylor's map of the same year (1816), it shows a proposed 2,800-foot (850-metre) pier springing from the Churl Rocks. (Some of the Churl Rocks can still be seen under the George IV Obelisk and in Moran Park.) This official plan for the pier followed the design suggested by Toutcher and most of the earlier pamphleteers. In the following year, however, the new plan proposed by Rennie appeared. It showed the pier situated farther east, in its present position.

The entry of John Rennie, the great Scots engineer, into the discussion and design of the harbour eventually changed the whole concept and scale of the project. It was he who conceived the idea of the two embracing protecting piers which form the harbour that exists today. The combined voice of ship captains like Toutcher, the traders, an engineer like Rennie, and the Harbour Commissioners persuaded the government to accept an altogether larger-scale undertaking than originally conceived. But government approval had to be won in stages. The proposed East Pier was first extended to 3,800 feet (1,160 metres) and then to its present 4,230 feet (1,289 metres). Later, in 1820, permission was given to construct the West Pier, which finally reached a length of 5,080 feet (1,548 metres).

John Rennie, 1761–1821. Engineer, portrait by Sir Henry Raeburn. Rennie was born in Scotland in 1761, and worked with the noted firm of engineers Boulton and Watt before he became an established canal engineer. He came to Ireland in the early 1800s to advise on the building of the Royal Canal. He was involved with the construction of Howth Harbour, and the Custom House docks in Dublin, as well as many important docks and bridges in England.
(National Galleries of Scotland.)

The West Pier, which matches the East Pier in its external curving contour, ensured that tides bearing sand and silt would be forced across the harbour mouth so that deposits could not accumulate in or near it. In order to protect the harbour from north and northeasterly swells, Rennie designed two short projecting arms that ran inwards, leaving a narrow entrance of about 450 feet (140 metres) at the harbour mouth. Engineer William Cubitt, however, suggested the construction of a 1,200-foot (365-metre) protective breakwater out to sea, to span and shelter the harbour entrance, thus allowing it to be broader and more easily accessible. The question of exactly how the pier heads should be completed and how wide the mouth should be provoked endless debate and disagreement among the Harbour Commissioners, engineers and seamen. Rennie's death in 1821 only added to the indecision, which lingered over this question for the next ten years. When the Board of Works took over responsibility for the harbour in 1833 they wrote: 'on assuming the direction of these works we found some embarrassment arising from the want of a definite plan for their future progress.'

In the end, neither Rennie's original plan for a narrow harbour opening nor the breakwater scheme proposed by Cubitt were adopted. Instead, rounded pier heads were constructed, leaving a wider harbour mouth of 750 feet (230 metres) and a vulnerable opening to the northeasterly seas, which continued to bedevil the harbour until the recent construction of the effective (but ungainly) marina breakwaters. The nineteenth-century piers enclosed an area of 251 statute acres (1 square kilometre), creating what the guidebooks for the rest of the nineteenth century described as one of the finest artificial harbours in the world. It is still, without doubt, an exceptional harbour. However, in the last fifty years, there has been persistent infilling of the harbour and covering-over of original features of cut stone for utilitarian purposes, left in crude rock and concrete and obscuring what were once open views. If the harbour were just another construction of clumsily dumped rock armouring and concrete, it would not matter but Dún Laoghaire is nothing like this, being both a harbour and a great monument. Because the harbour is an amenity and a working port, its status as an architectural monument is often overlooked.

The technical achievements of the harbour building are remarkable and were all carried out without the benefit of modern lifting equipment and hydraulic power. The bases of the piers were each 310 feet (95 metres) broad and were constructed of blocks of Runcorn Sandstone, each 50 cubic feet (1.4 cubic metres) in volume. From 6 feet (2 metres) below water and upwards, granite was used. At the top, the pier was to be 53 feet (16 metres) broad with a 40-foot (12-metre) promenade on the inner side and an 8-to-9-foot (2.4-to-2.7-metre) parapet wall to protect the upper promenade. Still today

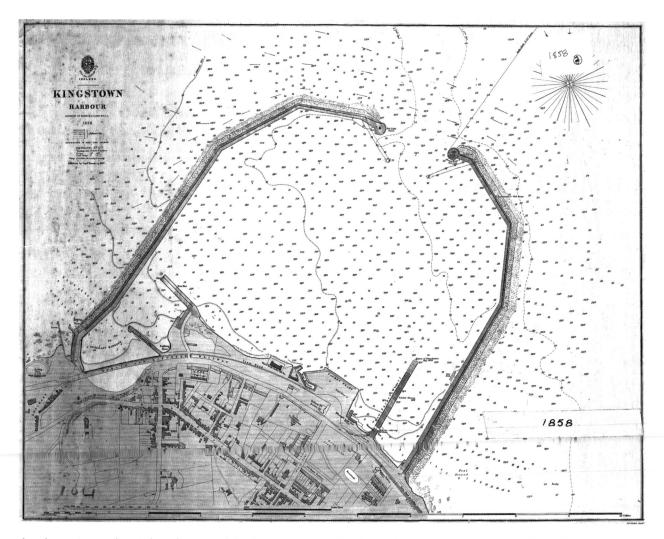

the sheer size and weight of some of the largest granite blocks in the piers is awesome. Some of the stones of the extra-high parapet at the exposed elbow of the East Pier are enormous, yet they are carefully laid and interlocked. Some of the largest blocks, often well over a metre square, were used for the edge of the piers and for the protective upper parapet. Massive wedge-shaped stones can be seen in the parapet, which create a strong interlocking wall. Many of the stones bear the regular chisel marks of the quarryman and the holes that facilitated lifting them into position. Even the long, sloping 'sea pavements' of the backs of the piers were very carefully laid and jointed. All the parapet walls are gently sloped to counter the force of the sea. Even the interior walls of the piers are slightly battered so that the entire construction gives an impression of eternal solidity and strength. Despite this, a former lighthouse keeper recalls a terrible storm in 1916 when the East Pier was almost breached and massive boulders from the back of the pier were

The 1858 chart of Kingstown harbour shows it in its 'finished' state, complete with its rounded pier heads, Victoria wharf across the breast of the harbour, the new Carlisle Pier and traders' wharf, which forms the Outer Coal Harbour. The harbour was to remain like this until the 1970s.

Right: The Boyd Monument was erected in 1863 to commemorate Captain Boyd of the naval guardship Ajax who drowned while trying to rescue the stricken crew of a coal boat smashed against the back of the East Pier.
Below: Steps and bollards are just some of the many examples of remarkable granite stonework to be found around the harbour. Now bearing a slight polish after 200 years, they are a testament to the outstanding design and skill of the stonemasons who made them. The cast-iron bollard (left) at the end of the West Pier bears the date 1845.

hurled by the waves onto the promenades, making great craters in its surface.

In an estimate prepared by Captain Toutcher for a 3,600-foot (1.1-kilometre) pier, by far the most expensive item was the underwater work of laying caissons, watertight chambers of Runcorn Sandstone that facilitated the construction of the foundations, which at 40s per cubic yard would cost £160,000. By contrast, the cost of all the masonry work was estimated at £36,000. From the total Toutcher deducted £80,000 for the granite that he had obtained free from Dalkey.

In June 1817 a contract for cutting and transporting stone for the harbour was drawn up with the stone contractor George Smith, who had already supplied stone from Bullock for Howth Harbour. At first, as we have already seen, the stone was taken not only from Dalkey, but also from Glasthule, and from what would become the pond in Moran Park at the Churl Rocks. The stone from Dalkey was transported to the harbour by a funicular railroad made up of six trucks joined together by a continuous chain. The weight of the descending trucks pulled up the empty ones. Each truck could carry 25 tons of granite. By 1826, 250 wagons of stone were being delivered each day. Traces of the metal track, as well as the grooves worn by the cables in the stone, can still be seen in Dalkey Quarry and in the boundary wall of Dalkey Lodge, while the pathway bordering the present railway has preserved the name 'The Metals'.

The minutes of the Harbour Commissioners record many interesting facts about the lives of the labourers who cut and carted stone. In 1823 there were 1,000 workers, some with their families, living in huts on Dalkey Commons without any sanitary facilities or running water. Generally, about 700 men were employed in the work at the quarries and on the piers. Outbreaks of typhus and cholera as well as injuries were commonplace, and in the early days of harbour construction no medical treatment was available. The Kingstown Dispensary, run by Charles Duffy, a surgeon, was finally opened in 1831 and a temporary cholera hospital at Glasthule was set up.

It must have been a grim existence. Ordinary labourers earned very little, about 10s or 12s a week; a foreman earned 15s. Many were paid by tickets or by arrangement with hucksters and publicans, until the commissioners finally ruled that the men were to be paid in cash only. It is not difficult to imagine the hardship of the labourers and wonder how they managed to exist on the pittance they earned for a tough day's work. Nor is it hard to understand why on several occasions there were riots and strikes, as in 1815 when Smith, the stone contractor, tried to cut wages and was personally threatened.

Some employees fared better. An assistant engineer earned about £300 per year. Head engineers earned much more. Thomas, a resident engineer, lived at No. 4 Crofton Terrace. This terrace had been erected by James Crofton, one of the Harbour Commissioners, who let his houses to professional people engaged at the harbour. Jeremy, the Tide and Port Surveyor, lived at Seamount off Clarence Street where a small terrace still stands overlooking the harbour.

In 1817 Lord Lieutenant Whitworth laid the first stone, the whereabouts of which remain a mystery. It was accompanied by a coin of the realm, ten previous days' news-papers, and an inscription that read, 'In the hope that it may be the cause of life to the seamen, wealth to the citizen, Revenue to the Crown and benefit to the nation.' After the ceremony, a breakfast was served for 300 guests in a tent that had been specially erected near the new pier.

From then on the progress of the harbour was quite rapid. Between the laying of the first stone in 1817 and April 1820, 2,285 feet (700 metres) of the East Pier were com-pleted. Three years later it had reached 3,350 feet (1.02 kilometres). The West Pier, begun in 1820, was already 1,600 feet (490 metres) long by 1823, and by December 1827 had reached 4,140 feet (1.3 kilometres) in length. The completion of the pier heads with their lighthouses lingered on into the late 1840s and, although a bill was issued in 1822 proclaiming the existence of a lighthouse on the East Pier of the 'Royal Harbour of George IV at Kingstown', it was only a temporary wooden structure, which was moved seaward as the pier was extended. There were frequent incidents where ships nearly hit the unfinished pier head because the lighthouse was too far inshore. The present East Pier lighthouse, built with sharply cut granite masonry, was finished by 1847. The completion in 1859 of Carlisle Pier as the new mail packet terminal brought the construction work to a close and by 1860 the harbour was considered complete. Carlisle Pier remained the busiest berth in the harbour for over a century and had a depth of 17 to 20 feet (5 to 6 metres) and quay walls measuring 760 feet (230 metres) on the east side and 571 feet (175 metres) on the west side.

The Dublin Builder of 1863 reported that the whole scheme had then cost £1 million – a very substantial amount in Victorian terms. Between 1800 and 1875 Kingstown Harbour received the lion's share of large sums spent on east-coast harbours. Howth cost about £400,000, Donaghadee £170,000, and Dunmore East £120,000. Opponents of Kingstown Harbour never lost an opportunity to criticise its effectiveness or question the huge expenditure. General maintenance was continually necessary. In 1880, for example, 27,000 tons of sand and mud were removed and 907 yards (830 metres) of heavy sea pavement were set on the exterior of the piers as reinforcement.

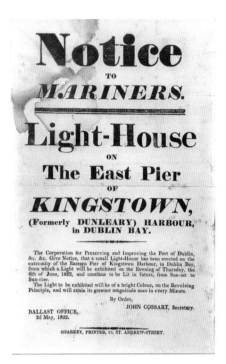

Notice
TO
MARINERS.
Light-House
ON
The East Pier
OF
KINGSTOWN,
(Formerly DUNLEARY) HARBOUR,
in DUBLIN BAY.

The Corporation for Preserving and Improving the Port of Dublin, &c. &c. Give Notice, that a small Light-House has been erected on the extremity of the Eastern Pier of Kingstown Harbour, in Dublin Bay, from which a Light will be exhibited on the Evening of Thursday, the 6th of June, 1822, and continue to be Lit in future, from Sun-set to Sun-rise.

The Light to be exhibited will be of a bright Colour, on the Revolving Principle, and will attain its greatest magnitude once in every Minute.

By Order,
JOHN COSSART, Secretary.
BALLAST OFFICE,
2d May, 1822.

SHARKEY, PRINTER, 23, ST. ANDREW-STREET.

Far left: A Notice to Mariners published in 1822 informed mariners of the placing of a light in a timber tower that could be moved seawards as the construction progressed towards the extremity of the pier.

Left: An 1860s photograph shows Carlisle Pier (completed in 1859) equipped with an iron shelter to cover passengers and luggage at the train platforms. A royal navy guardship can be seen in the background.

The name 'Dunleary Asylum Harbour' reflects the fact that, from the outset, the harbour was not intended to cope with any particular kind of shipping. It existed as a refuge for ships bound for Dublin. By about 1830, a wide range of maritime activity had been seen in the harbour; fishing boats, naval frigates, royal yachts, colliers (coal boats), passenger paddleships, lifeboats, revenue cruisers, a convict hulk, merchant ships and yachts. There had also been shipwrecks (which were met with heroic action on the part of the lifeboat), one royal visit and a regatta.

The harbour was able to prove its utility as early as 1824: the figures for that year claim that 3,351 vessels took shelter in Kingstown. In 1835 a total of 2,000 vessels entered the harbour, apart from the regular mail packets, 57 men-o'-war and cruisers of the Navy. Its use as a harbour of refuge is evident from the fact that in 1845, of the 2,214 vessels that entered Kingstown, 1,117 then proceeded to Dublin.

The Boat Harbour, more recently called the Creek or the Depot, provided one of the first berths for small vessels in the new harbour. It was built in 1819 for £543 by two local contractors, Nugent and Tully. This little boat harbour was, it seems, mainly for the use of revenue personnel who later had their houses or offices nearby. It had a small boat slip, four sets of steps and a crane. The Boat Harbour was filled in and the houses were all swept away by the development of the new car ferry terminal in the early 1970s. The Boat Harbour is marked on an official plan of Kingstown Royal Harbour of 1823, which reveals many interesting details. For instance, there is a moored vessel called the *Royal Charlotte*, which may have been the Lord Lieutenant's. The *Royal Charlotte*, an armed yacht, may also have kept an eye on the harbour works since during the 1820s there appears to have been no permanent naval guardship. In 1832 we find the Master of the yacht, Mr Ellis, living in Rumley Avenue (now Mulgrave Street). As evidenced by a contemporary print, the yacht was flagship to the Dublin Regatta in 1828, the first significant yachting event in Kingstown Harbour. She appeared in a second print of the harbour that was published in the *Dublin Penny Journal* in 1834.

His Majesty's cruisers, such as the *Shamrock* and *William and Mary*, were also frequent visitors to the harbour. A Kingstown provisioner named Howard even advertised himself in 1832 as 'Grocer and Agent to His Majesties Cruisers'. In 1818 it had been projected that 'close to the pier head there will be a depth of water of twenty-four feet at the lowest springs which will admit a frigate of 36 guns or an Indiaman of 800 tons, and at two hours flood, a seventy-four may take refuge with safety.'

The Royal Navy always maintained some sort of presence in Kingstown, though the date of the establishment of a permanent guardship is unclear. From 1821, a convict ship (a hulk without masts) called *Essex* lay in the harbour. The *Essex*, which was pictured in the *Dublin Penny Journal* of 1834, held as many as 275 convicts awaiting deportation. Many of the convicts, both men and women, had been found guilty of very minor offences, such as stealing a handkerchief or a loaf of bread, and they came from all

The Depot, or Boat Harbour, was of early origin and is shown on an 1821 plan. With its many steps and boat slip, it was once used by revenue boats and small rowing boats to ferry people out to larger ships at anchor in the harbour. In this c. 1900 photograph, small yachts are being wintered on the quay.

The Depot in the 1970s, with Edith Byrne, daughter of Matt Byrne, who campaigned to protect the stonework of the harbour.

parts of Ireland, to await transportation to Australia or Tasmania. There they served out their sentence in prison labour camps. It was once suggested that the convicts be employed on the harbour works, but this idea was rejected by the Harbour Commissioners. The Master of the *Essex*, J. Lamb, was living at No. 4 George's Place in 1832. The convict hulk was still in Kingstown by 1835, for in that year a Royal Navy surgeon, J. Speer, came to live in one of the new houses in Sussex Parade (Marine Road). As Medical Superintendent of Prisoners, he was responsible for the health of the convicts. From the *Essex*, hundreds of prisoners had their last glimpse of Ireland and of the rapidly developing Kingstown.

W.F. Wakeman, a nineteenth-century tourist writer, describes the harbour of the 1860s in florid terms: 'Foreign men-o-war, gunboats, revenue cruisers, and a cloud of yachts of every size and character, from the 200 or 300 ton steamer which might circumnavigate the globe, to the butterfly cutter of the season, frequent the fine area of water embraced by its noble piers.'

A coastguard station, consisting of a tide surveyor, six tide waiters, a coxswain and four boatmen, existed at Dunleary as early as 1820. The coastguard's chief duty lay in attending to the 'examination of baggage and other goods brought by the packets' and also 'to visit and rummage' such ships as might be passing through the Dunleary station's district. The service was mainly concerned with smuggling, which was then commonplace, as the names of local hiding places and caves such as the Brandy Hole near Bullock suggest. On 26 April 1735, the *Dublin Weekly Journal* reported that the King's Officers had made a seizure of a large quantity of tea and brandy at Bullock and that the next morning, when the smugglers attempted to recover their goods, a great battle ensued, in which several were wounded on both sides and two of the smugglers were killed. In 1895 the Kingstown Coastguards had three vessels stationed in the harbour – the *Fanny* of 375 tons; the *Hind*, a yawl of 131 tons; and a 10-gun ship, *Flora*.

The rather limited trading and commercial life of Kingstown Harbour was always confined to its older and western portion. In 1835 there were twenty registered yawls, which imported coal, timber and iron and exported cattle, granite, corn and lead ore. The predominant commercial activity, however, was the importation of coal from places like Swansea and Whitehaven in south Wales.

THE KINGSTOWN HARBOUR MASTER

Among other early additions to the harbour were a reservoir (now Moran Park pond), a water jetty and pump house. The jetty was later incorporated into Carlisle Pier. Prior to this there had been complaints about the lack of a freshwater supply at the harbour. Water had to be fetched from Juggy's Well, a spring near Monkstown Hospital. In 1826 Captain Toutcher was made water master at the harbour. The direct rival of the enterprising Captain Toutcher was Lieutenant William Hutchinson of the Royal Navy, a man of equally high calibre and ability.

Lieutenant Hutchinson was appointed harbour master of the new Royal Harbour in 1822. He had previously held the title of harbour master of Bullock and Old Dunleary Harbour along with his jobs as clerk to the Chamber of Commerce, and inspector of quarries at Bullock. As superintendent of the pilot boats of Kingstown, Hutchinson also maintained his own boat and men. He had orders to supervise the pilots, watch over their conduct and report any who were 'habitually drunk'. He was also responsible for the life-boat stationed at Sandycove. After 1826, he acted as agent to the mail packets for which he was paid fifty guineas per annum in addition to the half pay he continued to receive as a lieutenant in the Royal Navy.

The appointment of Hutchinson as harbour master of the new harbour irritated Captain Toutcher, who had applied for the position and sought official recognition and remuneration for his devotion to the harbour project. He maintained that Hutchinson, who lived 2.4 kilometres away at Bullock, could hardly fulfil so many appointments and duties. It seems clear that Hutchinson's appointment as harbour master was 'encouraged' by his uncle, who was on the Ballast Board, and was also favoured by the Harbour Commissioners. It was nevertheless an excellent choice, for Hutchinson maintained a record of thoroughness and efficiency in all his duties throughout his long career. Like Toutcher, he was completely dedicated to the harbour. A unique watercolour, which survives in the Gillman collection of Dún Laoghaire memorabilia, bears the title 'View of Kingstown harbour drawn for Captain Hutchinson RN 1851 (Harbour Master)'. Although in very poor condition, it gives accurate and detailed information on the state of the harbour, the town, the yacht clubs and the vessels in the harbour. It also illustrates one of Hutchinson's pilot vessels.

Unofficial pilotage, or 'hobbling' as it was called, was commonplace. 'Hobbling' consisted of venturing out in Dublin Bay in small boats in the hope of acting as pilot to arriving ships. As recently as 1934, three Dún Laoghaire men – Millar, Shorthall and Pluck – were drowned while hobbling.

No detail escaped Hutchinson's thorough organisation. In 1835 *Wilson's Dublin Directory* noted that 'a stomach pump for the restoration of suspended animation' was kept in the office of the harbour master. On rough days, a blue flag was flown from his office, indicating that the normal boatmen's fares for transferring passengers to and from ships could be doubled. (In 1860 the normal fares were: 6d for a single passenger with luggage, 1s for a return fare, and 2d for children and labourers.)

In 1817 special harbour constables were appointed. They wore a uniform of a blue cloth jacket with red cuffs and cape, grey pantaloons, blue waistcoat, grey coat and glazed hat.

Hutchinson's greatest achievements were in life saving and the running of the lifeboat service. A beautiful silver teapot was presented to him by the Ballast Board in recognition of his part in the rescue of the crew of the *Ellen*, which foundered at Sandycove in 1821. In 1829 he received the RNLI Gold Medal for his courageous rescue of the eleven crew members of the *Duke*, which had been wrecked on Sandycove Point. But he was instrumental in saving many other crews: a decade earlier he had helped save the *Pandora* after she broke her moorings in Dublin Bay.

Among the most numerous victims of shipwreck were the small colliers, which were invariably poorly maintained and equipped and under-crewed by their profit-hungry owners. Anchors and cables were often quickly lost, and the crews left helpless. For these colliers, which ran all year round from places like south Wales and the Mersey, shipwrecks were commonplace. In 1861 G.R. Powell published a small booklet entitled *The Gale*, which relates in full the story of the drowning of twelve men at Kingstown in February of that year. Three vessels, two of them colliers, *Neptune* and *Industry*, were wrecked on the back of the East Pier. Even more astoundingly, thirteen colliers and brigs sank inside the harbour. On the same day there were eight additional wrecks at Howth and another fourteen further down the east coast. The force of the storm in the Irish Sea made the main packet ship *Leinster* turn back

The harbour constables' office was a handsome but tiny granite building which stood on Victoria Wharf; it disappeared in the 1960s and is said to have been dismantled and stored in an OPW yard in Trim.

to Kingstown. It was perhaps due to the loss of so many vessels inside the harbour that three very modern Dublin-designed Mitchell screw moorings were laid in 1862 in place of the old ground chains.

During the gale, Hutchinson as harbour master and lifeboat coxswain tried to save what he could and was later, with Captain John McNeil Boyd and two others, awarded the RNLI Silver Medal. Captain Boyd, who was attached to the Royal Navy guardship *Ajax*, permanently at anchor in the harbour, went to the rescue of the crew of three on the *Neptune*. In the course of the rescue, he and his crew were drowned. Boyd, a Donegal man, was a mariner of the highest quality and had written *A Handbook for Naval Cadets*. A day of public mourning was declared in Kingstown during which a cannon salute boomed out at regular intervals. An estimated 7,000 people attended the funeral.

THE LIFEBOAT SERVICE

Some sources say that a lifeboat was installed at Dunleary by about 1810, while others talk of the transfer of the Sandycove boat to Dunleary in 1821 after the loss of the *Eliza*. It is significant that in 1808, when the brig *Olympus* ran into difficulties off Dalkey, the crew were saved by a lifeboat. One date is certain: in 1830 a Northumberland lifeboat was brought over by the Duke of Northumberland and stationed at Kingstown under the charge of Hutchinson. As an outcome of the tragedy brought about by the gale of 1861, a lifeboat house was erected on the Royal Slip at the foot of the East Pier. By June 1861 this handsome boathouse of rustic granite blocks was under construction. Stone pediments in the form of gables surmount the arched openings at each end. This new boat shed housed the Kingstown lifeboat in such a way that it was always in readiness to put to sea. It should be remembered that these lifeboats were large and heavy, and were propelled solely by oar or sail power, usually in adverse conditions.

In 1876 the lifeboat rescued the crews of two ships, the *Vesper* on the Kish Bank and the *Leonie* near Bray. On the return trip with the rescued men, however, the lifeboat itself capsized and four were drowned. In 1878 the Kingstown lifeboat successfully rescued the entire crew of the Austrian brig *Olinka*, which had come from Rijeka on the Adriatic and was wrecked on the Kish. And in 1881 an entire crew was saved from a wreck on the North Bull sands. But the most tragic event in the lifeboat's history occurred on Christmas Eve 1895 when the boat was sent to the rescue of the *Palme*, ashore at Seapoint. The lifeboat capsized with the loss of all fifteen crewmen. A stone memorial situated opposite the present lifeboat station records the names of the men, many of whose descendants still live in Dún Laoghaire.

*A great crowd at the
traders' wharf for the official
launch of the new lifeboat
Dunleary, inaugurated in
1898.*

In 1919 the Dún Laoghaire lifeboat station received a petrol-driven lifeboat to replace its sailing and rowing boat, which had so often battled out in gale conditions to shipwrecks as far off as Bray Head or the Kish Bank. In 1925 the new lifeboat *Dunleary* went out to the Burford Bank in gale-force winds and saved all forty-six crew members of the German square-rigger *Hamburg*, which had run aground on passage from Melbourne carrying 3,500 tons of wheat.

In 1938 a new diesel-engine lifeboat, the *Dunleary II*, came into service. This boat rescued the forty-seven crew members of a Norwegian freighter, *Bolivar*, which had run aground on the Kish Bank and dramatically broken in two in a gale in 1947. In 1967 Dún Laoghaire received a 44-foot (13-metre) steel lifeboat, the *John F. Kennedy*, which was capable of a speed of 14 knots and was in every way excellently equipped. Since 1862, when records of the lifeboat's activities began, hundreds of people have been saved by the efforts of its voluntary crews. Its secretary in the latter part of the twentieth century was Dr John de Courcy Ireland, a noted historian, educationalist and maritime expert, who endlessly sought to raise public awareness of the importance of the lifeboat and coast-watch services.

In 1845 Lieutenant Hutchinson settled into a new harbour master's house, now Moran Park House, built near the reservoir in the area of the Churl Rocks. He remained in Kingstown till his death in 1881 and is remembered by a plaque in the Mariners' Church which he had supported and which now appropriately houses the National Maritime Museum of Ireland. Later the harbour master lived in what used to be the Harbour Commissioners' house. The house used not to be well known for it was hidden behind the town hall and stands back from Crofton Road. It was approached through an entrance that lay between two rows of well-built Georgian-style cottages which were erected for harbour employees. All of the cottages were swept away in 2005 to prepare the site for development. On a harbour plan of 1821 there is a small image of the Harbour Commissioners' house, showing it situated behind the stone yards and commanding a good view of the harbour. In 1820 the stone contractor George Smith was given the contract to build this house for a mere £330. Toutcher in his memorandum writes, 'I proposed that Board Room House to be built where it now stands but disapproved of the plan of the house, particularly the staircase.' This is interesting, for the Harbour Commissioners' house does contain a very unusual staircase. It is semicircular and

The Harbour Commissioners' house, with its neoclassical stone portico, is set back from Crofton Road.

projects out at the rear of the house and is surmounted by a tower with a clock and signalling turret. The boardroom, which spanned the front of the house, has good plasterwork decoration. This house, built in the neoclassical style which was then popular elsewhere in Ireland, represents the first serious piece of architecture in the new town. A heavy Doric portico of two granite pillars supports a balcony from which the whole harbour could be surveyed. Though the architect remains unknown, it is likely that the design was produced by one of the harbour engineers. When the Dún Laoghaire Harbour Company was formed, this became its headquarters and the building was carefully restored. Subsequent development on both sides have altered the ground level and left the building situated at the top of a rather disconcerting ramp.

George Smith, as the stone contractor to the harbour, clearly had access to an unlimited supply of granite. By about 1820 he had built a house for himself, which he called very appropriately Stoneview, now situated in Clarinda Park. A little later he built Granite Hall, which he let to wealthy tenants. These two houses and the Harbour Commissioners' house were all impeccably constructed in ashlar blocks of Dalkey granite. Smith and his son Samuel also erected cottages for some of his employees along the seafront to Sandycove. The area was called Newtownsmith. He built more cottages on Glenageary Hill, which are still known as Sam Smith's Cottages or The Seven Houses. Even in these modest cottages, details of good granite masonry can be seen and the centre house has a pediment feature with a blind lunette window. The Smiths also built Granite Lodge, a two-storey house at the corner of Tivoli Road and Glenageary Hill, and Ashgrove Lodge in which George's daughter and her husband, Bargeny McCulloch, lived. Ashgrove was a pretty two-storey house with Regency-style latticed verandas, but it was demolished to make way for a new evangelical church.

HARBOUR ARCHITECTURE

By 1863 the harbour had received a variety of architectural furnishings – a battery or fort, an anemometer, a coastguard station, a seamen's reading room, a harbour constables' office a  pump house and a lighthouse and keeper's dwelling. Moreover, from 1860 onwards, a large naval vessel known as the guardship was permanently at anchor in the harbour. During the 1860s, HMS *Royal George*, a large three-masted frigate, was moored in the harbour where it made an imposing sight and it can be seen in many of the early photographs of the period. Later in the century a number of naval steamships, such as the *Belle Isle* and the *Melampus*, were well known for their striking profiles. Besides the naval ships, Glasthule battery, a small fort similar to the remaining one at the Forty Foot, had been built to protect the coast. The battery stood near the site of the former baths next to the East Pier. The building of the harbour rendered it useless since it then stood far inshore. In 1843 it was occupied by 'a former Drum-major of the Royal Artillery, who is in the habit of taking lodgers, and keeps the place in a state of dilapidation'. In the same year, the Board of Works agreed to demolish the old battery and build a new one at the end of the East Pier. However, the stone facing of the pier heads was only begun in 1842 and still no battery appears in prints of the harbour dating 1850. It is only in 1860 that G.R. Powell was to write in his guide, 'round the lighthouse has been lately built the Kingstown fort, a small but powerful defence should an enemy show himself within range'.

The granite-built East Pier lighthouse, with its circular accommodation at ground level for the lighthouse keeper.

This East Pier battery, circular in form, was superbly built of substantial blocks of ashlar granite, the tops of the walls being sloped to deflect shot. The fort was equipped with gun platforms on three different levels, the highest facing out to sea. A particularly fine set of steps was erected at the very end of the pier to provide access for naval rowing boats to the fort. The battery was once equipped with high-calibre guns, a powder magazine, and 'a means of heating balls to white heat'. It never saw action, fortunately, and was used mainly for firing salutes. The battery is now open to the public

View from the East Pier lighthouse in 2010, showing the garrison living quarters. Beyond we see the Dún Laoghaire skyline before the addition of the Lexicon Library, with the Dublin mountains in the background.

every day and the large Irish flag flown there is a welcome sight for all sailors. It is entered by a deep barrel-vaulted passageway which leads to the beautifully built East Pier light house, constructed about 1047 to the designs of George Halpin, engineer to the Ballast Office. A spiral stair inside the granite structure leads to the lantern and balcony which affords excellent views of the bay.

The anemometer on the East Pier is yet another example of the skill of the stonemason, and the stonework looks as crisp today as if it were just finished. By monitoring wind speed and direction, it made a significant contribution to safety at sea. The anemometer is no longer in use and the rusting mast has caused bad staining on some of the granite masonry.

The supply of water to ships is an important service in any harbour, but by 1820 the former Churl quarry had filled up with water and was piped to a short jetty at the springing point of today's Carlisle Pier. A small square pump house with a central door and cornice is shown in a print in the *Dublin Penny Journal* but it has since disappeared, probably at the time of the building of Carlisle Pier (1853–55). (It is visible in the print on p. 31.)

The coastguard station, which stands near the Coal Harbour, appears to have been built in the 1840s and features a short, square tower, somewhat Italianate in manner. A small boat slip, pier and granite-built boathouse as well as a rocket house stand just seaward of

Above: The anemometer on the East Pier. The design was perfected by Professor Thomas Robinson of Trinity College Dublin. When built in 1852, it was one of the first in the world. The little granite building, which adopts a severe Greco-Egyptian style, is reminiscent of a family mausoleum.

Right: The inscription on a telescope presented to the Sailors Reading Room by G.E.W. Dalton in 1877.

the coastguard buildings. In 1837 there were five officers and thirty-eight men responsible for the coastguard stations from Kingstown to Wicklow. Kingstown later became the depot for the entire east Irish coast. Other harbour buildings included the Sailors' Home or Seamen's Rest. According to G.R. Powell, this facility saved countless men from 'many a temptation, and much loss of money and character'. It was a low building, erected on Victoria Wharf in about 1870. Until its demolition in the 1960s, it was the first home of the National Maritime Museum. The object of the Seamen's Rest, or Reading Room as it was also known, was to lure sailors away from the evils of drink and encourage reading and recreation. Swearing or improper language, gambling, card playing, drunkenness and smoking were not permitted there.

In the mid-1850s a stone-built lighthouse was erected on the West Pier. The circular pier head around the lighthouse is paved with granite blocks, laid in concentric circles, and is a striking piece of craftsmanship (see p. 8). A separate dwelling was later constructed for the keeper. This fine cut-granite house was built in 1863 by a contractor named Stapleton, who was highly praised in *The Dublin Builder* for his workmanship. The stone for the house was cut and worked on the spot by the contractor. A notable feature around the top of the house is a thick cornice in the form of a roll-moulding. Unfortunately, the house has been blocked up for many years.

John Rennie, the designer of Dún Laoghaire Harbour, was acclaimed for his practical engineering skills elsewhere in Britain and Scotland before he ever came to Ireland. He designed several Irish harbours and always succeeded in producing useful and attractive structures. The remarkable curved stonework of the pier heads, the broad double-level

The Navy Steps, located to the side of Victoria Wharf (now Ferry Terminal pier) in front of the Royal St George Yacht Club still exist. The beautifully constructed double flight of steps provided access for pinnaces to ships of the Royal Navy anchored out in the harbour. It is also likely that these steps were the point of embarkation for the many nineteenth-century convicts who were ferried out to the hulk or prison ship to await deportation to Tasmania.

walkways, the strong protective parapet walls, the many cantilevered steps and sloping granite stairs leading to the water, the sculptural quality of the drum-shaped granite bollards, even the roughly hewn sea pavements at the bunks of the piers, the boat slips and quaysides, not to mention some of the now lost or buried features of the harbour like the Depot, are all testament to both the skills of design and stonemasonry of the time. The many cut-stone steps or stairs of the harbour are worthy of particular attention, in the way they are recessed into the walls and canted out as they descend. The former Navy Steps (above), once part of St Michael's Wharf, still remain but are now inaccessible. The Depot or Revenue Boat Harbour also remains intact but buried beneath the now-obsolete car ferry parking lot near the entrance to the marina. Perhaps it will one day be unearthed and reclaimed – who can tell what the future holds? As the urban world in which we live succumbs to more and more infill and concrete, the remaining traces of bedrock, cliffs and stones seem more important in the way in which they connect us to the origins of our land.

Despite the obvious qualities of such stonework, it was in the past often simply dumped, buried or concreted over. Now, fortunately, there is a general awareness of the irreplaceable nature of such features and an understanding of the time-consuming labour and incredible human effort required to quarry, transport and position all these massive stones.

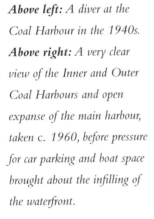

Above left: A diver at the Coal Harbour in the 1940s.
Above right: A very clear view of the Inner and Outer Coal Harbours and open expanse of the main harbour, taken c. 1960, before pressure for car parking and boat space brought about the infilling of the waterfront.

LOST ACTIVITIES OF DÚN LAOGHAIRE HARBOUR

The presence of a Royal Navy guardship in Kingstown Harbour in the 1800s has already been noted. This practice was discontinued in about 1904, as the following year the Urban District Council passed a resolution 'that the attention of the Admiralty be directed to the loss sustained to Kingstown through no guardship being stationed in the harbour'. Nevertheless, in 1906 and again in 1907 the Atlantic Fleet visited Kingstown, mooring in Dublin Bay while its officers attended a grand ball held in the Pavilion. The visits of the royal yacht to Kingstown in 1900, 1903, 1904 and 1911 also provided pomp and spectacle for the town. A naval base and auxiliary patrol office were stationed at Victoria Wharf in 1917. The Dublin-built gunboat HMS *Helga* was frequently stationed at Kingstown. In April 1916, she was brought up the Liffey to shell Bolands Mill and Liberty Hall and in 1918 she was engaged in action with German U-boats. Following independence, the *Helga* became the Irish fishery patrol ship *Muirchú* and represented the first and principal vessel of the Irish Navy. Her successors, the *Macha*, *Maeve* and *Cliona*, were often in Dún Laoghaire after 1946. Vessels of the Irish Navy continue to visit the harbour today.

Although Dún Laoghaire Harbour's geographical situation and the town's residential nature have prevented it from becoming a major commercial port, it could have been developed as a centre for building ships and boats. In 1905 plans were submitted to the Kingstown Urban District Council to erect a boatbuilding shed at the back of the West

Pier. In the early 1950s the Dalkey Shipyard operated on this site, employing forty-five men in the building of pilot boats, cutters and harbour tug boats. The shipyard filled orders from Izmir and Istanbul and was about to undertake a Polish order when it was closed in 1954–55. Part of its boat slip still lies derelict off the West Pier. Small boats and yachts have also been built at Dún Laoghaire, although the popularity of fibreglass eventually contributed to the closure of many old boatyards including Doyle's, Clancy's, Atkinson's and Mahony's.

As the twentieth century progressed, Dún Laoghaire Harbour saw several of its major activities decline and disappear. The twentieth-century reliance on oil brought about the end of coal importation at Dún Laoghaire, as the smaller companies vanished. The fishing fleet also suffered a decline, as trawlers moved to better fishing grounds and better-equipped ports. However, an ungainly looking icehouse was erected on the Coal Harbour quay in 1972.

For years, three blue-grey dredgers – *Saxifrage, Sisyphus* and *Fag-an-Balach* – were familiar fixtures in the harbour, working chiefly at the mailboat pier. Today all have been scrapped. Their coal-fired steam engines must have been among the last to operate in the country; that of the *Saxifrage* is preserved in the National Maritime Museum. Yet another loss to harbour life is the departure of the Irish Nautical College from Dún Laoghaire. Founded in 1889 as the Dublin School of Navigation, the Nautical College moved to Dún Laoghaire in 1953. It provided a state-recognised education for professional seamen.

From time to time, pleasure boats and launches have run excursions from Dún Laoghaire to Howth Head, Dalkey Island, Killiney Bay and Bray. The *Western Lady* was popular in the 1960s and before that the *Larsen* and later the *Merry Golden Hind* provided pleasure cruises. However, the most attractive of all was the *Cynthia*, a paddle steamer built originally for pleasure cruising at Margate but finally operated at Dún Laoghaire by Hewitts until she sank in 1933. The *St Bridget*, operating from the East Pier, continues the tradition today and is very popular with excursions to Howth and Dalkey Island.

THE IRISH LIGHTS

The vessels of the Irish Lights have moored in Dún Laoghaire Harbour since the 1870s. The lightships, painted red but once black in colour, lay at anchor off the West Pier and used to quietly contribute interest to the harbour. One of the lightships, the *Albatross*, served as a training headquarters for the Sea Scouts.

Early photographs of the harbour often feature the gracious paddle steamer *Alexandra* and her successor moored in the East Pier bight. The *Alexandra* was an inspection vessel of the Irish Lights Commissioners. The *Tearaght* was also well remembered; she broke her moorings in a gale in 1916 and was battered against the East Pier until she sank.

The grey-and-white tenders of the Irish Lights, including the *Granuaile*, *Atlanta*, *Ierne* and *Isolda*, were frequent visitors to Dún Laoghaire in the 1960s and 1970s, but these were replaced by a large tug-like vessel, the *Grey Seal* and, more recently, another *Granuaile*. These vessels collect or deposit buoys and supplies at the waterfront depot, established here in 1875. The present depot maintains buoys, lights, beacons, markers and other equipment needed by the Irish Lights for the entire Irish coastline. Naturally, the two lighthouses at Dún Laoghaire are also under the care of the Irish Lights. As early as 1831, harbour master Hutchinson had sought financial aid to erect a fog bell on the East Pier. A manually operated bell hung for a long time in a wooden tower near the East Pier lighthouse. Sometimes a gun was used as a fog warning. By 1920, however, foghorns had been fitted to both lighthouses and the bell and gun were

A peaceful scene from the 1960s shows yachts on their moorings with an Irish Lights vessel beyond. This area is now occupied by the marina.

abandoned. Now both lighthouses are fully automated. In 2005 the Irish Lights moved from their premises in Dublin into purpose-built headquarters at Dún Laoghaire Harbour. The striking circular building with its sea-green tinted glazing, which echoes the shape of many navigational buoys, was designed by Scott Tallon Walker Architects (see photograph on p. 237).

The Kish is by far the most remarkable lighthouse in Dún Laoghaire's history. Work was begun on it in the Inner Coal Harbour in 1963. The first base built for the lighthouse broke apart in a gale and had to be towed from the Coal Harbour to Greystones where it now forms part of the south pier. The lighthouse was completed at St Michael's Wharf in 1965 and towed by three tugs to the Kish Bank on a calm June night. The principal contractors, Christiani and Neilsen, constructed this telescopic concrete lighthouse to designs based on Swedish prototypes. It contains comfortable accommodation for three and replaces the lightship which formerly was manned by about eight. A helicopter pad provides the means for rapid transport to or from the mainland.

Below left: The Kish lighthouse in Dún Laoghaire Harbour.

Below right: The Irish Lights vessel Granuaile, with the spire of the former Mariners' Church, now the National Maritime Museum, and the Lexicon Library to the left.

In 1992 the control and management of the harbour was transferred from the OPW to a limited company, which was comprised of councillors and local business interests. Five years later it received the status of a semi-state company, along with eight other ports but without the support of any regular state funding. Much attention was at first directed to the rebuilding of the ferry terminal, which was completed in 1997 and received an award for its design. The terminal building is today still in very good condition, but lies unused.

For many years much discussion took place with regard to developing a marina at Dún Laoghaire, and various plans were vigorously promoted by private interests. In 1992 a hydrographic survey of the harbour was carried out. It examined the geology of the seabed and addressed other issues, such as silting, in the context of future uses. A new harbour police boat named the *William Hutchison* was put into service.

In 2001 the new and very substantial marina was finally opened, and in the same year the Harbour Company decided to replace the destroyed Victoria fountain with an exact replica, which was unveiled in 2003. The Harbour Company continued to carry out exemplary conservation works in 2006 by restoring the East Pier bandstand and in the following year by resurfacing the pier itself. This ambitious project involved replacing the old concrete promenades with a semi-polished concrete surface containing seashells and pebbles. The result is most attractive and is appreciated on a daily basis by the thousands of people who walk the pier. In 2008 the old Harbour Commissioners' house, sometimes called Harbour Lodge rather than Harbour Office, was carefully restored as the Harbour Company's headquarters.

During the late 1990s Carlisle Pier, then almost 150 years old, became redundant and no clear agreement could be reached as to how it might be best used. In 2003, following an architectural competition, four ambitious schemes were shortlisted, including dramatic glass structures from architects such as Heneghan Peng and Daniel Libeskind. In the heady days of the economic boom, nobody gave much thought to mere details, such as cost or maintenance. Plans included a museum and an aquarium and, though very striking, were at odds with the Victorian character of the town. As it happened, the Lexicon Library would later adopt aspects of Carlisle Pier designs.

In 2018 the Harbour Company was disbanded and responsibilities taken over by Dún Laoghaire–Rathdown County Council.

Chapter 3

KINGSTOWN: INFANT CITY OF
THE STEAM AGE

The view of Dún Laoghaire from Killiney Hill is always evocative, although today houses stretch back towards the Dublin Mountains and green spaces are disappearing. In 1835 a correspondent for the *Dublin Penny Journal* described it as follows: '... beneath is Kingstown, an infant city, built in the most ornamental style, and still enlarging into dimensions of maturity, stretching away beyond its picturesque piers, the most picturesque bay in Europe spreads for miles'. About ten years earlier another writer had predicted

This romantic painting, dating from about 1850, shows the newly completed Kingstown Harbour and Dublin Bay in the background. Below the jagged rocks of Dalkey Quarry lie Dalkey village, Bullock and Sandycove and a chimney whose steam engine once powered the Atmospheric Railway.

that, 'the village will, probably at no distant day, expand into a town of much fashionable resort'. He was right. In one decade, 1825 to 1835, Kingstown changed from an old village into a new town. Apart from the construction of the new harbour, three important events stand out as responsible for this growth: the royal visit of George IV, the establishment of the mail packet service at Kingstown, and the opening of the Dublin-to-Kingstown railway line.

The royal visit to Dunleary in 1821, with its consequent name change to Kingstown, focused public attention on the new port and earmarked it for future development. Five years later, the establishment of the Kingstown-to-Liverpool mail packet service (and the later addition of the Holyhead service) secured the town's position as the principal mail and passenger link with England. The opening of the first railway line in Ireland between Dublin and Kingstown in 1834 greatly enhanced the town's potential as a resort or watering place. Thus by the mid-1830s Kingstown had become a desirable place to live. It was a centre of communication with the latest and fastest means of transport both on land and sea, meeting at one of the world's newest and finest artificial harbours.

ROYAL VISIT

Perhaps one of the most spectacular occasions in the early history of the harbour was the visit of King George IV in 1821. Dónal Ó Suilleabháin in *Ó Kingstown go Dún Laoghaire* describes in detail the preparations made for the king's arrival at Dunleary, where a pavilion, flags and banners, and Royal Slip stood waiting. (The Royal Slip was built in the inner angle of the East Pier, where it still exists.) Instead, he arrived without ceremony at Howth and only after a month's visit, when he decided to return home, did he visit Dunleary, leaving his name to the harbour and his title to the new town. A proclamation issued in 1821 records how King George IV, 'at the head of the Royal slip at Dunleary, now KINGS-TOWN', made his farewell speech. An engraving of the king embarking at Dunleary shows how rapidly the harbour was progressing. Amidst scores of yachts and ships, and a profusion of rigging and bunting, the more or less fully extended East Pier can be discerned, though it as yet lacked its masonry quays, promenades and walls. The print depicts all the usual worthies, such as the Lord Lieutenant, Lord Mayor of Dublin, nobility and gentry and some curious guests, including one 'Mr Kent on his aquatic velocipede' – a sort of half bicycle, half paddle board! There is also 'Commodore O'Brien from Kilrush on his Lilliputian yacht' – a dinghy, then unusual, rigged in the style of a big yacht. The king travelled to and from Ireland on the paddle steamer *Lightning*,

which was subsequently renamed *Royal Sovereign*, commanded by Captain Skinner. One of the Admiralty's best captains, Skinner was an early advocate of steam power in ships. (He unfortunately drowned off Holyhead in 1832 when he was swept off his steam-driven mail packet ship.)

An obelisk, called the George IV Testimonial, was erected near the harbour on Queen's Road in 1823 to commemorate the king's visit and the renaming of Dunleary. Built for £550 to the design of the stone contractor George Smith and engineer John Aird, it was later described by Thackeray (1874), perhaps unfairly, as 'a hideous Obelisk, stuck on four fat balls and surmounted with a crown on a cushion (the latter were no bad emblems perhaps of the Monarch in whose honour they were raised)'. Evidently, the persons responsible for blasting off one of the four 'fat balls' in the 1970s shared Thackeray's opinion. An iron support inside the ball saved the monument from collapse, and it was later repaired. The monument also records the laying of the first stone of the harbour in 1817 and the names of all its commissioners and engineers. The shaft, 15½ feet (4.7 metres) long, was cut from a single piece of granite, extracted from the quarry at Sandycove. An early print of the monument (see p. 31) shows that it originally stood perched between two rocks with a gap (now filled in) beneath. It also shows the railings around the base of the obelisk to be much higher, but levels have changed over the years and rock was removed when shelters were created beneath in the 1950s.

Above left: On 3 September 1821, King George IV departed from Ireland after a month-long stay. He left in great fanfare from the partially built harbour, which was then renamed the Royal Harbour at Kingstown.
Above right: Marine Parade, formerly Queen's Road, runs across the harbour frontage allowing fine views of the piers and bay. Seen here with the obelisk of 1823 and before the recent introduction of cluttering street furniture.

In 1816 the newly completed Howth Harbour received the first steam paddleships of the Irish Sea. These mail packets, as they were called, belonged to the Admiralty and carried mail and passengers between Howth, Holyhead and Liverpool. The packets used Howth until 1826 when they transferred to Kingstown, and a regular mailboat service plied the 103-kilometre route between Dún Laoghaire and Holyhead in Wales for a century and a half.

During the 1820s, the Harbour Commissioners regularly received applications from private steamship owners for permission to berth at Kingstown. Among such vessels were the *Ivanhoe* and the *Emerald Isle*. As early as 1821 a levy was proposed of 5d per passenger and 10d per horse and carriage to be paid to the Harbour Commissioners. Nonetheless, the commissioners seemed reluctant to allow this on a permanent basis.

In 1825 the need for a jetty for the Liverpool packets was discussed by the Harbour Commissioners and by 1827 a wharf had been built for £1,516. This wharf projects slightly from the East Pier and may still be seen near the present bandstand. At first, the wharf was reserved for the use of the Admiralty's mail packets (it seems that either the Admiralty or the Post Office had paid for the wharf). In 1828 the director of the City of Dublin Steam Packet Company, Mr J. Watson, applied for permission to use the Admiralty's packet jetty on the East Pier but was refused. The Admiralty continued to carry post office mail until 1850 when a new contract was made with the City of Dublin Steam Packet Company.

In 1837 the new and more commodious Victoria Wharf was constructed across the breast of the harbour. Named after the newly crowned Queen Victoria, the wharf accommodated packet boats and later Royal Navy troopships. Here in 1854 a famous and sad embarkation took place: 20,000 troops left Kingstown for the Crimean War. They returned in 1856 in much diminished numbers. This 150-metre wharf, later called St Michael's Wharf, and now buried beneath the redundant ferry terminal, gave direct access to the new railway station. This convenient arrangement was bettered only by Carlisle Pier, where passengers stepped straight off the ship onto the train. However, in January 1981, this efficient rail link was abandoned and the track filled in. A large cast-iron shed gave shelter to the passengers. This shed was engulfed by an ugly two-storey structure

THE PIER, DUN LOAGHAIRE

which formed the mailboat terminal for many years. The entire pier was cleared of buildings in the early 2000s and the iron shelter was also demolished.

The new Victoria Wharf enabled shippers like the City of Dublin Steam Packet Company to get a footing in Kingstown. It is a point of pride that for seventy years, between 1850 and 1920, this Irish concern ran with impeccable efficiency and safety one of the world's most impressive mailboat services. In 1850 they bought the *St Columba* and the *Llewellyn* from the Admiralty and, with two other vessels, ran a passenger service between Kingstown and Holyhead with an average passage time of four to five hours. The company also took over the mail service in that year. Soon there were calls for even more efficient quayside arrangements with a direct railway link. The present Carlisle Pier was erected to meet this need. A chart from 1857 shows very clearly the half-finished state of the new Carlisle Pier. When it was opened in 1859 a new contract was formed in which the passage time was reduced to three hours and forty-five minutes, with a penalty of 34s for every minute late. Four new vessels, all paddle steamers, the *Ulster, Munster, Leinster* and *Connaught*, each capable of 17½ knots, were built and came into service in the early 1860s.

Four new screw-propelled ships, also named after the four provinces, were commissioned in 1896 to replace the older paddle mailboats, and their average passage time was reduced to under three hours. They made two sailings a day, leaving Kingstown at 6.45am and 7.15pm.

In 1860 G.R. Powell wrote of Carlisle Pier, 'It has been but opened recently and is found a great convenience to mail and express steamers', adding, 'the centre is a groove into which run the special trains'. The idea of bringing the train out onto the

Above left: The captain of one of the four steam paddleships introduced in the 1860s confidently steers his vessel into Kingstown Harbour c. 1890. Note the sailor on the left operating the telegraph to instruct the engine room.

Above right: A queue of passengers and well-wishers at the mailboat was a familiar sight as many Irish people emigrated from Dún Laoghaire. This postcard of about 1960 shows a crowd stretching from Carlisle Pier all the way in front of the Royal St George Yacht Club.

A painting of the harbour c. 1860 by Richard Brydges Beechey (1808–95) showing a regatta day at the Royal St George Yacht Club. There is much interesting detail in the picture including the magnificent yachts and elegant spectators, the small paddleship ferry to Dublin, the numerous rowing boats, not to mention the granite steps, boat slips and other architectural features of the completed harbour.

pier to meet the passengers must have seemed a very advanced idea at the time. To the Victorian traveller, the eleven-hour journey from Dublin to London must have seemed an incredible feat.

A very interesting service was initiated in 1861 when a group of Kingstown residents, who were dissatisfied with the railway, took 'practical steps to remedy their grievances by starting opposition steamers and omnibuses'. From June 1861 two steamers – the *Kingstown*, bought for £3,600 and the *Dublin* costing £4,400 – plied regularly between the Custom House Quay and Kingstown. These steamers were described as being 'after the American fashion of deck over deck', and were painted white and green. One contemporary writer praised the steamers for their inexpensive fares and the luxury of being able to walk about and exchange the shelter of the saloon for the sea air. But the same writer also complained of the coal smuts, advocating cleaner-burning coke, and criticised the lack of accommodation for non-smoking passengers.

In the following year, *The Irish Builder* noted that, 'the advantages of sea communication between Dublin and Kingstown appear to be now fully established … and any question as to the seaworthy qualities of the "Kingstown" was completely set at rest last Easter Monday when, although it blew a whole gale throughout the day, she performed her trips with ease and regularity.' During the summer the *Kingstown* made evening excursions to Bray and Ireland's Eye. While it is hard to believe that the steamers could break even competing with the railway, their presence in Kingstown confirms that the town had time and money to devote towards leisure and novelty.

During the First World War, the *Ulster, Leinster, Munster* and *Connaught* (the latter was withdrawn in 1916 for use as a government troopship and later sunk) sailed regularly between Dún Laoghaire and Holyhead. They were obliged by their contract with the Post Office to maintain sailing despite the action of German U-boats in the Irish Sea. In 1917 the *Leinster* was narrowly missed by a torpedo, but on 10 October 1918 she was not so lucky: she was torpedoed 25 kilometres out from Kingstown and sank in ten minutes. Five hundred and one lives were lost, but 256 survivors were brought back to Kingstown by British destroyers. Many Dún Laoghaire people lost friends and relatives. (One survivor, a Mr T. Connolly, presented the National Maritime Museum in Dún Laoghaire with a large model of the *Leinster*.) The *Leinster* had had previous ill luck. In 1902 she rammed and sank the Kish lightship *Albatross* in thick fog, but fortunately there was no loss of life.

In 1920 the service was taken over by the English-run London North Western Railway (L&NWR, later London Mail Steamers, which became British Railways, later to be rebranded as Sealink). They introduced four new ships to the route – the *Anglia, Scotia, Hibernia* and *Cambria*. The *Cambria* and *Hibernia* survived the Second World War and were replaced in 1949 by newer mailboats of the same names, which disappeared from Dún Laoghaire Harbour only in 1976. The four ships of 1920 could sail at 25 knots, but the new *Cambria* and *Hibernia*, which were much larger than their predecessors, could make only 21 knots. They were among the first mailboats to have fully covered decks. The *Hibernia* was built by Harland & Wolff in Belfast and could take about 2,000 passengers. These ships were supplemented by the *Princess Maud*, an elegant but uncomfortable ship.

The mailboats have always been a subject of interest for Dún Laoghaire people, whose conversation was spiced by tales of a ramming of the pier or a long wait off the harbour during

The painter Admiral Beechey managed to capture a serene moment when the Leinster *entered Kingstown Harbour in 1868. The onlookers include a group of fishermen and a white naval pinnace.*

Above left: The mailboat Anglia *ploughs into a heavy sea on leaving Kingstown Harbour.*

Above right: The dainty Princess Maud *moored alongside Carlisle Pier, pictured in the 1960s.*

fog or gales. It was a long-standing Dún Laoghaire tradition to watch the departure and arrival of the mailboats: the mailboat turning or wearing round the wood-piled Carlisle Pier was a sight known to all. During the Second World War, the *Cambria* was attacked by a seaplane with torpedoes but escaped being hit.

In 1965 British Railways introduced a car ferry service between Dún Laoghaire and Holyhead, which meant that cars could be driven directly onto and off the ship instead of being lifted into the hold by crane. In that year the *Holyhead Ferry I*, which accommodated 150 cars, commenced sailings to Dún Laoghaire where she docked at a large temporary terminal, unfortunately sited on the East Pier. This arrangement caused much traffic congestion and inconvenience at the foot of the East Pier and around the National Yacht Club. Eventually a more permanent ferry terminal was built at St Michael's Wharf. The new car ferry ran simultaneously with the regular mailboat sailings and was augmented from time to time by other British Railways car ferries, such as the *Dover, Normandia* and *Caledonian Princess.* The success of the car ferry both contributed to and was the result of a tourist boom in Ireland that began in the 1960s. Paradoxically, the same boom and the fashion for bringing one's own car led to the decline of Dún Laoghaire's hotel trade. In 1951 there were eighteen established hotels in the town; half a dozen in 1981 and just two left by 2022. The latest challenge for these remaining hotels

Opposite top: *The almost completed Kish lighthouse moored off the East Pier in 1965, just before being towed out to the Kish Bank, and the mailboat Cambria at Carlisle Pier.*

Opposite bottom left: *Loading the mailboat: before the advent of car ferries, a limited number of cars were lifted by crane into the hold.*

Opposite bottom right: *The first car ferry was accommodated on the East Pier with a temporary ticket office, customs shed and ramp. Photo taken c. 1966.*

Above: *For a century, a train link met the mailboats on Carlisle Pier and transferred passengers to the city. Photo taken c. 1960.*

was, of course, temporary closure and the subsequent lockdown restrictions during the Covid-19 pandemic.

Plans for a large car ferry terminal in 1964 met with much opposition as they meant that the public would be deprived access to St Michael's Wharf, the old Depot Harbour and boat slip would be filled in, and the old Sailors' Home, then the Museum and headquarters of the National Maritime Institute of Ireland, would be demolished. However, as it seemed the most suitable site, the scheme went ahead. A new projecting pier with double berths, a large terminal building, a customs shed and offices for the harbour master were erected. Two large tarmac areas were provided for the arrival and departure of vehicles. The new pier was erected on circular concrete pillars, some of which, after only ten years, began to disintegrate in an alarming manner. However, the whole scheme was carefully executed and well planned, with a minimum of damage to the harbour environment. A sense of scale was preserved and some landscaping carried out. The new terminal was inaugurated in 1969.

The last large traditional ferry was the *St Columba*, which combined passenger, car and lorry traffic services between Dún Laoghaire and Holyhead. The *St Columba* was introduced in spring 1977 and could accommodate a peak load of 2,500 passengers and 335 cars or 36 forty-foot lorries. Though it lacked the grace of older ships, with its strange funnel and boxy superstructure, it provided comfortable seating and accommodation for all its passengers. *St Columba* cost £19 million (around €174 million today) and her average speed was only 19½ knots. The opening of the stern and bow allowed for greater speed and facility in loading, discharge and turnabout, though it could not make use of the existing ferry pier and ramps. An elaborate new ramp and ugly elevated roadway from Carlisle Pier to the car ferry terminal (erected by 1977 to facilitate the *St Columba* ferry) in front of the Royal St George Yacht Club was much criticised as an unjustifiable duplication of existing facilities and the structure was eventually removed.

In 1993 a high-speed catamaran ferry, the *Stena Sea Lynx*, came into service, which in turn was replaced just two years later by an even bigger high-speed ferry, the *Stena Explorer*. The new ship, which was also a catamaran, a boxy and most unnautical-looking vessel, could carry 375 cars and 1,500 passengers and could make the passage to Holyhead in ninety minutes – the fastest time since regular sailings began in the early nineteenth century. This ship was also to be the last ferry to sail between Dún Laoghaire and Holyhead. A completely revamped ferry terminal was designed in 1994 and further infill of the harbour took place to provide hard standing for cars and lorries. The new building, which was sensitively designed and fits in with the harbour environment, has sadly lain vacant since the closure of the ferry service in 2015.

THE DUBLIN-TO-KINGSTOWN RAILWAY

By about 1830, the imminent growth and prosperity of the new town must have seemed secure for in the following year the Dublin and Kingstown Railway Company issued shares to finance the construction of the first railway line in Ireland – one of the earliest commercial railways in the world. It opened in 1834 and was in full public use by 1835, at a cost of £340,000 (around €25 million today). The coming of the railway greatly enhanced Kingstown's potential as a resort, although the original intention had been primarily to create an efficient and cheap system of transporting merchandise to Dublin and only secondly to provide fast and safe transportation to Dublin for passengers of the mail packet ships.

The idea of a canal link between Kingstown Harbour and Dublin Port had received much attention and even some support. In 1825, for example, the engineer John Killaly proposed building both a large ship canal across the sands of Dublin Bay and a railway. Both plans were scrapped because of their costliness. By 1831, however, plans for a railway had won government approval and shareholders were invited to invest in the new company.

By June 1834, the railway was 'in a very advanced state' and by December it was opened to the public, with trains making the 9-kilometre journey in fifteen minutes. For

This special print issued during the 1840s by the printer Kirkwood illustrates ten views of Ireland's first railway and a route map. In this era just before photography, we see a topographical account or record of the railway, with embankments running through the sea in places, and the two new stations at Westland Row in Dublin and at Kingstown.

the fifteen months ending June 1836, an average of 4,000 passengers a day were carried, at single fares of 1s, 8d and 6d for first, second and third class respectively. The carriages were considered superior in comfort and finish to any in the British Isles. Mr Pierce Mahony of Gresham Terrace, legal advisor to the Dublin and Kingstown Railway Company, tried without success to bring over a royal party for the opening ceremony. However, the railway inauguration was celebrated with the publication of a set of prints made from drawings by the noted artist Andrew Nichol and accompanied by a full description of the railway. Some feeling of the excitement and novelty of Ireland's first railway is conveyed by this extract:

Hurried forward by the agency of steam, the astonished passenger glides, like Asmodeus, over the summits of the houses and streets of our city – presently is transported through green fields and tufts of trees – then skims across the surface of the sea, and taking shelter under the cliffs, coasts among the marine villas, and through rocky excavations, until he finds himself in the centre of a vast port, which unites in pleasing confusion the bustle of a commercial town with the amusements of a fashionable watering resort.

Dublin Penny Journal, December 1834

The first station stood at Salthill near Kingstown, but as early as 1836 the line was extended across the old harbour to its present terminus. A silver salver was presented by a group of citizens to one of the town's foremost developers, Mr T. Gresham, in recognition of his efforts to oppose this extension of the railway into Kingstown. The opposition obviously felt that such a noisy, dirty, modern contraption would scar the pleasant environment of Kingstown's new water-front. A compromise was reached and the railway did not cross in front of Gresham's new hotel and terrace of houses and the station did not obstruct his view of the harbour. The railway was extended, involving, as has already been mentioned, the demolition of the old Dunleary Coffee House and the Martello tower, as well as the division of the old harbour. In 1844 a second, experimental railway line known as the Atmospheric Railway was laid between Kingstown and Dalkey. The train operated by a suction pipe but was not very successful and the line was taken up ten years later. This project had prompted residents to object to Parliament in 1843 as they felt it would detract from their properties. However, the railway extension was kept in a low cutting where it would obstruct no views from the terraced houses.

LOCOMOTIVE ENGINE—DUBLIN AND KINGSTOWN RAILWAY.

The Hibernia, *one of the remarkable steam engines that pulled the trains, illustrated in 1834.*

The Kingstown Railway Station building, now Hartley's restaurant, stands at the bottom of Marine Road. In 1840 the board of the Dublin and Kingstown Railway Company resolved to build a new station to replace the seemingly inadequate 'Station House and Parcel Office'. The noted architect John S. Mulvany was appointed to prepare designs and estimates. Considerable debate arose over whether the building should be sited at the end of or beside the railway line. But by 1842, a contract was made with a builder named Roberts to erect the present station house at the end of the line for £2,800. This small one-storey building was completed in the mid-1840s. The granite facades are excellently executed, and Mulvany's usual play of architectural surfaces and planes is combined with a simple yet strong design. Mulvany inherited this neoclassical simplicity from the master James Gandon, architect of some of Dublin's finest buildings. One particular detail, a garland-draped roundel above each exit to the platform, is especially 'Gandonian' in style. The recessed entrance bay of the main facade, with its two clean-cut Ionic columns, was one of Mulvany's favourite compositional devices. The arrangement of the other facades, with pilasters and arcading, recalls Italian palace architecture of about 1500 –

The handsome Kingstown station house was completed by 1844 to the designs of J.S. Mulvany. The architect had to invent a new type of building and chose an Italianate villa as his model, quite in keeping with the neighbouring yacht clubs which were then evolving and which he also had a hand in designing.

an appropriately dignified style for such a new and perhaps not yet entirely respectable mode of transportation. The plan was simple and efficient, comprising a central ticket and parcel office in the main hall and flanking waiting rooms, which led onto the platforms by staircases. The most impressive surviving feature of the large terminal shed, completed in 1853, is its huge supporting wall. On the harbour side it is articulated horizontally by a vast granite cornice cantilevered into the wall and vertically by pilasters of jointed masonry. This fittingly powerful Italian palace-style cornice and wall helped conceal the iron and smoke of the steam age. The Kingstown station house is one of the finest secular stone buildings in the town. Railway sidings were later constructed to connect the traders' wharf, the Irish Lights depot and Victoria Wharf with the main rail network.

The Industrial Revolution played no small part in the early development of Kingstown and, as we have seen, the steam packet ships and the construction of Ireland's first railway were groundbreaking advances in the field of transport. Even aspects of the quarrying and delivery of stone to the harbour and the laying of stone blocks were assisted through advances in technology. The existence of the mailboat in Kingstown was as important in the nineteenth century as Dublin Airport is to the country today, and the royal visit of 1821 set the seal on the trajectory of the town and harbour, and triggered the rapid programme of building and expansion into surrounding areas.

Chapter 4

BIRTH OF A SEAPORT TOWN

HOUSEBUILDING AND THE VICTORIAN STYLE

Most of the detached houses of the area began to appear in the early nineteenth century, though as we shall see there were some eighteenth-century houses in Dalkey and in the hinterland of Dún Laoghaire. There were a few older farmhouses and the occasional residence, such as Corrig Castle, already in existence. The noted excursionist Thomas Cromwell, who visited Dunleary before 1820, described the new growth of houses in the area: 'Indeed from the pure air, dry soil and bold coast of this vicinity, Dunleary has become generally preferred as a summer residence to places nearer Dublin – the villas lately erected around are distinguished by no common degree of neatness, or even elegance.' By 1837, Samuel Lewis observed that, 'the immediate neighbourhood is thickly studded with elegant villas and handsome residences of the wealthy citizens of Dublin'. These quotations and the evidence of early maps of the area, such as Taylor (1816) or Duncan (1821), both point to the increasing residential popularity of the south side of Dublin Bay in the first decades of the nineteenth century, even before the harbour had been started. In 1800 a Dublin speculator erected Montpelier Parade, a large terrace of three-storey houses, in what was then comparatively wild countryside between Blackrock and Monkstown. The first terraces in Kingstown were built around 1832. These houses followed the form and style of earlier Georgian houses in Dublin, though they were less elaborate and had cement-rendered facades instead of brick ones. Certain features remained in vogue up till the 1850s, such as the steps to a pillared

*Above left: Holmston House, a fine early Victorian residence built in Kingstown's hinterland, still stands but has lost its once-extensive grounds. **Above right:** Lodge Park, off Tivoli Road, is one of the few surviving detached houses in Dún Laoghaire of early nineteenth-century date. **Below left:** The terraced houses of Adelaide Street followed the Dublin Georgian model of two or three storeys over basement and were ornamented with pillared doorcases and fanlights. **Below right:** Originally called Myrtle Lodge, then Echo Lodge, this house became a Dominican Convent in the mid-nineteenth century. Photographed here in the 1990s, it is now the site of Bloomfields Shopping Centre and the studio of Dance Theatre Ireland.*

front door and the leaded fanlight. The usual layout consisted of kitchen, scullery and coal cellar in the basement, reception rooms at ground-floor or first-floor level, and bedrooms above or in the return, or back extension. Some houses had a coach house and stables but, as the century progressed and public transport improved, they became less commonplace.

The detached residences described by Cromwell might have been houses such as Corrig Castle, Corrig House, Fairyland and Echo Lodge. Corrig Castle was known as the oldest house in the town for it dated back to the time of Rocque's maps of the mid-eighteenth century. It stood at the head of Northumberland Avenue, a vast imposing building with a battlemented roofline and rough Tudor-style mouldings. The clumsy 'medieval' style of this rambling mansion was probably the work of the nineteenth century, but little is known about its origins. The castle was subdivided into two residences during the nineteenth century and housed Belgian refugees during the First World War. It was demolished in about 1938 and a small estate of bungalows was built on the grounds. Just east of the castle was Corrig House, of late Georgian type, built in about 1815. It was plain in style and consisted of two storeys over a basement. Corrig House remained a private residence until the 1880s when it became the Corrig School and was much altered. It was originally approached from George's Street by a long and stately drive, which subsequently became Corrig Avenue. The house, with its two gate lodges, have all been demolished.

Echo Lodge was also built around this time and was already standing in 1816 when it appears on Taylor's map as Myrtle Lodge. It was later incorporated into the buildings of the Dominican Convent off George's Street Lower. Two large wings were added to the house after its purchase by the Dominicans in 1847. The Georgian-style house and Victorian convent buildings were demolished to make way for the Bloomfields Shopping centre. Fairyland, at the top of York Road, still remains but in much altered form. Built before 1816, it was once a Georgian-style brick house, and was the home of architect and builder John Semple, who with his son is credited with the magnificent later remodelling of Monkstown Church. It is now cement rendered and is a residence of the Christian Brothers. Several houses situated about the top of York Road also date from this early period. Airhill seems to have originated as a farmhouse, and Racefield probably took its name from the old race fields or courses once located nearby. Opposite Racefield on Tivoli Road is a pair of charming four-windowed houses known as Tivoli Parade. They appear on Taylor's 1816 map and their Georgian-style facades are fronted by handsome wrought-iron railings. Most of the large houses of nearby Tivoli Terrace South were built in the 1830s and, standing on high ground, all possessed fine views of the bay. Tivoli House, for example, was a plain detached residence with a pillared front door. In 1835 it was occupied by Alderman Arthur Perrin. It was demolished in 1977.

Lodge Park and Primrose Hill, both situated near Tivoli Road, are further examples of the town's first detached houses and date from about 1830. Such houses were always occupied by what were known as the 'first' residents of the town, generally wealthy professional people. The well-known grocers and spirit dealers Findlaters, who would eventually have a chain of shops all over Dublin, at one time owned Primrose Hill, a house of irregular plan with Regency character. During the 1820s, a wealthy priest, the Rev. B. Sheridan, took up duties in St Michael's Church and built Lodge Park, a house with elegant stucco additions, such as a lion and urns. Lodge Park was set in extensive grounds in which the three houses of Durham Place were built in 1840 and the large St Joseph's Orphanage was erected in 1860.

The two finest houses of Kingstown were built by George Smith, the stone contractor for the harbour. Smith, as we already know, had access to as much fine Dalkey granite as he wanted and with it he built two residences: Granite Hall and Stoneview.

Stoneview stands overlooking the centre of Clarinda Park, now divided into separate residential units, and Granite Hall (or Fortwilliam as it was sometimes known) stood eastward of Glenageary Hill on the elevation above the harbour. Both houses were erected about 1821. George Smith moved into Granite Hall, while his son Samuel lived at

Stoneview. Stoneview consists of a two-storey central block flanked by wings whose ends are curiously curved. The quirky neoclassical detailing of the fine masonry is noteworthy. For example, the central bay of the house is crowned by a curious pediment and the entrance columns are tucked into a recess in the facade. These strange stonework features are also found in the Harbour Commissioners' house, which Smith also built.

Like Stoneview, Granite Hall was characterised by neoclassical severity. Once again, plain recessed columns ornamented the front door. The facade featured two bow-shaped end bays. When demolished, some of the curved masonry was used in improvements at Sandycove Harbour.

Granite Hall was repute to have cost George Smith upwards of £10,000, an enormous sum for the period. The vast expense is indicative of the quality of this large two-storey house, the finest in the town, which was unfortunately demolished in the 1950s. A handsome gate lodge with a good neoclassical portico of fluted pillars survives on Glenageary Hill. During the 1830s the Commissioner of the Metropolitan Police, the Right Honourable J. Lewis O'Ferrall, took the house and it passed to his daughter, widow of the O'Conor Don, an ancient Irish family from County Roscommon. In the 1920s the grounds were cut back for the building of Rosmeen Gardens. They were further diminished when M.P. Kennedy, the next owner of Granite Hall, built Rosmeen Park.

The existence of these detached residences, from Granite Hall across to Tanyland, marked the development of a building line along the elevated rear of Kingstown. With the exception of the two Smith houses, the others were constructed of rubble stone and were faced with Roman cement. The absence of brick in construction and decoration may be explained by the ready supply of unwanted stone which would have been left over from the harbour works.

The earliest recorded Kingstown addresses of well-to-do Dubliners can be traced in the street directory of 1832. By this time some of the first terraced houses had been built. Near the harbour, the two-storeyed terraces of Roby Place and Sussex Parade (Marine Road) were already occupied, mainly by professional people, including lawyers, surgeons and naval captains. During the early 1830s, a great many wealthy residents maintained both Kingstown and Dublin addresses. In Sussex Parade, for example, an attorney named Farley and an agent for Globe Insurance named Patterson both had Dublin addresses. The eight houses of Sussex Parade, the town's first terrace, line Marine Road, the principal thoroughfare which rises from the harbour. They are of a simple two-storey-over-basement plan. The entrances are decorated by the traditionally Georgian arrangement of stone columns and fanlight. The hall and rooms are small in scale but more space is created in the return – this projection at the rear was a common device in all Kingstown street building for the rest of the century. The presence of quite sizeable front gardens, often close to the busiest localities, is a special feature of the town, which emphasises the strongly residential atmosphere of Dún Laoghaire.

With the establishment of a more efficient mail packet service to Holyhead by the 1830s there was a growing demand for overnight accommodation in Kingstown. One of the earliest and most substantial buildings to be erected in the town was Hayes's Royal Hotel, which opened for business in 1828 and was originally referred to as Mr Gresham's Hotel. He was already well known as the owner of the Gresham Hotel in Dublin and his investment in Kingstown was certainly a vote of confidence in the new town and harbour. The new hotel was three storeys over basement in height and twelve windows wide, with steps up to a double entrance of fluted Doric columns. With its small-paned

The houses on Marine Road are set back from the road, with No. 4 presenting an elegant arched gateway to the front garden.

windows it had all the appearance of a large Georgian house, but it contained many bedrooms and private drawing rooms with sea views. At the rear, there was superior five-stall stabling for livery with lock-up coach houses. There was also a large coffee room and smaller parlours, which were used for dining. An advertisement in *The Freeman's Journal* of 7 August 1828 stated that a turtle, weighing 80 lb (36 kg), would be served for dinner along with 'the most superior wines'. A bill from the hotel dated 1838 gives an idea of the cost of staying there overnight. An apartment cost £1, wax lights 2s, two dinners 8s, two children's board 7s, two maids' board 3s 6d. The same gentleman racked up a bill of more than £40 for post horses over a period of three months, which included the hire of pairs of horses and the washing of carriages.

Not everyone was impressed with all aspects of the new town: the topographer D'Alton, writing in 1838, bemoaned the haphazard development of the new town, but excepted some of the new terraces: 'Amongst which, Gresham Terrace, with the Royal Hotel, a spacious, elegant and well-conducted establishment, is particularly striking, having in front a fine plot of ornamented ground, with a terraced walk over looking the busied sea.' Gresham Terrace was built by the hotelier Thomas Gresham at a cost of about £35,000 (about €2.5 million in today's money). A square, which would have incorporated the present Royal Marine Gardens, Pavilion Gardens and Moran Park into one formal park, was planned for the front. But Victoria Square, as it was to be called, never materialised. Instead, in 1834 the town commissioners were empowered to purchase lands 'for the purpose of being adapted as public walks and gardens'. The residents of Gresham Terrace were to pay a special levy towards the square, but would receive a key free of charge. Other inhabitants would have to pay 20s per annum for use of the park. At these rates, it was hardly a 'public' park. Interestingly, the 1834 Act which established the town commissioners was drawn up by Pierce Mahony, a solicitor who owned one of the Gresham Terrace houses and was involved with the railway.

Gresham Terrace ran at right angles to Sussex Parade, and was demolished in its entirety in 1974 to make way for the new shopping centre. Its nine houses, which were aligned with the old Royal Hotel, occupied the most commanding site in the town. The terrace was designed in 1832 by George Papworth and was completed and fully occupied by 1838. The roofline was ornamented by a fine Georgian-style iron rail, some of which was saved at the time of demolition by Mr D.H. Gillman and was part of his extensive Dún Laoghaire collection. In order to make the best of the view, the houses were built high, consisting of three storeys over a basement and a flat-roofed viewing promenade. As already noted, the facades of the Gresham Terrace houses followed the pattern in Dublin with its rows of Georgian houses, though various features that were soon to become typically Victorian are in evidence. Firstly, in place of brick the facades were surfaced in Roman cement, allowing scope for applying thick but simple window mouldings and

A print advertisement for Hayes's Royal Hotel. The hotel's construction in 1828 was an early vote of confidence in the new town and harbour.

HAYES'S ROYAL HOTEL, KINGSTOWN.

banding on the lower storeys. With very few exceptions, all fashionable houses built in Kingstown up to the end of the century were finished in the same Roman cement, which was either left in its natural dull grey or was soberly painted in a natural stone colour. (A contemporary lease of De Vesci Terrace states that all houses were to be painted thus.)

Gresham Terrace was always occupied by the well-to-do and gentry. In the 1830s Earl Annesley, the Lord Bishop of Dromore, Major General Sir Edward Blakeney, Earl Norbury, Gibton, Glascott Symes MD and the Rev. G.H. Wall lived there. In her book, *Green and Gold*, Mary Hamilton paints an evocative picture of how life was ordered within the rooms of such houses:

> … a cool, green-walled drawing room; a solitaire board, with its brown and gold shot marbles, standing on the bottom shelf of a walnut what-not; a musical box that played tinkling tunes, its works visible through a glass top; hanging from the bell-pull Aunt Caroline's straw workbag with 'Mentone' embroidered across it in vivid wool ... In the mornings my aunts would sometimes spend an hour or two sewing, in what they called the Breakfast room – the room was never used for breakfast, but was kept for needlework and writing – here Aunt Caroline would sit at her rosewood davenport, penning innumerable letters to relations in her small, neat hand ... in the afternoons at Kingstown Aunt Caroline would take us visiting. We would climb up the high steps of house after house calling and leaving cards on people, many of whom were out.

Such were the occupations of many a lady resident of the new Kingstown terraces.

In the 1840s a succession of terraces sprang up all over Kingstown. Haddington Terrace, 'with its bower windows and tasteful Elizabethan architecture', was begun in 1835. It stood on high ground between the Mariners' Church and the seafront. Three years later the terrace was finished, although it was extended from eight to twelve houses in the 1840s. It is hard to appreciate what the topographers Lewis and D'Alton, writing in 1837 and 1838 respectively, meant by 'Elizabethan'. They presumably referred to the early use of wood-panelled bay windows or oriels which were applied to two storeys of the facade. Such bay windows became an almost standard feature of Kingstown houses in the 1860s and 1870s. These windows permitted sidelong vistas and for this reason were to become very popular in houses on avenues which otherwise lacked sea views. The device, derived from Tudor architecture, was originally popularised in English seaside resorts, such as Brighton. The composition of the terrace as a whole may be seen in Newman's print of Kingstown (early 1850s) where each end house and the two centre houses

project forward. Each of the front doors is treated with a very handsome projecting Ionic portico, while the plain windows were originally ornamented with hood mouldings. It is regrettable that two of the houses were demolished in the late 1970s. However, the facade of the new building approximately reproduced the features of the rest of the terrace, so avoiding an unsympathetic interruption of the visual integrity of the whole seafront. Much more intrusive interventions would later come which were to break the Victorian harmony of the Dún Laoghaire skyline.

Apart from the dignified seafront terraces, many shorter rows and terraces of distinctive houses were erected in the 1830s along and near George's Street. For example, by 1834 six houses at Mellifont View, five at Merville Place, two at Mount Clarence and six at Anglesea View had been erected along George's Street Upper. These were generally medium-sized, double-fronted, two-storey houses and though they were plain, they usually managed to muster some kind of pillared doorway which was intended to evoke an air of Georgian grandeur for their middle-class occupants.

An unusually pleasant feature of Dún Laoghaire's main street is that, like Marine Road, it remains partly residential with well-kept front gardens of flowers, shrubs and trees. Mount Haigh, Mount Clarence and Leinster Terrace preserve this feature, although Anglesea Place and its long railed front gardens was swallowed up by the construction of

Part of architect George Papworth's elevation of Gresham Terrace. Situated at the centre of Kingstown beside the Royal Marine Hotel and St Michael's Church, it was regarded as the best address in Kingstown.

Lee's, the town's first department store, which opened in 1906. Merville Place disappeared in stages: first with the erection of the Adelphi Cinema and later with the demolition of the rest of the terrace in about 1970.

Streets such as Northumberland Avenue, Mulgrave Street, Patrick Street and York Road present a mixture of one- and two-storey, plain-fronted Victorian houses. These are usually enhanced by good iron railings, fanlights and columns about the door. The columns were usually made of timber and were painted. Here, the cottage type is also noteworthy in featuring large-scale architectural elements, such as big window frames and doorways, which were calculated to aggrandise what were really quite small and ordinary dwellings. Sometimes these houses appeared as a one-storey building at street level, but rose to two storeys in the return. Examples of these are to be found in Mulgrave Street. The houses of Northumberland Avenue, however, belong to a different category as most have basements, and the front doors are approached by a flight of broad granite steps. They are simple in character and vary in height and size, but combine to produce a pleasant residential avenue of unassuming and well-mannered Victorian houses.

Mulgrave Mall is a terrace of eight double-fronted houses at the top of Northumberland Avenue. They are similar to those of Sussex Parade, two storeys over a basement, and are set well back from the road. Built in 1838, they are plain, except for their doorways of classical columns and attractive fanlights. Nos 34–35 Northumberland Avenue, known as Mount Irwin, comprise two houses with small-paned, tall-proportioned windows, which give them a Georgian appearance.

Below left: An attractive wrought-iron gate in the pattern of crossed arrows, from Brighton Avenue, Monkstown. Similar gates were erected elsewhere such as at the houses of Rus-in-Urbe, Glenageary Hill.
Below right: The delightfully quirky curved flight of steps at Northumberland Avenue allows for a tradesman's entrance below. This house served as the premises of G.A. Stevens, the noted firm of house removers.

Mulgrave Terrace East and Rus-in-Urbe are located at the top of Mulgrave Street and on Lower Glenageary Road respectively. Though erected in about 1843, they perpetuate the plain but elegant Georgian style which was popular in the 1830s.

The hilly slope of Dún Laoghaire's hinterland produces a varied effect in the streets and avenues which, like Northumberland, Adelaide and Corrig, run inland and upward from the sea. The houses and groups of houses are staggered in height as they mount the hill. The descent of these uphill streets, such as Glenageary Hill or York Road, presents another pleasing aspect of Dún Laoghaire – the appearance of a sea view in the distance. The intense building activity of the 1830s and the assured development of the town was witnessed by the fact that a Dublin-based business, M.M. Dowling's Timber and Slate Yards, had moved from the city to Crofton Place by 1839. The Top Hat Ballroom was erected on the site of Webster's Flag, Brick and Marble Yards. Webster, whose business was flourishing in the 1850s, built the adjoining brick terrace known as Webster's Place.

This classic Victorian terraced house, with stucco front, pillars and fanlight with decorative railings and ironwork scrolls on the window sills, made its appearance in Kingstown in about 1840.

It can be seen therefore that by the early 1840s Kingstown had experienced a house-building boom and much of the character of the present town had already been laid down.

DEVELOPMENT OF THE NEW TOWN

As we have seen, the initial growth of the new town began near Old Dunleary. As early as 1817 new buildings clustered around the crossroads of George's Street, York Road, Cumberland Street and Clarence Street. By this time the layout of present-day George's Street, Marine Road, Park Road and Crofton Road was already established and is shown in Rennie's plan for the harbour of 1817 (see p. 19). Tivoli Road, Dún Laoghaire's oldest thoroughfare, was probably formed in medieval times as part of a route between Monkstown and Bullock castles. It was more recently known as 'the back road'. Until the 1830s there was much random building between Tivoli Road and the harbour, concentrating along and off George's Street. In 1826 the writer of an Irish guide, *The Beauties of Ireland*, noted the rapid growth 'in every direction' and commented on the general bleakness of the place. But he added that, 'the sea views present some of the boldest features of the bay, in combinations highly picturesque'. It was this obvious potential for exploiting the view which drew the first serious developers to Kingstown.

The 1831 census reported that there were 5,736 inhabitants in Kingstown. At that time the town was still without any planned development. In 1834, however, an Act was passed 'for paving, watching, lighting, regulating and otherwise improving the town of Kingstown,' eighteen town commissioners were elected by the ratepayers and were empowered to control many aspects of the town's development. This body, which first met in the old Royal Hotel, was financed by a levy raised on the town's property owners, excluding the Harbour Commissioners. The town commissioners had authority to regulate the width of streets and to organise their paving, naming and cleansing. They could 'enter into agreement relative to the line, direction or mode of erecting, altering or building of any houses', in any existing street or future street in the town. Furthermore, 'no old building is to be altered or new building to be erected, without notice (of five days) to the Clerk of the Commissioners'. They also had the power to control extensions and projections from buildings, such as bay windows or balconies, and they laid down specified thicknesses (9 inches (23 cm) for brick and 18 inches (46 cm) for stone) for party walls between houses and buildings. The commissioners could levy fines and demolish buildings that contravened the set regulations. Though many of these enactments, such as those regarding sanitation and the fire service, remained unsatisfactory until the end of the nineteenth century, in general the Act was successful in improving the streets and buildings of the town.

The general spaciousness of Dún Laoghaire's streets was much improved by the commissioners' power to have irregular or projecting buildings set back in line with houses or the rest of the street. Prior to 1834, people could build where and how they liked. It is also interesting that the use of thatch was forbidden, even for outhouses. In the slums of Kingstown, such as those near York Road Lower and what is now Convent Road, the commissioners were less particular about enforcing these enactments. Some of these districts remained unsanitary webs of cabins and third-rate dwellings until the turn of the twentieth century.

Street names in Kingstown contributed much to the image that had been established by the first royal visit of 1821. Much of the town's nomenclature had its origins in English titles and honoured various lord lieutenants of Ireland. Streets and terraces bear the names of the Marquis of Anglesey (1828), Duke of Northumberland (1829), Earl of Haddington (1834), Earl of Mulgrave (1836), Earl of Eglinton (1852) and Earl of Carlisle (1855). Similarly, the names of the Dukes of Clarence, Cumberland, Sussex, Connaught, York and Wellington were used, as was that of Queen Victoria; terraces were named after the developers Gresham and Crofton and the town's ground landlords, Longford and de Vesci. Kelly's Avenue and Rumley Avenue were named after local families. Thomas Rumley, once president of the Royal College of Surgeons, was born in Dunleary where his father worked for the Revenue Commission. In 1832 he diagnosed a case of cholera in Kingstown, for which he was stoned by the inhabitants. In the mid-nineteenth century, Rumley Avenue was renamed Mulgrave Street and Kingstown Avenue became Patrick Street. Paradise Row, in the middle of a poor area, became Convent Road at about the same time. More exotic names like Tivoli and Rus-in-Urbe were suggestive of Italy and the finer airs of the Mediterranean. Excepting the original Dún Laoghaire, or names like Glenageary or Corrig, only a few other Gaelic-based names exist. For instance, a long-forgotten townland name for what became Royal Terrace – Kilahulks – survives only in an old lease. The profoundly English-derived nomenclature of Dún Laoghaire is a noteworthy part of the town's history and of its Victorian personality.

No part of Dún Laoghaire's past has disappeared or changed more than its shops and businesses. None of the earliest shop buildings survive, but some are known from old photographs and prints. J. Kavanagh, 'Apothecary and Chemyst to the Lord Lieutenant', established in 1825, was one of the town's most noted businesses in the nineteenth century. The firm had two beautiful shops: the first was later occupied by Perry's Yacht Chandlers and the second, located on George's Street Upper, stood opposite Dempsey's Butchers. Both shops were well decorated with stucco and ironwork and were lavishly embellished in the 1850s. The older shop, which was described in 1880 as 'an elegant structural feature of the thoroughfare', is pictured in a billhead of the 1850s (see p. 84). Its delicate arched windows were filled with new plate glass and framed by Corinthian pilasters. Above, a large royal escutcheon was flanked by windows with broad mouldings and projecting corners while the roofline was made up of a stone balustrade and pediment. The second shop displayed an equally ornate array of stucco pilasters, cornices, urns, an elaborate

From top: A late nineteenth-century cast-iron inspection cover, stamped with the initials of Kingstown Town Council; T.W. Little were plumbers and sanitation engineers in Kingstown; municipal coat of arms of Kingstown Town Council.

All street names were to be 'fixed, placed, marked or painted on some conspicuous part of some house, wall, corners or entry' by the town commissioners, who also had responsibility for numbering every shop, warehouse and building in the town.

royal coat of arms and an ironwork balcony. The George's Street Upper premises remained as a chemist until the 1950s, although it had been passed from the Kavanagh to the Corbett and then the Suche family. There are only two remaining shopfronts in Dún Laoghaire which in their upper facades recall the elegance of Kavanagh's chemists: the upper storey of No. 70 George's Street Lower, the former Pier Inn, displays ornate quoins, pilasters, elaborate window surrounds and roofline urns. Similarly the upper part of No. 41 George's Street Lower contains rich decorative mouldings. At one time, many of the shops in Dún Laoghaire were ornamented in this manner, and here and there old signboards and carved wooden consoles survive. It is regrettable that the tradition of harmonious frontages was so disregarded in many twentieth-century replacements, though in recent decades the standard of design has generally improved. Overlarge and unsympathetic signs that do not fit the overall facade were all too common. Many shopfronts still bear no relationship to the storey above, or to their neighbours, and the job is left to builders or carpenters with no design experience. The attractive integrity of all the old shops was created by a sensitivity to scale and detail and the use of restrained decoration and colour.

From the early 1830s, Kingstown boasted a wide variety of shops including several victuallers, taverns, boot- and shoemakers, and grocers. In 1832 there was also a chandler, a linen draper, a confectioner and three chemists. The establishment of the mail packet service at Kingstown no doubt created the confidence to establish, almost simultaneously, three very substantial hotels. In 1830 it was considered the most expensive place in Ireland for food and lodging. Hayes's Royal Hotel and Kelly's Kingstown Royal Harbour Hotel were the town's first hotels. About a year later, a Mr Rathbone established the Anglesea Arms Hotel, which overlooked the harbour on Crofton Road. Kelly's Hotel in George's Place is a plain two-storey house, once occupied by the engineers of Dún Laoghaire Corporation. By the mid-1830s they were joined by several others, some an amalgam of 'Hotel, Tavern, and Coffee House'. In Old Dunleary, for instance, the new railway gave rise to the modishly named Dublin and Kingstown Railway Hotel and Tavern, an establishment which subsequently became the Salthill Hotel.

The publican's trade was undoubtedly boosted by the presence of so many harbour employees, for there were always plenty of vintners and taverns in Kingstown. By the early 1830s, there were several noted public houses, including Long's Royal Harbour Tavern, Frost's Hibernian Tavern and Dockerall's King's Arms Tavern, and other premises under the still well-remembered names of Smyth, Leonard and Rooney.

In 1834 the noted firm of Alexander Findlater established an Irish and Scotch Whiskey

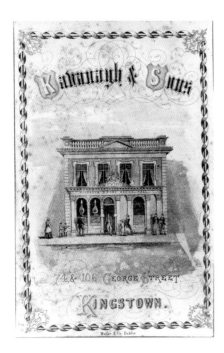

Store in Kingstown – a shop that became the town's most high-class grocer, a position it retained until the introduction of supermarkets in the 1960s. Findlaters catered for a new class of resident: the occupants of the terraces and detached houses at the back of the town. Equally, the arrival in 1836 of a merchant tailor, run by McComas and Sons of Dublin, indicated that a substantial well-to-do clientele had already settled in the town.

A great number of craftsmen, tradesmen and small shopkeepers also settled in the town and, by 1839, there were in George's Street Lower alone: nine vintners and taverns, five shoemakers, ten grocers and provisioners, three victuallers, five bakers, four dairies, two carpenters, seven drapers, tailors and clothes shops, one apothecary, two plumbers, two confectioners, two glass and delph stores, two poulterers, two surgeons, two painters, a saddler, a stationer, a tallow chandler, a hairdresser, a cooper, a dyer, a gun maker, a bell-hanger and even a painter of miniatures. Another new street, Kingstown Avenue (now Patrick Street), was well populated by a similar class of tradesmen, including ten shoemakers. Though the town commissioners were empowered to establish markets 'for the sale of all kinds of flesh and other raw victuals, fish and live or dead poultry or game, butter, herbs, roots, fruit, or garden stuff' and had the right to fine anyone who had 'unwholesome provisions exposed for sale', no market house was ever built. To this day, a covered public market place is wanting, a much-needed facility which could perhaps be accommodated in the new Myrtle Square public space.

Above left: An elegant illustrated trade card for J. Kavanagh.

Above right: A photograph of the late 1890s showing the junction of George's Street with Marine Road, with the highly ornamented premises of Redmonds' wine merchants on the corner. A profusion of carved brackets, gilded lettering, canopies and decorative ironwork was the norm in these Victorian shopfronts. Window displays and large retractable awnings were a feature of the street.

*Above left: Findlaters'
remarkable three-faced public
clock, dating from the early
1900s, was a landmark in
Dún Laoghaire until its
disappearance in the 1970s
when the building was sold to
Penneys.*

*Above right: Findlaters'
original premises at the corner
of George's Street Lower
and Sussex Street (now
Eblana Avenue), displaying
a handsome two-faced clock,
c. 1890s.*

CHURCHES

Dún Laoghaire has been graced by a great number and variety of churches. By the end of the nineteenth century, the town and its close surroundings had three large Roman Catholic churches, five of the Church of Ireland and four more of separate denominations. Several of these congregations owed their origin to the maritime tradition of the town. It is claimed that before the first St Michael's Church was built in 1824, masses held on the convict hulk *Essex* were attended by members of the public. However, since the *Essex* housed convicts awaiting deportation, it seems unlikely that members of the public would have been allowed aboard. Alternatively, Kingstown parishioners had to go to the nearest Catholic church at Cabinteely. The Scottish engineers who supervised the harbour works were Presbyterians, and they established their first church on York Road in 1828. The first Methodist church was set up in 1836 by Torbay fishermen who had settled here. In the same year, an Anglican church, specially dedicated to the seafaring community, was opened and called the Mariners' Church.

St Michael's, Kingstown's oldest and most centrally situated church, dating from the 1820s, was a plain rectangular building adjoined on the northeast by a simple square stone belfry with corner buttresses topped by pinnacles. In 1869 the church underwent the first stage of enlargement and embellishment. The architect of the new church was J.J. McCarthy, who had erected such fine Puginesque Gothic churches as Maynooth College

Chapel and Armagh Cathedral. Low aisles were added and a clerestory of small pointed windows, filled with tracery, was inserted into rough-textured stone walls. The transepts and chancel were extended in 1892 and the original square tower had to be demolished. The new chancel walls were richly decorated with murals and marble shafts and a beautiful east window was presented by the Crosthwaite family. The facade displayed two matching turrets.

The spire is the only part of St Michael's which remains today after the tragic destruction of the church by fire in 1966. A collection of photographs taken of the ruins of the burnt-out church reveals that the external structure was very little damaged by the fire, although the columns of the nave were seriously degraded. No doubt a different decision would be taken today and the Victorian church would probably have been restored. The spire, with its simple profile, free of cluttering pinnacles, was designed by J.L. Robinson and was added in the 1890s. The spacious apertures of the bell chamber, which are filled with tracery, and the smaller opening of the tall spire, contribute to the elegance which makes it the town's most memorable landmark. A major conservation project was undertaken in 2004 after it was discovered that some of the carved Portland stone tracery and mouldings in the tower and spire were rapidly decaying. St Michael's was in many ways similar in style to Glasthule Church, built in 1867. Both reflect the designs of Pugin, who had formulated an appropriately Roman Catholic style of Gothic based on French prototypes. This style distinguished itself clearly from the English Gothic that Protestant churches generally adopted. Glasthule, for example, displays the typically French rose window in its highly ornamental cut-stone facade.

The first Presbyterian church on York Road was a rectangular building, whose facade has a fine stone cornice and three large round-arched windows finished with granite mouldings. This church served the Presbyterian community until 1863 when the present church just across the road was completed. A large granite slab in the grounds of the new church records the completion in 1828 of the old one. This handsome building is now a

MARINE ROAD. DUN LAOGHAIRE (KINGSTOWN)

A postcard of the 1920s showing St Michael's Church on Marine Road, Dún Laoghaire. The clean, uncluttered appearance of the street is striking.

Below left: The dramatic scene of firefighters attempting to quell the 1966 fire at St Michael's Church.

Below right: The dazed public watched in dismay as St Michael's Church burnt.

training centre and was latterly used by Dún Laoghaire Vocational Education Committee and served for a time as Dún Laoghaire College of Art. The foundation stone for the new church was laid in 1861 and the contracting firm of Cockburn was employed as architect and builder, and was instructed to reproduce exactly Rathgar Presbyterian Church, which it had just completed. Cockburn, who had built some of the best Victorian buildings in Ireland, including Carlow Courthouse, had also built the houses of nearby Vesey Terrace, the Congregational Church on Northumberland Avenue, St John's at Mountown, and had the contract for the Royal Marine Hotel.

The design of the new Presbyterian church is interesting. It was raised up above a ground-floor hall, a measure that not only economises on space and heating but also, by lifting it up off the ground, gives the whole building added grace. The plan is comprised

of a short chancel, slight transepts and a nave with a gallery to the back under which is the entrance vestibule. The entire exterior is executed in jointed stonework and is vertically articulated by buttresses and tracery-filled Gothic windows. The stone tracery of the large east window and at the base of the spire is particularly refined. The elegant tower and spire are carefully proportioned and light in feeling, the ashlar stonework of the needle-like spire contrasting nicely with the rougher masonry of the tower.

In June 1863 'the new Scotch church at Kingstown' was officially opened by a visiting preacher, the Rev. Vernon White of Liverpool, who was paid 30s for his travelling expenses on the steamer. Amongst those who had endowed the church building was the well-known Findlater family, who lived nearby in The Slopes, a large house set in beautiful grounds (sadly, demolished in 1978). Both the old and new Presbyterian church buildings are set back in grounds with trees, and create pleasant breaks between the houses on York Road.

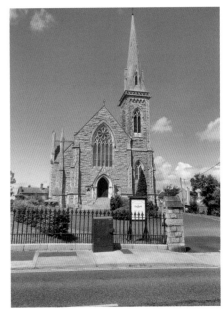

Above left: The old Presbyterian church on York Road became the premises of Kingstown Grammar School in the 1880s.

Above right: The elegant Presbyterian church of 1863 is an attractive feature of York Road and is an identical twin of its sister church in Rathgar.

Below: The foundation stone of the Scots Church, dated 1828.

In 1836 Kingstown's two churches were augmented by three new Protestant establishments: one Methodist and two Church of Ireland. As already mentioned, the first Wesleyan Meeting House was erected by Devon fishermen on Northumberland Avenue. Although there seems to be no record of the original church's appearance, it was rectangular in plan and was probably an unremarkable building. The present church was designed in 1903 by a Dublin architect named Beckett. It is a plain cross-shaped building of a restrained Early English Gothic style and was calculated to seat 250. Scots Philanthropist Andrew Carnegie subscribed £150 towards the new church, which cost £5,300. A tower was planned to rise over the present entrance vestibule, but sadly it was never built; such a tower would have greatly enhanced the character of Northumberland Avenue.

A tower and spire were also planned in 1886 for Christ Church on Park Road, but it too did not materialise. Christ Church, or the Bethel Episcopal Chapel, was begun in 1836 when the Rev. W. Burgh took out a lease for a site on Longford Terrace (Park Road). The chapel is shown on the 1843 Ordnance Survey map as a plain, rectangular edifice, then called the Free Church. In 1869, following the Act of Disestablishment by which the Protestant Church of Ireland became independent of the Anglican Church, the Bethel was renamed Christ Church and was allocated a parish. In 1871 the whole church was remodelled in a rather routine Gothic style. An attractive cast-iron ridge which crowned the roof was removed in the 1980s.

'In the year 1835, the want of an Episcopal church, contiguous to the harbour of Kingstown, for the benefit of sailors in men-of-war, merchant ships, fishing boats and

yachts, frequenting it, was much felt.' So ran a circular issued by the Mariners' Church in the mid-1860s when the building was about to be altered and beautified. The church, which was opened in 1837, was no handsome structure, as is clear from an early engraving, which clearly depicts its barn-like appearance. The Mariners' first chaplain, the Rev. R.S. Brooke, described it as 'large and gaunt, lofty and ugly, a satire on taste, a libel on all ecclesiastical rule, mocking at proportion and symmetry, but spacious and convenient'. The church consisted of a nave and two transepts, which were built to a great height in order to accommodate no fewer than two tiers of galleries. Only one gallery, however, was actually built because the church was considered acoustically poor.

Between 1862 and 1867 improvements were carried out which left the church in its present form. In 1867 a beautiful triple lancet window, made by Wailes of Newcastle and copied from the Five Sisters window in York Minster, was erected. The addition of the tall spire not only graced the church but also introduced a welcome vertical spike into Kingstown's predominantly horizontal rows of terraces. The spire's tense and sober elegance is created by its smooth convex profile, devoid of any projecting crockets or gargoyles, and by its small belfry openings and star-shaped apertures. The exterior of the church was embellished with the addition of granite pinnacles and castellated coping along the gables and roofline. A new chancel was added in 1884 and the three tall lancet windows had to be moved west. The newly fitted church was given a pitch pine roof to replace the plaster ceiling, while red Cork marble, Caen stone and grey marble were variously employed in the making of the pulpit, reading stall

The silver trowel presented to Mrs William Wallace in 1903 on the occasion of the laying of the foundation stone of the new Methodist church on Northumberland Avenue. The Wallaces were successful coal merchants with an office and yards in Old Dunleary.

Below left: *The handsome rose window of Christ Church on Park Road, which stands to the west of the People's Park.*

Below right: *The original Mariners' Church, opened in 1837 and now incorporated into the present building, was a large and bleak structure but it served its purpose until the 1860s when improvements were made.*

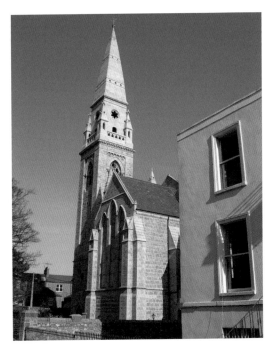

Right: The Mariners'
Church, situated at the end
of Haigh Terrace, showing
the later nineteenth-
century additions of spire
and chancel which so
dramatically improved
its appearance. The main
entrance stood on Adelaide
Street where fine railings
and Tudor-style frontage
still remain.

Far right: A detail of
the fine stained-glass
window in the chancel of
the Mariners' Church,
which was inspired by
the medieval Five Sisters
window in York Minster.

and chancel arch. Mary Hamilton, recalling her childhood visits to the Mariners' Church, describes her grandmother dressed for church in black dress, cape and bonnet, carrying a black leather-bound Bible. She remembers the crews of Welsh and Cornish fishing smacks who:

> flocked for Divine service and remained afterwards to sing hymns … the church held well over a thousand. By our time the Mariners' Church had gathered apart from the seamen, a general Congregation, and with the expansion of Kingstown the parish had become one of the wealthiest in the Church of Ireland. But I remember fishermen there, and the crew of the *Bellisle* and later of the *Melampus* marching into church and taking their places in the side aisle.

During the 1850s, William Vesey, brother of Kingstown's ground landlord, Lord de Vesci, came to live in Kingstown and built for himself the striking Glandore House near the top of York Road. In 1858–59 he set about erecting a church on the grounds of the house. St John's, as it was called, was built in anticipation of a growing Protestant population. By 1860, the nave and tower were completed and the church was opened. The church was never regularly filled, and it was eventually sold in the 1980s to a group dedicated to celebrating the Latin Mass.

St John's adopts the usual cross plan and features plain Early English Gothic window mouldings. However, in its general corner setting with trees and railings, it is a well-proportioned building of high-quality stonework. The present tower, with its rather stumpy roof, was intended to bear an elegant spire, but it was never realised, probably because of the subsidence that occurs in the sandy soil of the area. The church itself suffered minor cracks during construction and the adjoining Glandore House had to be built on solid granite foundations for the same reason. By 1869, a school building, which carefully harmonised with the proportions and texture of the church, was built nearby, together with a sexton's house. The first organ was bought at the second Great Exhibition, in 1865, held at Earlsfort Terrace in Dublin.

In 1863, with the growing population, three separate Catholic parishes were formed between Dalkey, Ballybrack and Glasthule, and Father John Harold set up a temporary wooden chapel in the grounds of Ballygihen House. The first stone of St Joseph's Church in Glasthule was laid in 1867. The striking Gothic-style church with its steep roof was built in the French style to the designs of Augustus Welby Pugin and George Ashlin. A planned belfry and spire were never built.

While the Quaker community established a Meeting House in Monkstown in 1832, two other denominations founded churches in Kingstown. The Kingstown Independent Church on Northumberland Avenue was established in 1849 on a site lately occupied by Lee's Carpet Shop. In about 1860 it became the Congregational Church. It was a small stone-built church with a tower, and some of its stonework can still be seen in the wall of the adjoining lane. In 1911 the Plymouth Brethren erected a small red-brick church about halfway up Northumberland Avenue. It is extraordinary that this avenue once housed three separate congregations of varying non-conformist persuasions.

The multitude of different churches in the town reflects the variety of creed and outlook of its population. Two of these churches have closed, the Mariners' and the Congregational, and a small seamen's 'Bethel' or chapel has disappeared from the Coal Harbour. In the old Garda barracks, which was once a convent of the Poor Clares, there was a very fine groin-vaulted Gothic chapel. The convent, which appears on a map of the neighbouring Royal Hotel of about 1830, was demolished in 1992. There are also chapels attached to the convents of the Little Sisters of the Assumption on York Road, St Michael's Hospital and in the now-demolished Dominican Convent. Though these

When the Mariners' Church closed due to declining numbers and the presence of four other Church of Ireland churches all in close proximity, it was appropriate that, in 1978, it became the home of the National Maritime Museum.

chapels are not particularly noteworthy, the oratory in the grounds of the Dominican Convent is remarkable. Its interior was exquisitely painted by the artist Sister Concepta Lynch in a decorative Byzantine and Celtic style. The unusual murals, inspired by illuminated manuscripts such as the Book of Kells, were planned and begun in 1920. It is the only relic of the convent to survive the construction of Bloomfields shopping complex and is the subject of a beautiful book, *Divine Illumination,* published by Dún Laoghaire–Rathdown County Council in 2019.

Kingstown witnessed two main church-building phases: one in the 1820s and 1830s and the second in the 1860s when many of the earlier structures were rebuilt. Apart from the ancient graveyard at Carrickbrennan in Monkstown, there were no burial grounds attached to any of the churches built in nineteenth-century Kingstown. It seems probable that the ground landlords did not wish to permit burials in their new and very residential town. The cemetery at Deansgrange was established in 1863 and contains many fascinating memorials to former residents of Kingstown. In particular, the Roman Catholic section near the main avenue boasts many beautifully carved Irish high crosses, dating from the later Victorian period, while most of the memorials in the Protestant section are of the plainer slab type. These monuments reflect the success of the new middle class in the Kingstown area – regardless of religious background – and the changing social and political scene of the nineteenth century.

Chapter 5

An Elegant Victorian Watering Place

YACHTING AND SAILING

'At the Royal Yacht Clubs the crème de crème of the aristocracy and gentry assemble during the Kingstown Regatta, which generally takes place every August. The usual gaiety of the place during this aquatic carnival is much increased by the brilliant appearance of the harbour, which contains an immense assemblage of elegant pleasure vessels of every size and rig, from the ship and steamer of 500 tons burthen to the yawl of only ten.' (Gaskin, 1869)

Kingstown's reputation as a town of leisure and fashion was greatly enhanced by the maritime activity of royal visits, the Royal Navy and private yachting. During the late nineteenth century, yachting was important to the town not only because it attracted the nobility and the wealthy and their magnificent yachts, but also because it drew crowds of visitors and spectators from Dublin at weekends and on regatta days. Contemporary guidebooks extolled the splendour of such occasions, describing in detail the military bands, the naval guardship covered with bunting, and the numerous visiting vessels. They wrote expansively of the graciousness, space and wealth exhibited by the harbour and its yacht clubs and by the town with its fine terraces and seafront hotels. This scene is reflected in the many fine photographs which were taken in the second half of the nineteenth century. Since its invention only a few decades before, photography

Above left: The Misses Gibton on their tricycles on the end of the East Pier. As this c. 1870 photograph shows, the East Pier was a popular place to promenade – and to cycle. The ongoing works are visible in the rubble in the background.

Above right: A stereoscopic photograph of c. 1860 shows the East Pier thronged with walkers, many of them decked out in their best outfits and top hats. Now, over a century and a half later, the pier is just as popular.

quickly became popular and by the 1890s there were numerous glass-plate pictures of the harbour, its ships and yachts. Many of the better-quality photographs were turned into lantern slides, which were used to give talks and lectures.

Yachtsmen were not slow to appreciate the superb qualities of the new harbour. The earliest-known regatta in Kingstown was arranged in 1828 by Lord Errol. Yachting continued to be the preserve of aristocrats and the very wealthy until the end of the nineteenth century when more modest boats and classes of boat became available. Among the competitors in the 1828 regatta, for example, were the Marquis of Anglesey's *Pearl*, Colonel Madden's *Ganymede* and Lord Errol's *Liberty*. The first commodores of the two new yacht clubs in Kingstown were the Marquis of Conyngham and the Marquis of Donegal.

Though yachting was not a new sport in the nineteenth century, its popularity spread after Britain's victory over the French in 1815 and the advent of prosperity and peace at sea. Several of the major English clubs were established in the 1820s and 1830s. Their Irish counterparts did not trail far behind: the first Royal Irish Yacht Club was founded in 1831. It is also a well-known fact that the Royal Cork Yacht Club, founded in 1720, is the oldest in the world. The first Royal Irish Yacht Club was dissolved and a new entity, the Kingstown Boat or Yacht Club was established in the early 1840s. It received the patronage of Queen Victoria in 1845 when a royal warrant was granted and it became the Royal St George Yacht Club. The following year, a second Royal Irish Yacht Club was formed at a meeting in the nearby Anglesea Arms Hotel and it too received royal patronage. The queen presented a prize known as Her Majesty's Plate for the regatta held annually by the two clubs. The regatta was hosted by the clubs on alternate years. In 1849 sixteen yachts competed for the trophy. The membership of both clubs was exclusive and select, and was drawn from the gentry and well-to-do all over Ireland. The Royal St George had over 400 members in 1845 but very few of them actually lived in Kingstown. The large yachts of such members were usually manned by paid crews who sailed them around the 'British Isles', berthing them at various places, such as Cork, Kingstown, Belfast Lough or the Clyde. The membership of the Royal Irish Yacht Club came more from the professions and also from the ranks of noted Catholic and Quaker businessmen – people who might not have been accepted by the landed gentry of the Royal St George Yacht Club. But 'The Irish', as it is still called, had the support of the Lord Lieutenant and had its own titled dignitaries in the person of its first commodore – the Marquis of Donegal.

With such a membership, elegant and permanent premises were required by both clubs. The Royal St George's first clubhouse was completed in 1843 on a site obtained from the Harbour Commissioners. When seeking permission to build their clubhouse, the building was actually described as a boathouse to the Harbour Commissioners. It was designed by John. S. Mulvany, who was also the architect of the nearby railway station, and indeed most of the lower floor was taken up with a boathouse. He produced a compact

An early photograph (c. 1880) showing the graceful façade of the Royal St George Yacht Club. All harbour-front buildings had to conform to a one-storey height restriction so as to preserve the views from the terraces of the town.

A plan of the late 1840s illustrates how the yacht clubs were built over the rocky foreshore and here we see the extended form of the Royal St George Yacht Club.

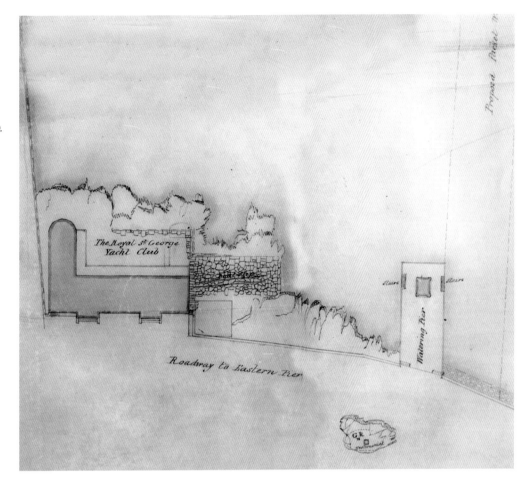

and elegant building, which stood on the harbour front near the George IV Obelisk. A contemporary map and print (above) illustrate the first and little-known form of the original clubhouse – the first purpose-built yacht clubhouse in Ireland. It consisted of a single floor or piano nobile built over a basement, with its three principal rooms elevated over the harbour. The origins of the design stem from the Palladian villa. The clubhouse was originally entered through a projecting portico of two Ionic columns held between plain pilasters and the old hallway is now a cloakroom. It was built by a leading Kingstown contractor called Masterson, and the railings were provided by Fielding's iron foundry (whose work can also be seen in Corrig Avenue, see p. 118). Club membership had increased to such an extent by 1844 that the architect George Papworth was employed to carry out what was to be a very clever and well-conceived extension. This extension involved accurately duplicating the original portico at the other side of a deep recess: a screen of paired Ionic columns flanked the new entrance. A handsome terrace was built on the seaward side and a refined facade of slender columns was placed on the main

front, giving an air of grandeur appropriate to the club's purpose and membership. It is remarkable that Dún Laoghaire can boast four yacht clubs of which three are notable monuments of Victorian architecture. It is also interesting that all of them, excluding the Dun Laoghaire Motor Yacht Club (founded 1965), were not permitted to occupy harbour 'land' and had to be constructed over the water or on reclaimed land, presumably in case the Harbour Commissioners required the space for commercial or naval activities. All of the earlier clubhouses had to conform to a single storey height, like the railway station or Seamen's Rest, so as not to obstruct the views from the terraces behind. The Harbour Commissioners would not allow 'any building to be raised, which might, by shutting off the sea prospect, deteriorate the Terraces'.

The Royal Irish Yacht Club's house is of particular interest as it was also one of the world's first purpose-built yacht clubs and has been very little altered since it was built. It was completed by about 1850 and its plans, elevations and details were illustrated in the English magazine *The Builder* in 1851, which gave special attention to the design of the waterfront facade. The architect, John Mulvany again, was an adherent to classicism and clothed his clubhouse in a neoclassical skin. The striking colonnade that screens the darkened recessed area of the main facade is composed of eight crisply modelled Ionic columns. The treatment of the other facades takes the form of alternating panelled pilasters and windows, against a wall texture of horizontal banding. The seaward elevation is well set off by its rustic stone terrace wall, which is pierced by round windows and finished with a stone cornice and parapet. The plan is straightforward and practical: the five principal rooms enjoy the harbour view and the service areas are confined to the rear.

Above left: The generous plasterwork cornice of the library in the Royal St George Yacht Club with its ivy-leaf decoration. No expense was spared in the decoration and furnishing of the Victorian yacht clubs.
Above right: The well-maintained facade of the Royal St George Yacht Club is an important feature of the harbour.

The boathouse and terrace of the Royal Irish Yacht Club (c. 1880s) overlooked the centre of the harbour. Architect Mulvany excelled himself by producing a perfect Italianate villa by the sea, the expense of which left the club in considerable debt for many years.

Although finished in Roman cement, the clarity and sharpness of line and modelling is reminiscent of Mulvany's stone railway station house.

In the club's first charter, members undertook to survey and report on the state of the Irish fisheries. Perhaps it was because of this intended service that members of the Royal Irish Yacht Club had the unusual honour of being permitted to fly the blue ensign of Her Majesty's fleet, with a crown and harp incorporated into it.

In 1857 a third 'Royal' club was founded at Kingstown. The Royal Alfred Yacht Club was established principally to foster good seamanship: its 'fleet' was led by a captain on cruises and races were organised. The club attracted a prestigious membership. The Duke of Edinburgh, for example, patronised and sailed with it in 1866. The Royal Alfred still flourishes, but remains homeless as it prefers to channel its funds into developing racing and prizes. It was the Royal Alfred that commissioned the first Dublin Bay 24-footer in

Opposite: The Royal Irish Yacht Club seen from the pontoons of the marina.

1937. These beautiful yachts, of which there were once eight, were a feature of sailing in Dún Laoghaire in the second half of the twentieth century. They had long overhanging sterns and elegantly swept bows and carried such names as *Adastra*, *Arandora* and *Fenestra*. The seven Dublin Bay 21-footers were an older class of gaff-rigged yacht and were not unlike their smaller sisters, the 17-footers, in appearance and rig. They were specially designed for racing in Dublin Bay and first appeared in 1903. Like the later 24-footers, they were designed by Alfred Mylne and had graceful lines. Three of these classic yachts have been meticulously restored along with their original gaff rig and cream-coloured sails and made their reappearance in Dún Laoghaire in July 2021.

One of the giant yachts that visited Kingstown for the regattas at the turn of the nineteenth century. The spectacle of these gracious superyachts with their long spars, gaffs, topsails and multiple jibs drew large crowds of spectators to the piers.

The Dublin Bay Sailing Club was founded in 1884 and, while also 'homeless' like the Royal Alfred, it has always remained in the forefront of yachting and racing at Dún Laoghaire. During the summer months, the club continues to organise weekly races for all sizes of yacht.

The third-largest clubhouse on the modern harbour front, standing between the Carlisle and East Piers, is the premises of the National Yacht Club. This club bore many other names in its early years including the Absolute Club and the Kingstown Harbour Boat Club. The building was erected in 1870 for £4,000, to a design by architect William Stirling. Since the building could not interrupt the public thoroughfare along the harbour front, it was erected on a granite vaulted base projecting out over the water. Stirling's design for the exterior of the club was a hybrid French chateau and eighteenth-century hunting lodge or garden pavilion. Both are composed of units of three pedimented bays containing rounded windows and blank roundels. The continuity of these elements with the elegant chimney stacks of the building gave it a certain grace and unity. An early drawing of the building shows viewing balconies on the roof and on the waterfront facade. The modern addition of a much-needed forecourt has obscured a large part of the original seaward base of the building and it is now hard to imagine the steps which once descended, Venetian-style, from a central doorway into the water where a punt waited to ferry members to their yachts.

An early photo (c. 1880) of the National Yacht Club, taken not long after the completion of the clubhouse when it was called the Absolute Club, shows how it was built out over the water, its rooms commanding fine views of the harbour.

The architectural legacy of no fewer than three magnificent purpose-built Victorian yacht clubs on the waterfront in Dún Laoghaire is unparalleled anywhere else in the world. All three have suffered from continued infilling of their own waterfront to create space for smaller yachts and winter storage, understandably perhaps, but much to the detriment of their original setting where they overlooked the water. The existence of these buildings, with their original furnishings still mostly intact, is another cornerstone of the unique heritage of Dún Laoghaire Harbour. They also have the merit of being distinguished architecturally as their classical style suits their purpose, something that cannot always be said for such buildings elsewhere, where bizarre Tudor concoctions were thought right for sailors! The late 1960s saw the establishment of the Dun Laoghaire Motor Yacht Club (DMYC), reflecting the need for a club that catered for owners of all types of boats, including those owned by racing and fishing enthusiasts. While the clubhouse is an uninspired building, it occupies a delightful site on the West Pier directly overlooking the Inner Coal Harbour. When the

The restored Dublin Bay 21-footer yacht Garavogue. Seven of these yachts were built between 1903 and 1908 and it is planned to restore all of them and keep them racing in Dublin Bay.

DMYC was established, it provided an alternative to the more formal traditions of the older clubs. Happily, much has changed and all of Dún Laoghaire yacht clubs have become more informal and devote much time and energy to promoting the sport, especially among the young.

Almost 200 years of yachting tradition has produced many notable sailors: Henry Scovell of Ferney, Stillorgan with his yacht *Atlanta*, Charles Putland of Bray with the *Enid*, and William Jameson of Montrose with *Erycina* were all well known in nineteenth-century Kingstown. Later yachtsmen such as Haffield from Dalkey, Pim from Glenageary House, and Dr W.M. Wright were also familiar. Mr Herbert Dudgeon of Glandore House on York Road, a noted yachtsman and commodore of the Royal Irish Yacht Club, is also remembered for the unfortunate occasion when his fine yacht *Mabel* sank on its moorings in the harbour. The yachting activities of the harbour produced considerable employment for boatmen, deckhands and yacht club staff. Many family names such as Cooper, McDonald and Doyle have long been associated with the yacht clubs and harbour life. In the early 1900s, James Clancy of Crofton Avenue was among the few very skilled

An unbelieveably slender profile and massive sails enabled these yachts to reach great speed, but they required a professional crew of at least twenty-five to manage them. Such yachts were owned by royalty or 'captains of industry' and made their appearance at the most fashionable events in Britain and the USA, to race at Cowes, on the Clyde or at Kingstown. The races were arduous, covering over 80 kilometres in a day, but the prize money was substantial. In 1896 the Royal St George Yacht Club offered eighty sovereigns to the winning yacht in the largest category. Here we see the finely tuned yacht B2 surging past the end of the East Pier.

yacht- and boatbuilders in the town while John Atkinson of Bullock produced many Dublin Bay 17-footers and other fine yachts too. At the same period, James Doyle and his daughter Maimie were noted boatbuilders and produced many Water Wags. These yachts were built in their yard on Clarence Terrace. Michael Mahony, who trained with the Doyles, went on to establish his own boatyard on Patrick Street. The first recorded sailmaker in Kingstown was J. Storey of George's Street who was in business in 1840. R. Perry's yacht chandlers and sailmakers was established at 114 George's Street Lower in the early 1900s and remained the main suppliers of canvas and rope, sails and chandlery up until the 1980s.

During the first half of the twentieth century, the term 'yachting' slowly disappeared in favour of 'sailing'. The change in terminology reflected the great change that took place in this sport after 1914. The enormous private steam yachts and the huge 12-, 15- and 23-metre sailing craft which graced the harbour in the early 1900s had completely vanished by the 1930s. Those incredible visiting yachts, such as *Shamrock* or *White Heather*, required lavish amounts of time and money to maintain, rig and sail. Most yacht owners today could not afford to employ a paid crew, which on the largest yachts might number twenty or more, although the occasional modern giant sailing craft have made their appearance in the harbour. These new boats, called superyachts, are like a hybrid between a huge dinghy and some type of stealth ship, having black sails and hull and a towering mast. However, for most people, smaller, more manageable boats are the norm. Now that the sport of sailing has become so popular, there are masses of different classes and types of boat and sailing craft, all capable of being handled by a small crew or even solo. Many

The tattered racing flag of Britannia.

Left: A salute is fired from the deck of King George V's yacht Britannia. Britannia raced in the Kingstown Regatta of 1896 and in others of the early 1900s. The harbour is thronged with spectators in every sort of punt or rowing boat. These spectacular events continued until the outbreak of the First World War in 1914.

Below: The cutter Merrymaid at the Kingstown Regatta of 1906 with a locally built Water Wag at her bows. The Water Wag is about 4 metres long, thus giving an idea of the enormous height and length of the cutter. Such visiting yachts had no engines, so they must have been quite tricky to manoeuvre.

of the older traditional classes of keelboat and dinghy continue to be sailed, such as the Glens or Dragons. Dún Laoghaire Harbour provides a base for hundreds of sailors and boat users from all walks of life.

After the last great 'revival' regatta of 1930 which was attended by the giant yachts, the sport gradually declined. Regattas were revived after the Second World War, but with the reduced size and scale of yachts which are familiar today. A special survival from the great yachting days remains nevertheless. The indigenous Dublin Bay Water Wags, Mermaids and 17-footers have all survived as racing yacht classes. The Water Wag, designed and sailed first in Killiney Bay at Shankill, then later in Dublin Bay, was the world's first one-design dinghy. The first Wag was built in 1878 and a regular racing fleet was soon established. This demonstrated, perhaps for the first time, that yacht racing was not a rich man's sport only: in 1900 a new Wag cost only £16. Gray's, the only surviving, well-established boatbuilders in the town, are especially expert in clinker-built boats, including Wags and Mermaids. The Water Wags have seen a remarkable revival and now over thirty boats might turn out to race on a summer evening. The 18-foot Mermaid, which is really a large version of a Wag, was being raced in Kingstown in the 1890s. In 1898 the first of a fleet of mainly Howth-based 17-footers were built. This class is almost completely intact with sixteen yachts and maintains the old gaff rig. The Dublin Bay 21-footers were first built in 1903; they eventually abandoned the bowsprit and gaff rig, and were successfully sailed with a modern rig. The fleet was all but abandoned in the 1980s and a similar fate befell the Dublin Bay 24-footer class. Another class, the 25-footers, has completely disappeared.

Below left: Water Wags racing in the Royal Irish Yacht Club Regatta of 1909.

Below right: All yachts, including dinghies, started and finished their races in the harbour, c. 1965.

Above left: Sailing for youngsters was introduced in Dún Laoghaire in the 1960s, as seen here with a colourful fleet of Optimists off the stern of the mailboat.

Above right: A Dublin Bay 24-footer makes a sharp gybe at the West Pier (1960s).

Since the Second World War, many international classes (all timber-built, of course) became popular, including Dragons (keelboats), Enterprises, Fireflies and Herons (dinghies). It used to be an extraordinary sight in the middle of Dún Laoghaire to see the Dragons hauled slowly up Marine Road and Patrick Street to Mahony's yard where they spent the winter. Since 1965, there has been an endless production of new classes and boat types, most built of fibreglass, and this of course led to the demise of the traditional boatbuilder. The Dublin Bay Regatta Week used to attract crowds of visiting yachts, spectators and tourists, but it was eventually abandoned. In 2005 a 'Dún Laoghaire Week' was established for all the clubs' sailing events, eventually to become known as the Volvo Dún Laoghaire Regatta. The event was held every second year in the first week of July and attracted over 400 boats and over 2,500 sailors. Unfortunately, it could not be held in 2021 due to Covid restrictions. The regatta is advertised as Ireland's biggest sailing event.

Yacht racing is still organised by the Dublin Bay Sailing Club on weeknights and Saturdays during the summer. The great regattas of fifty years ago and earlier had always featured rowing races in which, for example, local postmen raced the mailboat's sorting staff. There were also competitions for fishermen, Irish Lights men, Sea Scouts, Board of Works and township employees, and of course, boatmen and paid hands. The hire of

A heavy naval transport boat, powered by oarsmen, is raced in the harbour during a regatta, c. 1906.

rowing boats was once very popular and the Rogan family once kept such boats at the old lifeboat house slip at the East Pier, where it became known as Rogan's Slip. The tradition was continued by the Coopers until the 1960s. Unfortunately, rowing boats are no longer available for hire at Dún Laoghaire and those at Bullock Harbour are being discontinued.

Right: These sturdy rowing boats at the East Pier slip were available for hire from the Cooper family for many years in the mid-twentieth century.

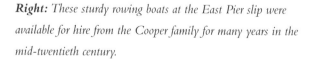

Chapter 6

SEAFRONT HOUSES AND TERRACES: 1840–1860

The 1840s saw a decade of steady development in Kingstown. The devastating and tragic effects of the Great Famine of 1847–52, which so depleted the population of the rest of the country, did little to alter the prosperity and development of Kingstown. In 1831 there were 5,736 inhabitants; in 1841, 7,500; and by 1851, the number had almost doubled to 10,500. A demand clearly existed among the Dublin well-to-do and new middle classes for new houses in Kingstown which the railway had placed just a twenty-minute journey away from the grime and bustle of the city. The growth of Kingstown was further boosted by the building of the Menai Straits railway bridge in Wales in 1850. This completed the London-to-Holyhead railway line and gave added speed and efficiency to the Dublin–Kingstown–London service.

Queen Victoria's departure from Ireland via Kingstown in 1849 stamped the seal on Kingstown's status as a truly Victorian town of fashion. Her visit was recorded in a well-known steel engraving published by Cranfield, copies of which once hung in nearly every house in the town. A lesser-known colour print by Lesage was also issued. In it the harbour is pictured crowded with ships and yachts flying flags and bunting, and the piers packed with spectators.

Prints of the queen's visit clearly show the completed rows of seafront terraces. Most of these elegant houses were built during the 1840s and coincided with the establishment of the yacht clubs on the waterfront. They were generally two or three storeys high, with handsome front doors and fanlights and were approached by broad stone steps fronted

by a neatly railed garden. The first developments, which took advantage of the sea view, were the Crofton, Roby, Gresham and Haddington Terraces, all built in the 1830s. Crofton Terrace was built by the Harbour Commissioner James Crofton and was rented to engineers and captains involved with the harbour works. The terrace stands above the railway and near the bridge to the Coal Harbour and contains a number of attractive ship motifs. Some of the houses have railings in the form of capstans and the door of No. 5 is ornamented by a projected hood decorated with buttons reminiscent of a canopy over the entrance to a ship's wheelhouse. The houses of both Crofton and the adjoining Connaught Place are notable by each being different from the others. Although they conform to the same street line and are two or three storeys in height, they present a varied array of bay windows, plain windows and heavily architraved windows, doors with pillars and fanlights and others with consoles and heavy frames. The effect is one of variety within an overall integrity of scale, materials and colour.

Albert Terrace, adjoining Connaught Place, comes as a complete surprise as it consists of three small one-storey houses ornamented in the same way as the larger houses and fronted by railings. On the corner of Albert Terrace and Kelly's Avenue is an attractive one-storey building with arched windows. Externally, its elegance is created by its simple but generous moulding and its handsome proportions, while inside there is rich

A contemporary print by Cranfield of Dublin depicts the departure of Queen Victoria on the royal yacht, the paddle steamer Victoria and Albert, *from Kingstown Harbour, with people crowding dangerously around the new East Pier lighthouse.*

plasterwork and unusual and colourful hand-painted mirrors. In 1870 this was called the Yacht Tavern and was owned by Miles Kelly. Next along the seafront is the building which was once the Anglesea Arms Hotel. The hotel was established by Alex Armstrong in about 1834, but it was run for most of the nineteenth century by the Rathbone family. The first hotel building was erected in the 1830s and a six-bay block was added to the west side in the 1850s. The hotel maintained the style of the rest of the seafront terraces, using horizontal banding and window architraves. Finally known as the Royal Mail Hotel, the premises was later converted into large maisonettes called the Crofton Mansions. The two large blocks which composed the hotel are well maintained and currently converted into apartments.

Adjoining the hotel was Roby Place which was built in 1832 as four attractive Tudorised houses. It was demolished in 1978 and replaced by a new apartment block which attempts to combine modern function with an appearance that bears some relationship to the rest of the seafront. Though its rather squat proportions produce a certain heaviness, the painted cement finish respects the adjoining Victorian buildings.

Eastwards stands Charlemont Terrace, six houses constructed in about 1845 for a developer named Cornelius Egan. The Charlemont houses conform to the tall, elegant style adopted by Gresham and Haddington Terraces. It was a high-class terrace, set back from Crofton Road and originally fronted by handsome railings. The houses, with their first-floor drawing rooms, command views of the harbour and the bay. The presence of private stables or coach houses at the rear confirms the original status of the terrace. The owners of less grand houses had either to rely on the railway and later, the omnibus or else hire a hackney. Egan also developed the three tall houses comprising Victoria Terrace, which adjoined Haddington Terrace. They were built by 1843 in the now-familiar 'Marine Terrace' style. While all these houses were individually of no great architectural significance, the long waterfront of varied yet unified terraces was, and still is, very impressive from the harbour and from the sea. For this reason, these seafront terraces should be viewed as an ensemble and not allowed to be whittled away or altered. Neither should developments which are too high or too brutalist be permitted. Two of Egan's Victoria Terrace houses became Ross's Victoria Hotel, one of Kingstown's best establishments for many years. It boasted a 'winter garden' on the roof in the late nineteenth century. This hotel was demolished in about 1978 and was replaced by an apartment block.

The eleven houses of Marine Terrace were completed in 1843. They extended eastward towards the Glasthule Martello tower (now the People's Park). In the same year, developer and later town councillor John Crosthwaite added another attraction to the seafront by opening the Royal Victoria Baths in the corner of Scotsman's Bay. These baths offered both open sea bathing and hot and cold baths of salt- and freshwater. They were later bought by the town council who completely rebuilt them between 1905 and 1911 at a cost of £12,000 (a little over €1.1 million today). The baths have been undergoing another major rebuilding which includes a café and a statue of Roger Casement, but strangely no baths. In the 1850s Crosthwaite built a second bath at Salthill. The earliest baths in Kingstown were built in the Royal Hotel. As early as 1828 the owner, Mr Hayes, applied to the Harbour Commissioners for permission to run a pipe from the sea to his

Above: *A sugar bowl from Ross's Hotel.*

Left: *This Edwardian postcard of Ross's Hotel presents an artist's idealised view of the hotel and the view from its terrace. Howth Head has become quite Alpine and the Martello tower at Sandycove has grown taller by about 20 metres! However, the card captures the holiday-resort mood which Kingstown was trying to cultivate.*

premises. The presence of the baths was a sign that Kingstown was fast becoming a resort. It already had the attractions of several good hotels, a railway and mailboat service, and a harbour full of yachts and other sailing ships. The August regattas especially were becoming a noted social event, and many people rented houses in Kingstown for 'the Season' – the summer.

The Windsor and Martello Terraces were built in the 1840s and extended along the shore of Scotsman's Bay. Two of the Windsor Terrace houses bear unusually ornate facades with elaborate stucco window frames. The rest of the Scotsman's Bay seafront, known as Newtownsmith, had been developed in the 1820s by the stone contractor Smith in the form of low cottages, most of which were replaced by larger houses. During the late nineteenth century, there was considerable pressure to construct an esplanade between the baths and Sandycove, but the expense of the project forced its postponement. It was not until the twentieth century that the rocky foreshore that blocked the route to Sandycove was finally reclaimed and a concrete roadway constructed.

Glasthule has existed as a settlement of cottages, located at the mouth of a tiny stream, since the eighteenth century at least. A century later there were several groups of cottages, mostly probably thatched, which housed families employed on the harbour construction. The developing Glasthule was described by *The Irish Times* in 1862 as 'an unhealthy and low lying village with a dense hive of cabins or rather wigwam population'. Attempts were made to improve the situation by private individuals by the building of stone cottages with slated roofs, such as Perrin's Row, Chalmer's and Halpin's Cottages, but it was only at the turn of the century that things really improved when the Kingstown Urban District Council set about building new terraced houses.

At the other end of Kingstown, the 1840s saw the erection of another impressive terrace facing westward over Dublin Bay. De Vesci Terrace, named after the ground landlord, was built and occupied by 1846. The facades of these ten houses were finished in high-quality cement and stucco work in the neoclassical style. The hall-door porticos are supported by fluted Doric columns. The horizontal banding of the ground floor is commonplace, but the large wooden oriel or bay windows are, after those on Haddington Terrace, early examples of this feature. Each bay window is elegantly coped with a concave roof. The houses were among the best to be built in Kingstown. They had a fine situation, a high valuation and, like Gresham Terrace, a large planted park which belonged (and still does) to the residents. The idea of building terraces around a communal park or square was to become very popular in Kingstown after 1860, once sites with marine views had been built on.

RESIDENTIAL KINGSTOWN — THE VICTORIAN TASTE

The housebuilding boom in Victorian Kingstown reflected the growth of a new comfortable middle class – a class that had not really existed before. Houses ranged from the quite ordinary and modest to the rather grandiose and ostentatious. Many Victorian houses in Dún Laoghaire feature curious decorative additions and extensions – small symbols of the new affluence of their owners. By the middle of the nineteenth century it became common practice to embellish older, plainer houses. These embellishments took the form of adding mouldings to plain windows or building porches onto flat-fronted houses. For instance, houses such as Beulah on Glenageary Road Lower and No. 43 Northumberland Avenue feature porches that were probably added some time after the houses were built. The Beulah porch is formed with round-arched windows and is covered by a small pointed and bracketed roof. This house, originally plain and flat fronted, has an unusual window in the gable under the chimney stack, which itself has been embellished with scrollwork. The Northumberland Avenue porch consists of a rectangular projection ornamented by corner pilasters and a frieze of garlands. The three houses of Mount Clarence Terrace were also greatly embellished years after their completion in 1834. Beautifully proportioned polygonal porches with plate glass windows and thick mouldings were added to each house, and all three were stressed as a terrace unit by placing a name panel on the roofline of the central house.

Pilasters, recessed panels, imitation stone quoins and bay windows were applied to many houses about the town, and rooflines were sometimes enlivened by urns, lions, eagles and the occasional figure. Thick stucco or cement cornices were often employed to aggrandise a fairly ordinary house. The supporting consoles or brackets around front doors were generally made of wood. A good example of this sort of ornament is found on the central house of Leinster Terrace on George's Street Upper which features a roofline panel decked with scrolls and a seated lion.

Mount Clarence House, Adelaide House and Nos 24 and 25 Adelaide Street were embellished with great licence, probably by a builder and plasterer named Slater, who lived in Adelaide House. All four houses were given porch and bay window projections richly covered with cornices, architraves, pilasters, consoles and ornamental flourishes in stucco plaster. The addition of two storeys on Mount Clarence House included a spacious new porch and entrance with a room above. The neighbouring Adelaide Street houses with their treble-windowed, two-storey rectangular bays are reminiscent of London

Above left: *Mount Clarence House, George's Street Upper, was extravagantly decorated in mid-Victorian times with stucco pilasters, brackets and fancy architraves and makes a striking match to its neighbour, Adelaide House.*

Above right: *Adelaide House, a substantial corner residence on George's Street Upper, represents the high Victorian taste and displays lavish stucco enrichments on the door and windows. It was for most of the twentieth century the home of Dr Roantree and his family.*

terrace houses. The rest of Adelaide Street is characterised by variety in house shape and window type, but all have handsome iron railings around their steps and short front gardens. Adelaide Street was built up between 1838 and 1848.

Many of Kingstown's fine ironwork railings, gates, balconies and fanlights were erected during those mid-century decades. Haigh, an iron founder, produced some neoclassical balconies and railings, a few of which have survived. The railings were based on a Greek key pattern instead of the usual rod-and-spike motif. There are at least fifteen different railing spikes in Dún Laoghaire based on the fleur-de-lis, traditional spearhead, African spearhead, floral or leaf cluster, and palmette patterns. These railings,

Decorative cast-iron railing spikes were used to ornament the front garden railings of most terraced houses in the Victorian period. These examples come from Corrig Avenue, Gresham Terrace (centre) and Crosthwaite Park.

fronting the town's gardens and bordering the steps of houses, are a source of great richness to Victorian Dún Laoghaire.

By about 1840, many lodges and small detached 'villas' had sprung up in and about the town in places near Glasthule and Tivoli Road. These houses were small, although inside they were sometimes quite spacious. The typical villa consists of one storey over a basement. The basement is usually sunken, and the entrance is approached by a wide flight of steps. The houses were made grand by the application of large-scale architectural features, including broad-framed windows, bay windows, a large front door with columns and other decorative accoutrements, such as pilasters and urns. Their names carried the suggestion of travel, leisure, good climate and picturesque situation: Rosina Castle, Seabank, St Helens (Sandycove), Bella Vista, Tivoli Villa, Summer Villa, Bagatelle, Airhill Cottage and Rose Villa. Tivoli Villa, on Tivoli Terrace East, was built about 1840 and is a good example of the type. It is pleasantly proportioned with large double-arched window frames that match the arch of the door. It is simply ornamented with unusual corner pilasters and tapering window mouldings and has a long front garden railing of an exuberant scroll pattern. Another attractive terrace of villa-style houses of the 1840s type may be seen at Brighton Vale in Monkstown where, close by the Martello tower, they enjoy fine views across Dublin Bay. Many of the fifteen houses are handsomely decorated with stucco flourishes and fine ironwork. There are many examples of larger villas on Alma Road, Queen's Park, Brighton Avenue and Seafield Avenue, where the basement is no longer below ground but is at garden level.

Avonville (No. 2 Tivoli Terrace South), Rossmore (No. 16 Corrig Avenue) and Nos 6 and 7 St Joseph's Terrace (Tivoli Road) are variations on the villa theme. Avonville is almost of Georgian simplicity and has a double entrance, which was designed to facilitate the passage of cabs and carriages. Rossmore features an unusual classical porch articulated by pilasters and a pediment.

Several terraces which adopted villa proportions and style are to be found elsewhere in Dún Laoghaire. These include Nos 9 and 12–16 Tivoli Terrace East, Nos 14–16 Corrig Avenue and Nos 19–25 Northumberland Avenue. They are pleasant intermediate-sized houses, lying between the two-storey terrace and the one-storey cottage in size and were well suited, due to their basements, to the inclined avenues and streets of Kingstown. The terraced houses of Charlemont Avenue off Crofton Road were completed in 1853 and are yet another variation on the villa theme; they are faced in brick instead of cement or stucco.

The smallest house type in Kingstown is no less deserving of attention. Such houses vary from plain cottages, which usually had good fanlights over the door, such as Nos

Throughout Sandycove and Dalkey there are many examples of the villa style of house, both detached and terraced. Here on Sandycove Avenue West, the windows, doors and chimney stacks are embellished with ornate brackets and rosettes. The two-storey return can be seen behind the main roof.

31–46 Mulgrave Street, to ornately decorated 'villa' cottages as those in Albert Terrace on Crofton Road or the twelve terraced cottages on the top of Mulgrave Street. These cottages are well set back from the road, have elaborately decorated door surrounds and a two-storey return at the rear. Normanby Lodge, also on Mulgrave Street, was built in about 1840. It was named after the Marquis of Normanby, heir to the Earl of Mulgrave, and was occupied by a Major Nicholson. It is an unusual one-storey house with curved flanking walls and accompanying stone urns. Some of the urns seem to have been moved down the street after the alteration of one wing. The attractive fanlight and front door are a normal part of the protracted Georgian style, but the elaborate ironwork balconies half a metre off the ground and the flanking wing make the house an appealing but rather extreme example of a miniature eighteenth-century mansion.

During the decade 1849–59 two large developments were undertaken. Corrig Avenue, formerly the private avenue to Corrig House, was built up with a mixture of terrace and villa-type houses, while Clarinda Park was formed in what were once the grounds of Stoneview House. The houses of Corrig Avenue, apart from Sydenham Terrace, were stepped up the hill, usually in detached pairs. These were solid two-storey-over-basement, flat-fronted houses ornamented in the familiar way with carved consoles and architraves around the windows and doors. The pace of development in the area was fast. In 1850 there were only fourteen residents but by 1859 there were forty. A number of mid-Victorian houses on the east side of Corrig Avenue, known as Guilford

Terrace, were blocked up for years and were eventually demolished. Corrig House was also replaced, by a dull residential block; its old gate lodges at the top and bottom of the avenue have vanished and the old assembly rooms, once a courthouse and later Shanahan's Auction Rooms, have been demolished.

Among the highest-quality houses to be built in Kingstown are Sydenham House and Nos 2–8 Sydenham Terrace on the west side of Corrig Avenue. They were built in 1859 by a local builder, Edward Masterson. Sydenham Terrace is made up of eight houses, which are composed as an architectural unit, possibly by the architect Darley or by the builder himself. Like those in De Vesci Terrace, the houses exemplify the neoclassical style. Masterson, who also built the Royal St George Yacht Club and Sorrento Terrace in Dalkey, maintained a very high standard of workmanship. Sydenham House and Terrace display fine granite steps terminated by panelled stone pillars surmounted by urns. The interiors exhibit unusually fine woodwork, while the front railings by William Fielding are of a unique spearhead design. Fielding's Lion Iron Works were located in Greek Street, not far from St Michan's Church in Dublin. The back gardens were furnished with a screen wall with niches for statuary or urns. Sydenham House itself, taking its name from the London gardens where the Crystal Palace was re-erected in 1853, possesses a handsomely arched and pilaster-ornamented carriage entrance.

By 1849, a few houses had already been built on Clarinda Avenue (later to become

Above left: The ornate entrance hall of Sydenham House on Corrig Avenue with elaborate architraves and overdoors, coloured glass fanlight and ceiling plasterwork. This standard of decoration was the norm in high-quality houses of Victorian Kingstown.

Above right: Two houses on Sydenham Terrace, Corrig Avenue. These houses were of generous proportions with large reception rooms and high basements, which allowed plenty of light into the kitchen and servants' area. Coal was stored in a cellar beneath the front steps.

Above left: Dún Laoghaire Bridge Club occupies one of the fine run of houses on Clarinda Park North. These terraced houses are distinguished by their double-height bow windows and typical Victorian detail of ornate brackets about the hall door, granite steps and cast-iron railings.

Above right: This fine house is part of Crosthwaite Terrace on Clarinda Park West. It was converted to educational use and is an example of one of the many short-lived private schools which at one time abounded in Kingstown.

Clarinda Park West). During the next decade, a three-sided square was formed as the terraced houses were gradually completed. Clarinda Park was developed for £80,000 (about €7.7 million today) by Mr P. W. Bryan, a wealthy wine merchant of George's Street who was said to have 'built upwards of 100 first class houses in Kingstown'. The earliest houses, Nos 8–11 Clarinda Avenue, were built in brick, which was unusual for Kingstown. They have typical Georgian fanlights and doors. Some of these houses, which were in perfectly sound condition, lay blocked up for years awaiting demolition. Apart from some flat stucco-fronted houses on Clarinda West, the rest of the park is uniform with its bay windows carried up two storeys. Eventually, four sections of terrace in this design were erected around Clarinda Park, including what was once called Bolton Terrace. Most of the terraces have a three-storey return but due to the drop behind Clarinda East, an extra storey was squeezed in at the rear, fronting onto Glenageary Road Lower. No. 21 Clarinda Park West is notable for its coach-house entrance, which is overlooked by a delightful baroque-style convex window, delicately ornamented in stucco. It is important for the integrity of the whole park that no house should alter the proportions or appearance of its frontage, let alone be demolished. The fine open park of Clarinda was for a long time the sports ground of Victoria School, subsequently Glengara Park School.

By the late 1840s, Kingstown had acquired some new large detached houses of note.

Gortleitragh was built for the Stewarts, the hereditary agents for Lords Longford and de Vesci, the landlords of the Kingstown estate. The estate office was located at 6 Leinster Street, while Lords Longford and de Vesci themselves lived on their estates in Counties Westmeath and Laois. (There is a popular legend that two young titled gentlemen assisted an elderly man on the sailing from Holyhead and that in time they inherited his land at Dunleary. The truth is more prosaic: the lands and castle of Monkstown, which belonged to Walter Cheevers in the late seventeenth century, were at that time sold to Michael Boyle, Archbishop of Armagh, and through the marriages of his two daughters the property came into the ownership of the Lords Longford and de Vesci.) There was little activity on the Longford and de Vesci estate in terms of building during the eighteenth century, with the exception of some detached houses and the new Church of Ireland in Monkstown, which was begun in 1785. However, all this changed after 1800, when new leases were made for the building of Martello towers and houses in and around Dunleary. With the commencement of the Asylum Harbour in 1816 and the imminent spreading of Dunleary, the outlook for the landlords looked very promising.

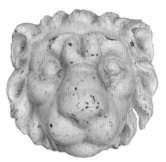

Above: An interesting feature of the cast-iron gutters of The Slopes were the lion masks that covered the joints.

Below: The entrance porch of The Slopes, a fine detached Victorian house that was demolished in 1978.

Gortleitragh House, which was completed by 1846, consisted of two storeys over a basement and looked out over Dublin Bay past De Vesci Terrace. A wing and large conservatory were added later and its terraced gardens were among the finest in the town. A surviving account book for the year 1856 shows that £102 14s was spent on the garden, £100 15s on the stable, £23 13s on coal, and £14 5s on gas. During the Second World War, the house was shuttered and empty because it had been the property of the German Embassy in Ireland. In 1955 it was demolished to make way for the flats at Sloperton.

The prosperous St Stephen's Green wine merchant and grocer Charles Smyth built the neighbouring house called The Slopes. It was later bought and remodelled by the Findlater family, who added a handsome porch and new rooms with an

Above left: *The old stables of Longford Lodge possessed a quirky charm, but were demolished when the house was converted to its present use as a nursing home.*

Above right: *Longford Lodge, photographed in the 1940s. It was later converted to its present use as a nursing home.*

elegant bow window projection. The house was demolished in 1978 and the only surviving remnant is a long snake-like staircase of cut granite.

Holmston House lay in extensive grounds and was approached originally by a long drive from Glenageary Hill. Two handsome granite gate pillars and a lodge remain at the bottom of the present Holmston Avenue. The house was first occupied by Patrick Reid and was held by his descendants until recently. It is a large block-shaped house of similar dimensions to Gortleitragh and has a heavy stone portico of Tuscan columns projecting over the front door. The house remains on a small piece of land and its finely timbered grounds are now known as Glenageary Woods.

Longford Lodge, the home of Glengara Park School up until 1992, is another important detached house. It was originally built in about 1843 with a southeast-facing entrance, but was later extended and its present, somewhat austere, north facade was added. An attractive cobbled yard and coach house once lay to the rear. It was for long the residence of the Cooper family, originally of Markree Castle, County Sligo. Longford Lodge possessed an unusual corner entrance on Glenageary Hill with rare asparagus-like iron gateposts. This ironwork was moved back to form a new entrance for the present nursing home, which has been operated in the house for many years.

Glandore House stands behind St John's Church near the top of York Road. This magnificent stone-built house was designed by Deane and Woodward in the Venetian Gothic

Glandore House on York Road is remarkable for its cut-stone features, tall chimneys, Gothic windows and decorative balconies.

idiom for William Vesey, a brother of one of the ground landlords. It is a large house of irregular plan with steep-pitched roofs and dramatic tall chimney stacks. Typical Venetian detail is found in the double windows whose Gothic arches are carefully contrasted in yellow sandstone and granite. The windows lead onto a small sandstone balcony, which is pierced with Venetian star patterns. In the 1890s the noted yachtsman Herbert Dudgeon bought the house from the Veseys. It was more recently the property of Mr J. Watson, the proprietor of the well-known Killiney nurseries. The house has latterly served as a nursing home and as a guesthouse. Although Glandore House survives, it does so only as a striking example of the problem of preserving an individual house while allowing its setting to be destroyed.

The quest for the survival of the larger old houses in suburban areas is always problematic as the extensive grounds on which they originally stood becomes ever more sought after for redevelopment. Though much has disappeared in the environs of Dún Laoghaire, the Victorian legacy is very significant. Most of these houses and terraces are now protected structures.

Chapter 7

SANDYCOVE AND BULLOCK

Oone of the best views of Dublin Bay's southern shore is from Howth Summit, where the full sweep of the Dublin and Wicklow mountains can be appreciated, with the region of Dalkey, Bullock and Sandycove below, now thickly populated with new houses and apartments dotted among those of the nineteenth century and earlier. The granite coast marks the limit of such building and leaves an attractive and varied shoreline of small harbours and bathing places.

SANDYCOVE'S ROCKY SHORELINE

Sandycove is a small sheltered harbour with a short pier, used originally to ship stone across the bay to the Liffey and Dublin Port. Quarrying for the South Bull Wall at the Liffey was begun as early as 1735 when it was decided to replace the original wooden breakwater with a stone structure. A certain amount of quarrying may have taken place along the shore of Scotsman's Bay as many of the rocks here are jagged from drilling and blasting, but there is no reference to this activity in documents or on maps. A great deal more quarrying took place at Sandycove Point when the Martello tower and battery were built. There was also a wall or jetty to the west (still remaining in front of Neptune Lodge) from which stone was loaded as well as the longer wall on the south side of the harbour itself. Later, the harbour was completed by the addition of a back wall and a pair of cantilevered granite steps. A finely crafted granite boat slip was added in 1864.

A lifeboat, some say the first in Ireland, was established at Sandycove in 1803 and it is depicted in a small engraving by Kirkwood of the 1840s. It was housed in a small covered

shed and had a short boat slip, both of which are more or less intact today. Sandycove is well known as a delightful swimming place, especially at high tide, but older people will remember when there were a few rowing boats belonging to local fishermen, such as Johnny 'Mackerel', moored there. Much quarrying took place around Sandycove Point and this can be seen around the Martello tower where it stands dramatically perched on cliffs of granite which have been hewn away. There were also several small quarries inland, such as that at Dundela Park where the remains of a pond were extant until quite recently. Here at Dundela, there were three small quarries, once accessed from both Castlepark Road and Albert Road. House names such as Quarryside in Elton Park recall this activity.

Sandycove Point was the scene of a number of shipwrecks, for instance in 1821 when a coal brig, the *Ellen*, came ashore on the rocks at the Forty Foot. At that time there was a lifeboat at Sandycove and the then newly appointed harbour master at Dunleary, Captain Hutchinson, rowed out to rescue the stricken crew. Tragically, four of his own crew were lost overboard. Almost a century later, in 1915, another ship (dramatically photographed), a large sailing barque called the *Inverisk*, dragged its anchor in a storm out in the bay and was driven ashore at the Ring rock near the boys' bathing place. The twenty-three crew all survived, some of whom were winched ashore by the coastguard.

An early nineteenth-century watercolour of the coast at Sandycove showing fishermen's boats, sheds and cabins. Howth is visible in the background.

Above left: The seafront road linking Dún Laoghaire to Sandycove was completed in the twentieth century and involved much reclamation and infill behind the concrete sea wall.

Above right: The Inverisk *aground at Sandycove Point in 1915. The ship was later floated off and repaired in the Liffey Dockyard.*

RESIDENTIAL SANDYCOVE

As we have already seen, the southern shore of Dublin Bay was quickly developed with houses and terraces from the 1830s onwards, and the Sandycove area was no exception. The land at Sandycove Point was held by the Crown while other parts of the shore were under the control of Dublin Port and Docks Board – or the Ballast Office – who had leased it for quarrying purposes. The first building leases in the area date from 1803, around the time the Martello towers first appeared, granted by the Proby estate, the ground landlords of most of Sandycove and part of Dalkey.

A number of detached villas such as Mornington House or St Kilda, which took advantage of the fine sea views, were built along with an assortment of cottage-style houses and terraces, examples of which may be seen on both Sandycove Avenue East and West. Other terraces of two- and three-storey houses were erected overlooking Scotsman's Bay and in prominent positions elsewhere. For instance, Munster Terrace, Cliff Terrace and Bayswater Terrace were built on the main road to Dalkey and afforded good sea views from their rear windows. Almost all these houses were built of rubble stone and were plastered in the Victorian manner with cornices and architraves, though there are a few exceptions where red brick was used, such as Breffni Terrace. The houses were typically two storeys

A tall, tapering gate pier at St Kilda's shows the stonemason's skill in working this hard stone.

high with granite steps leading up to a hall door, and were ornamented with the usual classical pillared porches and fanlights. In his books, such as *The Garden* or *The Sea Wall*, writer L.A.G. Strong evokes life in residential Sandycove in the early twentieth century. He describes through a child's eyes the houses and gardens with their cooks and housekeepers. He writes about a leisured way of life and spent much time himself fishing in the rock pools, boating and swimming at the Forty Foot.

The extension of the railway to Dalkey in the 1840s and the building of a station at Sandycove quickly boosted the popularity of the area. Many houses were built for renting during the summer season. The first edition of the Ordnance Survey, made in 1837 and published in 1843, already shows a substantial cluster of houses around Sandycove Road, at the bottom of Albert Road and on Sandycove Avenue West, including Sandycove Terrace. Albert Road is unique in that nearly all the houses are of the cottage style. By the 1860s, new streets had been laid out with a wide variety of terraced houses, cottage- or villa-style houses and some larger detached residences like Ballygihen, Gowran Hall and Beaufort Lodge. These latter houses were demolished in the 1970s and 1980s when their extensive gardens fell victim to property development. The nineteenth century leases, which had been granted from the Proby estate, led to a heated legal debate many years later in the 1960s, when some residents in Sandycove realised that, due to the type of lease they had, they did not actually own the bricks and mortar of their own houses. This was ultimately resolved by the passing of an amendment to the tenancy law.

Adjoining the Martello tower is a white-painted 'modern' house, which has an unmistakeable maritime flavour. Though its actual name is Geragh, it is more generally known locally as Michael Scott's house. It was designed by one of Ireland's best-known twentieth-century architects as his own residence. Scott picked a stunning site, and in his design echoed the curves of the Martello tower, adopting the international style of the 1930s. Some dislike it for its stark simplicity, especially on the seaward side, while others admire the way in which steel and concrete were used to create a ship-like elegance. Whatever one's preferences, the house, built in 1937–38, is a landmark in the history of Irish architecture.

Above left: *A fine pair of three-storey-over-basement houses on Sandycove Avenue West. Many similar houses and terraces were built in Sandycove during the 1840s.*

Above top right: *Ballygihen was one of a number of detached houses demolished during the 1980s to make way for apartment blocks. Its gardens, like that of its neighbour Gowran Hall, once ran right down to the sea. Part of a castellated granite gateway bearing the name of the house survives on the main road.*

Above right: *A typical early Victorian house at No. 5 Summerhill, which lies on the main road connecting Dún Laoghaire to Glasthule. The horizontal channelling of the ground floor, the Georgian-style windows and the pilastered door surround create an impressive facade.*

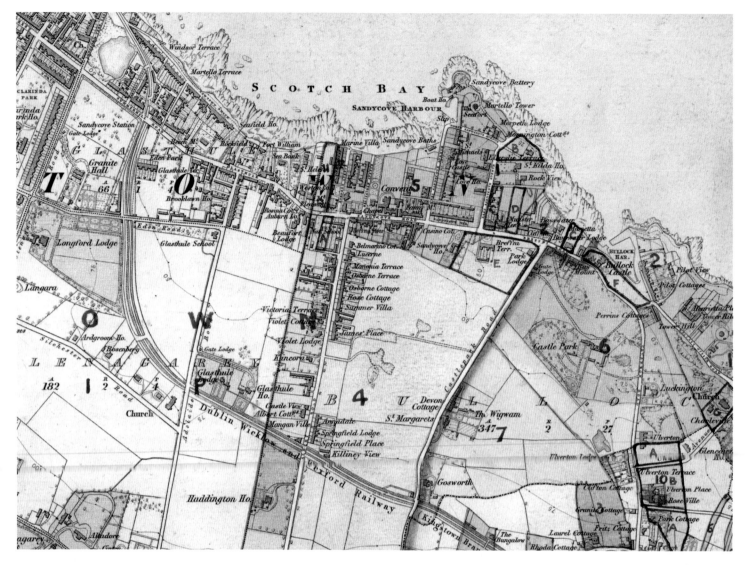

Above: A map of the Proby estate, showing how Albert Road was well developed by the middle of the nineteenth century.

Left: A view of Joyce's Tower and the Geragh from the sea, showing the quarried foreshore and the treacherous nature of the granite coast.

THE FORTY FOOT

The Forty Foot comprises some 200 metres of rocky foreshore at the tip of Sandycove Point and is possibly the most famous bathing place in Ireland. The presence of deep water at all stages of the tide and the pleasant surroundings, both natural and historic, have contributed to its popularity. A feature of the Forty Foot and Sandycove Harbour are the steps that have been carved into the rock itself and chiselled to provide a grip. The Forty Foot was for long the sole preserve of men and was financed and cared for from 1880 by a voluntary group called the Sandycove Bathers' Association. Further along the coast the Loreto nuns had a women-only bathing place, adjacent to their convent. Happily today, both sexes bathe together at the Forty Foot and the quaint rusty old sign 'Gentlemen Only' has disappeared.

Amongst the many improvements made at the Forty Foot since the late nineteenth century was the building of a substantial stone wall whose main object was to screen the naked male bathers from more innocent eyes, but it also afforded some shelter from southeasterly winds and rain. In 1909, following a challenge by the town council as to their rights of occupation, the Bathers' Association stated that they had spent upwards of £2,000 in making steps, carving rocks, affixing ladders, blasting dangerous rocks, building walls, covering sheds, concreting floor space and providing life-saving apparatus. A sheltered pool was created by blasting away much rock. Prior to this, as an early photograph of 1860 shows, Sandycove Point was much as nature and quarrymen had left it, with no easy access in or out of the sea. The Crown, as landlord of the tower and battery, and of the foreshore adjacent, ruled in favour of the bathers.

In 1891 one Francis Byrne was prosecuted for bathing after 9am without a costume and in 1906 another regular Forty Foot swimmer, Mr Carson, blatantly flouted the bye-laws and bathed and exercised naked. Carson's case was heard in the courtroom at Kingstown town hall and he was let off with a nominal 2s 6d for each summons rather than the fixed penalty of 40s.

A modest structure still known as Sandycove Baths stands in the corner of Scotsman's Bay by Sandycove Avenue West. As early as 1838, the writer D'Alton tells us that 'commodious hot and cold water baths' are located there. In the later nineteenth century they were described as the ladies' baths. Only traces of these early baths remain in the little cove, with stone steps and a low wall running out to sea.

A relic from the old days of the Forty Foot, this sign once read 'Forty Foot – Gentlemen Only'.

BULLOCK HARBOUR

The name Bullock is said to come from a Norse word meaning a haven, although a more popular belief is that it derives from a Gaelic word suggestive of the roar of the sea through rocks. Northeasterly storms still pound the coast here, and waves can surge right over the rocks past the remaining cottages and over the quay itself. Bullock Harbour, with its beautifully shaped stone quays and pier, remains one of Dublin county's most unspoilt amenities, despite various attempts to develop more houses and apartments there.

Large outcrops of high rocks lie to the east behind Bullock Harbour providing some natural shelter to the little haven. The rock is deeply fissured with long parallel cracks and grooves; in fact, this is a feature of all of the granite bedrock in this region. A dangerous submerged rock just off the harbour point, called Old Bulloch, is well known to locals and to the west there is an extensive and treacherous bed of sharp once-quarried rocks which are covered at high tide. These can be seen from Bullock Harbour and from the flight of granite steps at the end of Sandycove Avenue East.

In 1800 Captain Bligh of 'Mutiny on the *Bounty*' fame made an excellent survey

Above left: A mostly good-natured campaign on the part of women swimmers who wanted equality of bathing rights took place during the 1980s and 1990s.
Above right: Gentlemen bathers c. 1890 at the very same spot.

and chart of Dublin Bay (for which he deserves to be better known). In his report, he mentions Bullock: 'This is a dry harbour – It lies between Dalkey and Dunleary and has a quay on the West side, to which small vessels come to load with stones.' He also records the existence of the remains of an earlier wall or pier which once gave Bullock Harbour some protection from northerly winds. Off the entrance, which he says is bad, is a rock which can be seen at low water on spring tides, which he calls Old Bullock.

The present granite-built harbour was constructed in 1818 by the Ballast Board for the purpose of shipping stone across the bay. The Ballast Office managed the affairs of Dublin Port and in the early 1800s took leases on land at Bullock and Sandycove for the purpose of quarrying. Bullock Harbour is still under the control of the Dublin Port and Docks Board, which is 'descended' from the original Ballast Board. Stone was carted down the Ballast Office Road for shipment across the bay in small vessels called lighters.

Stone has been extracted from many places at Bullock, including the area at the back of the harbour where great rocks plunge into the sea and quarry marks and holes are still to be seen. These rocks are reached by a stone doorway that bears an illegible inscription. There was once a tavern at the bottom of Castle Steps known as Golden's Inn, which must have been popular with the stone carriers and sailors alike.

A boat slip, which lies in the inner angle of the harbour, is still to be seen but is partially submerged beneath a more recent concrete slipway. The principal quay on the east side is comprised of an elegantly curving wall that runs along to the pier and is made of coursed fingers of granite. The harbour is furnished with stone bollards and many strong iron rings for tying up. A most attractive feature of the roadway that runs along the western quay is the run of octagonal granite bollards and chains. An outer and often unnoticed quay is

Below left: This c. 1890 photograph of Bullock Harbour shows how it dries out at low tide. A timber crane or derrick on the pier was used to handle granite and coal.
Below right: Bullock pier and harbour, seen from the top of Bullock Castle, which gave the Cistercian monks a commanding view of all activities going on below.

known locally as the Ruin or Room and lies just outside the harbour mouth. It provided a place for larger vessels to berth when conditions were calm. Likewise, small ships could moor up on the outer side of the main pier to load stone or deliver coal, for which purpose two cranes once stood on the pier. For many years, a large coal store was operated at Bullock by the Downey family.

BULLOCK CASTLE

The attractive stone-built Bullock Castle stands guard over its picturesque harbour as it has done since about AD 1250. Built by the Cistercian monks of St Mary's Abbey in order to protect their fisheries, it is a small defensive castle with a narrow profile facing out to sea. The monks chose a commanding position and built a solid granite castle of modest size. It has stood the test of time, and is probably the best-preserved medieval structure of its kind in south County Dublin. Weston St John Joyce says that the monks extracted an annual toll of about 600 fish per boat from fishermen using the harbour.

A spiral staircase leads from the ground floor, with its vaulted undercroft, to the main space or hall above.

The castle was restored by the Carmelite Sisters for the Aged and Infirm, the current owners, during the 1960s and it was for a while open to the public. The battlements and

Above left: The surface of the pier at Bullock is made of cut granite and cobblestones on which horses could get a better grip.
Above right: Long fingers of granite on the pier at Bullock Harbour are very similar to those used on the Liffey's South Bull Wall.

cap towers, or lookouts, are all in very good condition. A carved stone head may be seen on the southern corner of the castle, beside the archway.

Bullock Castle was once surrounded by a substantial walled enclosure, later the castle gardens, which featured a small lookout, known locally as Garret's Tower. This tower, which stood near the castle steps on Ulverton Road, was dismantled in the 1890s. These steps, at one time a steep pathway, were the only way to access the harbour from the Sandycove direction until the mid-nineteenth century when the present roadway was formed to the west of Bullock Castle.

The castle is in a good state of preservation but it is not generally open to visitors. Nearby once stood a curious feature called the Rocking Stone, which was left stranded after the last ice age atop a granite outcrop, and which rocked easily. The Rocking Stone and a cromlech, or dolmen, nearby were said to have been quarried or broken up when the adjacent Martello tower was built. Both features were depicted by the noted topographical artist Gabriel Beranger in 1777. There was another rocking stone in the district, now long forgotten, that appeared on early Ordnance Survey maps in the back garden of a house near Fitzgerald's pub in Sandycove.

Bullock Castle and Harbour, c. 1890, with the Ballast Office Road on the right. Perrin's Cottages, seen at the foot of the road, were occupied by fishermen and employees of Alderman Perrin, one-time owner of the castle.

Top left: *The slender profile of Bullock Castle as seen from the sea. The precipitous rocks at the back of Bullock Harbour were a great danger to sailing ships.*

Top right: *The dramatic and dangerous rocks at Bullock, photographed in 2020.*

Left: *The 1867 Ordnance Survey map of Bullock (25 inches to the mile) shows in great detail the various cottages and quarries of the district, including some now-vanished houses such as those of Pilot View, Henrietta Place and the old house attached to Bullock Castle.*

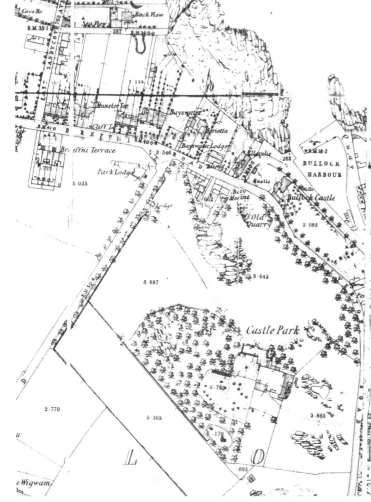

Bullock Castle appears in many paintings and engravings of the eighteenth and early nineteenth century. As early as 1698, Francis Place depicted it just prior to the erection of the adjoining house, but showing several thatched cottages in the vicinity. There was no harbour as we know it today and the grounds of the castle fell away to a steep and rocky shore. The creek at Bullock was, naturally, in continuous use from medieval times and in the eighteenth century there were many reports of confrontations between smugglers and the revenue officers.

Some time in the early 1700s a three-storey, gable-ended house was added to the northeast corner of the castle. A fine sketch from 1813, by Charles Pratt, shows it with a projecting porch and oval window in the attic pediment. A row of cottages backed onto the main road, and a defensive corner tower with an enclosing wall (or bawn) stood near the top of the castle steps.

Bullock Castle, photographed c. 1900, from a snow-covered Ulverton Road, is one of the best-preserved small castles in south Dublin.

The Crown lands of Dalkey, which included Bullock, were bought by Colonel Allen of Stillorgan in 1683 and by descent they passed to the Carysfort or Proby estate. In 1804 the house and lands of Bullock Castle were leased by the Carysfort estate to the Ballast Board for the purposes of quarrying. The board made improvements to both Bullock and Sandycove Harbours and used them to load granite for shipment across the bay to Dublin, where it was needed to repair the Great South Wall, or South Bull Wall, and build new quays in the port.

In 1817 the then 24-year-old William Hutchinson was appointed to supervise the quarrying and shipment of stone, to manage the lifeboat stationed at Sandycove, and to oversee the pilots at Bullock. He was paid £100 per annum and he had the use of Bullock Castle. Hutchinson, as we have seen in Chapter 2, was an important figure in the history of

Dún Laoghaire Harbour where he was later made harbour master. The eighteenth-century house was enlarged in Victorian times and a granite porch was also added where there was once an unusual letterbox in the form of a lion's mouth. It was demolished in the 1980s.

Bullock Castle with its now-vanished house, c. 1978.

The gardens of Bullock Castle once extended southwards to include all of the site now completely covered by the buildings of Our Lady's Manor. During the early 1960s the Carmelite Sisters for the Aged and Infirm, who are based in the USA, were invited to establish an institution in Ireland by Archbishop John Charles McQuaid. The new 100-bed block was opened in 1965 and further large extensions have been carried out which unfortunately dominate the harbour. The building project beside the castle involved the demolition of its adjoining eighteenth-century house.

CASTLE PARK AND OTHER HOUSES

On the Ordnance Survey map of 1867, the fields between Dalkey and Sandycove are still relatively undeveloped and small quarries dot the landscape. The most significant house on the map was Castle Park, formerly known as Castle Perrin, whose lands extended from Dalkey to Sandycove and included the quarries behind Bullock Harbour. The original house at Castle Park was probably built in the 1820s for it remains, with its late-Georgian windows, a recognisably earlier part of the larger house. By 1830, it was owned by Alderman Arthur Perrin, who lived in Bullock Castle and rented Castle Perrin to well-off members of the British administration in Dublin. It was Perrin who enlarged the house by building an imposing mock-Tudor mansion facing the sea, which is today the centrepiece of Castle Park School. A battlemented tower rises over the hall door, and the whole effect, with its grey rendered walls, is rather sombre. A large hall with an arcade in the Tudor manner is the most striking internal feature of the house, but all the rooms have elaborate plasterwork cornices and centrepieces.

Before the construction of Ulverton Road, the route from Sandycove to Dalkey passed along by Bullock Castle, and down a steep hill, now known as Castle Steps, behind Our

Lady's Manor, past a group of houses called Perrin's Cottages, and on to join the Ballast Office Road at Bullock. These four cottages were built by Perrin for his employees at Bullock Castle and Castle Park, sometime before 1837.

In 1851 the Right Hon. John Richards, Third Baron of Her Majesty's Court of Exchequer, was in residence at Castle Park, and some twenty years later we find another legal personality, the Hon. James O'Brien, Second Justice in the Court of the Queen's Bench, renting it.

A school was established here in 1904 by W.P. Toone, and in its early years attracted many pupils from England and abroad. The school has been diligent in preserving the surrounding fifteen acres of fields and trees but apartments are now being constructed in the lands.

A fine walled garden lies behind the house and is still very well maintained. The base of a small circular greenhouse, which originally had a rather elegant onion-shaped dome, may still be seen in the garden. The rather grandiose castellated Norman-style entrance on Castle Park Road, with its archway and circular towers, incorporates a gate lodge, which is of earlier date.

Amongst the various cottages that were once to be found at Bullock were the dwellings of quarrymen, fishermen and pilots. The Pilots' Cottages, built by the Ballast Board in 1807 at a cost of £10 each, consisted of a neat row of ten cottages, only three of which now survive. The pilots provided a valuable service to shipping in Dublin Bay. Their job was to sail out in small pilot boats, often in treacherous weather conditions, and guide ships safely up into the port of Dublin.

In the later nineteenth century the harbour was used by small coal boats making deliveries to Downey's coal yard there. Heavy iron rings, which were once used for ropes to winch the boats into the harbour, may still be seen. The coal was lifted in great baskets into the quayside

Top left: The rocky foreshore between Sandycove and Bullock where there is evidence of stone quarrying. A steep flight of steps descends to the sea from a lane at Sandycove Avenue East.

Left: The hall at Castlepark, in Tudor-Gothic style. The old house continues to operate as the focal point of a small private school.

sheds from where it was delivered by horse and cart to houses in the Dalkey area.

In 1911 there was only one pilot listed as resident in the Pilots' Cottages, but at Bullock Harbour there was also a fisherman, a lightship keeper, a seaman, three gardeners and a yacht- and boatbuilder named John Atkinson. Atkinson built many of the yachts known as Dublin Bay 17-footers, a number of which still sail at Howth.

Bullock is still of course a 'dry' harbour as there is no water at low tide. With its outstanding stonework and picturesque collection of small boats, is now used mainly for pleasure purposes but it continues to be home to a small group of crab and lobster fishermen and boat hire attracts visiting fishermen and divers who enjoy the coast around Dalkey.

Chris Lawless, the last of a long line of fishermen in Bullock Harbour, on his crab and lobster boat in 2021. The Smyths, Lawlesses, Cunninghams, Bradleys and Williamses were well-known seafaring families and many were volunteers with the Dún Laoghaire Lifeboat.

Chapter 8

DALKEY – A SENSE OF THE PICTURESQUE

Dalkey, once an important medieval trading town, remained a quiet backwater until the nineteenth century brought Martello towers, large-scale quarrying and the railway to its doorstep. The eighteenth century had seen little building in the district but some quarrying around Bullock Harbour. Dalkey, with its small coastal roads, many sea views and rocky bathing places, is imbued with a maritime quality. As a district, it has managed to retain its own special identity, one that is quite different from that of neighbouring Killiney or even Dún Laoghaire and though this is partly due to its position, it is mainly because its residents have, since the nineteenth century, so jealously fought to protect it. Castle Street, with its two castles, church, shops and houses, still preserves the quality of a small town. The railway makes a discreet appearance in Dalkey, passing through mostly in a cutting, then disappearing into a tunnel from which it emerges onto the dramatic coast of Killiney Bay. Most of the unique coastline has remained unspoilt because the scope for development has always been limited by presence of the sea on one side and Dalkey Hill with its public park on the other.

However, there has been consistent pressure to build apartment blocks and other houses on every available piece of land, never more so than at present, and sometimes to the detriment of the natural landscape and comparatively unspoilt coastline. It could be argued that this process began when the first large houses and terraces were erected in the middle of the nineteenth century, but at that time the scale and density of such projects was generally modest and the designs were usually ornamental. By comparison, today's

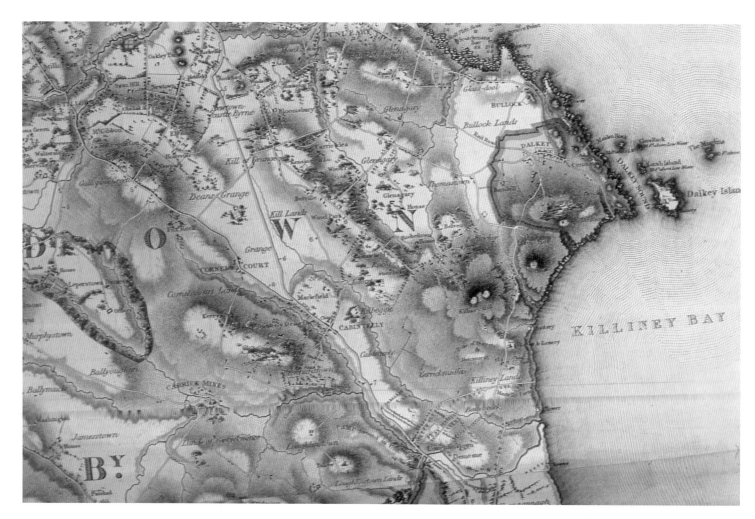

developers are often greedy to pack in the greatest number of residential units and scant regard is paid to the existing character of the place. Some of the crowded developments near Bullock Harbour are a case in point. Yet Dalkey has managed to keep its particular charm. Without doubt, the presence of granite, which is to be found everywhere, contributes to this. Granite was used in the building of the ancient castles and churches, the Martello towers, the local harbours, the Loreto Convent, the nineteenth-century churches and many houses, not to mention the miles of lovely stone walls.

One of the most colourful publications about Dalkey is James J. Gaskin's *Irish Varieties*, a book published in 1869 at a time when Dalkey was undergoing great change. Gaskin witnessed the Victorian transformation of Dalkey from an ancient village surrounded by fields and rocky scrub into a town with its own administration and a coastline dotted with many fine residences. In the space of approximately thirty years, commencing in about 1840, Dalkey saw rapid development. Houses and terraces sprang up here and

William Duncan's highly graphic map of County Dublin, made in 1821, shows well the extremely rocky and undeveloped nature of the coastline. Dalkey town is situated somewhat inland from the sea.

The tiny and picturesque Coliemore Harbour, with its granite piers, boat slip and walls, is almost hidden in the Dalkey coastline. The sheer rock at the back of the harbour was also quarried. The harbour is a favoured departure spot for fishing and boat trips to Dalkey Island.

there amid the rocky terrain; sites with sea views were eagerly snapped up. In comparison with Killiney, Dalkey seems to have a greater diversity of house types and there are many more cottages, small villas and terraces and the gardens are generally smaller. However, there was a distinctive taste for the picturesque in many of the grander new houses with a profusion of Italianate and Gothic features, such as battlements and towers. Perhaps this was partly inspired by the antiquity of the area with its ancient castles and ruined churches, although it was also in line with the more widespread nineteenth-century medieval revival. The grounds of Bullock Castle were surrounded by a castellated wall, most likely of nineteenth-century date and mock crenellations were soon to appear on other houses like Cliff Castle, Inniscorrig, Queenstown Castle, Castle Park and Monte Alverno. None of these houses, like Corrig Castle in Dún Laoghaire or Killiney Castle, had a connection with real castles but that was unimportant to their Victorian owners. The idea of adapting a castle to one's home and of recreating antiquity became popular in the nineteenth century. The new Loreto Abbey of 1843 was also built in the Gothic manner, as of course were nearly all churches of the period. Even the signal tower, or Telegraph, on Dalkey Hill was renovated by local landowner Warren to look like a castle.

The names of the new addresses and houses – Cape Sorrento, Vico, Mount Salus, Monte Vista, Nerano and Torca – are all suggestive of exotic foreign destinations and romantic connections. Sorrento was named in honour of the Bay of Naples, with which

Left: A pedestrian entrance near Monte Alverno on Sorrento Road demonstrates the fashion for Gothic-style architectural features.

Above: The castellated wall surrounding the gardens of Bullock Castle in this 1886 sketch reflect the Romantic movement's love of medieval-style features. (By permission of the Royal Irish Academy © RIA.)

Below: Iniscorrig, a large Tudorised house built of cut stone, stands overlooking Dalkey Sound and its own private harbour. But like many other coastal mansions it began as a fairly modest Victorian house.

Killiney is often compared. A few Irish names begin to appear on houses after 1840, suggesting a changing political mood and an interest in the Celtic Revival, and these include Rarc an Ilan, Cnoc Aluin, Carraig-na-Gréine, Bartragh, Tubbermore (names with a topographical origin roughly translating as Island View, Beautiful Hill, Rock of the Sun, Top of the Beach or coast and Great Well), and the name Coliemore itself. Coliemore Harbour, sometimes anciently spelt Colamore, was described in a sale document of 1844 as the ladies' bathing place and the plot of land to the northwest, where Coliemore Lodge was built, was sold for £1,100 – an example of the high prices paid for sites during the housebuilding boom in Dalkey.

DALKEY ISLAND

An aerial view of Dalkey Island. The Martello tower is visible in the middle, with the battery to the left and St Begnet's Church to the right (north).

Dalkey Island, with its ancient church of St Begnet, Martello tower and battery, is unique and unspoilt, a remarkable natural feature so close to a capital city of over a million people. When one sits at the back of the island among the seagulls' nests, long grass, bracken and rocks, looking out to the Irish Sea, it is hard to believe that the city is little over 10 kilometres away. The island, uninhabited since the last British soldiers left the fort in the nineteenth century, consists of twenty-two acres of rocky grassland, now grazed by goats

and rabbits. The name Dalkey can be translated as 'Thorny Island' and is derived from the Norse 'Deilg-Ei' or the Irish version 'Deilg-Inis', but some suggest that the name refers to the shape of the island rather than to its vegetation. It is true that the island has the shape of a tapering thorn or dagger and rises at the northern end of Dalkey Sound from small rocks and islands to substantial height at its southern end. The Martello tower and battery remain in very good condition, though the door to the tower is sealed up, preventing access to the magnificent views up and down the coast of the Irish Sea.

The ruin of St Begnet's Church is thought to date from the tenth century and is in remarkably good condition. It creates a bold profile on the island with its buttresses, or antae, at either end of the main structure, its square-headed, west-facing doorway and little belfry. The antae, which occur on a few other very early Irish churches, serve no structural purpose but are a design hangover from the ancient days of wood construction. During the building of the Martello tower in the early 1800s, workmen used the church as a place of shelter and built a fireplace in its eastern gable where, strangely, there is no evidence of an east window to be seen in the masonry. In the belfry there is a granite cross of Latin form, somewhat inappropriately squeezed into the space where a bell once hung. This cross was brought to the mainland in the 1950s and lay for a time in the garden of Queenstown Castle near Coliemore Harbour while a debate ensued over where it should finally rest. It was eventually brought back to the island and placed in the belfry. There

Below left: The Martello tower on Dalkey Island is an imposing structure built of cut-stone blocks. It is one of the largest towers built as part of the coastal defences of County Dublin in the early 1800s. Nothing had been built on the island since the erection of St Begnet's Church (seen in the background) in around the tenth century.

Below right: This c. 1880 photograph of St Begnet's Church shows the very primitive nature of its design and construction, in common with other early churches in places such as Glendalough and Fore.

is a strong case for relocating the cross in the church or nearby. An excavation that took place near the church in 1958 revealed burials from the sixth to the eleventh centuries, and fragments of thirteenth-century roof tiles from the church itself. Near the church are two crosses cut into the granite bedrock.

The ruined church in Dalkey village is also dedicated to St Begnet. Little is known about her: she was possibly a seventh-century Irish princess who achieved sainthood by dedicating her life to prayer. Her feast day is 12 November and her name may also have been given to the Bennett Bank or Begnet's Bank, north of the Kish lighthouse.

Near Dalkey Island's western shore is a freshwater well, marked on some maps as 'the Scurvy well', and its waters are said to possess curative powers. The well was probably last used on a daily basis by the soldiers who occupied the Martello tower and battery during the nineteenth century, but its waters are still drinkable.

There is little doubt that Dalkey was a place of very early settlement, and archaeologists have found evidence of a promontory fort on Dalkey Island. Promontory forts are usually located on a headland, with sea on all sides but one, where a fortified ditch would be constructed. A similar fort existed on Lambay Island. Bronze Age spearhead moulds, arrowhead flints and pottery fragments were found here. A fascinating find of a stone axe head, possibly dating from 4000 BC, was made by divers in 1991 nearby in the sea close to the Muglins.

The Muglins is a large barren rock to the northeast of Dalkey Island, and now carries a red-painted, cone-shaped lighthouse. It was the scene of an unsavoury eighteenth-century event. In 1766 *The Gentleman's Magazine* carried a report of two pirates, named McKinley and Zeckerman, who commandeered a ship sailing from the Canary Islands to

Below left: The new jetty on Dalkey Island, built to facilitate visitors.

Below right: The Muglins, is a haven for birds and a renowned fishing spot.

London with a large quantity of Spanish dollars, some jewels and other valuable cargoes. The pirates brutally murdered the captain and crew and threw the bodies overboard. They proceeded towards Ireland but were caught near Waterford and brought to Dublin where they were tried and hanged. Their bodies were first hanged on the South Bull Wall at Dublin Port but, following complaints from the public, the corpses were removed to the Muglins where they were hung up in chains!

THE KING OF DALKEY

In the late 1780s a satirical society was formed in a hostelry called The Palace, in what is now Dublin's Temple Bar area, and its president was elected with the grand title of 'King of Dalkey (island), Emperor of The Muglins, Prince of the Holy Island of Magee, and Elector of Lambay and Ireland's Eye, Defender of his own Faith and Respecter of all others, and Sovereign of the Most Illustrious Order of the Lobster and Periwinkle.'

Various proclamations of a political and satirical nature were issued and every summer, at least until 1797, a lavish ceremony took place on the island, including the coronation of the 'king'. The *Dalkey Gazette* described the scene on 16 August 1796: 'On Sunday morning, at the dawn of day, his Majesty King Stephen came in a private coach to The Palace, attended by their graces …' They set sail from Sir John Rogerson's Quay 'His Majesty's arrival [at Dalkey] was announced by firing of rockets, discharges of artillery and the most unbounded shouts of applause from the surrounding multitude …'

The events of 1798 may have put a different colour on these ceremonies. Though they were an occasion for fun and entertainment, there was undoubtedly a serious element of political satire.

MEDIEVAL DALKEY

The lands of Dalkey, Killiney and Shankill were granted to the Church in medieval times and the Archbishop of Dublin established a manor at Shankill to control these lands and collect dues from his tenants. In Dalkey, he had the right to collect a tax which consisted of 'a prise of fish', and could grant tenancies in the form of burgages. A burgage included a strip of cultivable land and many of them backed onto the town, where the tenant had the right to graze cattle or sheep on the common. It might also include an orchard or garden. In 1326 the archbishop granted thirty-nine burgages in Dalkey. Some of the present-day house plots and lanes in Dalkey reflect this ancient pattern of land use.

Above left: A Dalkey fisherman at Coliemore Harbour c. 1890 with one of his lobster pots.

Above right: A precariously loaded boat full of lobster pots is rowed into Dalkey Sound c. 1910. The deep waters of the rocky coast ensured a bountiful harvest of crabs and lobsters.

Right: An eighteenth-century map, made by Thomas Reading in 1765, showing the burgages or strips of land that had been leased to tenants for cultivation in Dalkey since medieval times. The town of Dalkey can be seen to the right.

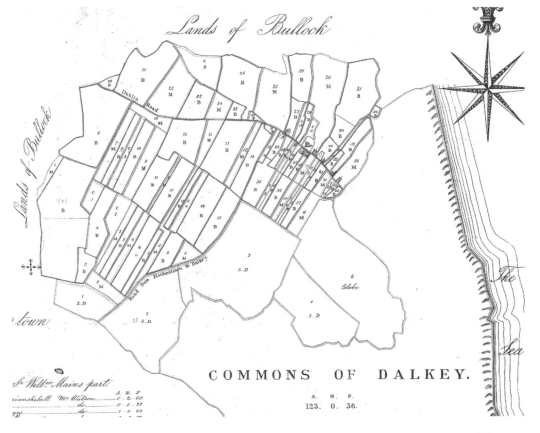

St Begnet's is a surprisingly large church with a long nave and chancel, reflecting the importance of Dalkey as a medieval town.

The king also held land in Dalkey, which in the fourteenth century he granted to Reginald Talbot in return for an annual rent of one goshawk. Such birds must once have been common around Dalkey, and it is interesting that the Hawk Cliff, near the Vico bathing place, was still to be found on nineteenth-century maps. However, Talbot found himself in trouble in 1369 when his goshawk was deemed to be 'un sound, un fit, and of no value – a fraud on the Court, and a grievous damage to the King' and he was fined!

There are two churches dedicated to St Begnet in Dalkey, one on the island, as already discussed, and one on Castle Street in Dalkey village. The latter, which stands beside the Goat Castle, is attributed to the ninth century with later alterations. In the graveyard there is a stone slab, inscribed with cup marks and concentric circles, one of the so-called Rathdown Slabs (also at Rathmichael and Tully churches) and almost certainly of pre-Christian date. These curiously carved grave slabs seem to cross the divide between pagan and Christian symbolism as some simply bear concentric circles and herringbone patterns while others hint at cross-type arms. Little can be said with certainty, but they may have Viking origins.

Dalkey was described in 1760 by John Rocque as 'Dalkey, 7 castles' and all writers describe it as a medieval town that once flourished as a seaport. Records show that large quantities of fish were caught off Dalkey and were exported to places such as Chester and Bristol. Charles V. Smith, in his excellent study *Dalkey – Society and Economy in a Small Medieval Irish Town* (1996), revealed that few records survive to document the extent of Dalkey's trade or its status as a town. He concludes that its origins were based on agricultural and fishing activities, and that from the fourteenth century onwards it was favoured as a place for vessels to unload part of their cargo before attempting to sail up the shallow River Liffey to Dublin itself. (Until the completion of the South Bull Wall in the 1760s at the mouth of the Liffey, and even after, Dublin Port was notoriously difficult for ships to reach in safety. The combination of prevailing westerly winds, shallow waters and a sandbank, which is still known as the bar, caused numerous shipwrecks. For this reason it suited many shipowners to unload some or all of their cargo at Dalkey.)

While Dalkey is frequently described as a port, we do not know of the existence of any quays or jetties, nor is there any mention of dues being collected by customs. There may have been an early quay at Bullock, as Bullock Harbour was for centuries under the control of the Cistercian monks of St Mary's Abbey in the city, and it was they who built the castle there.

Though Dalkey was once noted for its seven castles, only two now remain. They were built, it would seem, in the fifteenth century as fortified houses for merchant families. The castles were used to store valuable merchandise such as wine, and also provided some protection for the town against possible attack by the 'wild Irish'! The surviving castles are attractive late-medieval structures of moderate size, and have no very elaborate features

Dalkey's Castle Street in the 1920s, with Goat Castle, which was converted into a town hall in 1868. This is now open to the public and has a small museum and visitor centre attached.

such as carved chimneypieces or windows, which one would expect in a merchant town.

Charles Brooking's map of 1728 shows Dalkey's seven castles still intact, but forty years later, Peter Wilson reported that most of the town walls and one castle had been destroyed, leaving six. The Ordnance Survey map of 1843 shows only five surviving. The ruins were obviously considered by some to be a convenient source of building stone, and Wolverton Castle, which stood near the corner of Dalkey Avenue, was reportedly demolished by William Porter in the 1840s to provide material for building Tudor House. (The name Ulverton Road is a corruption of the name Wolverton.) Dungan's Castle stood opposite, almost at the corner of Ulverton Road, and belonged to a family of merchants who prospered here during the sixteenth century. The ruin of Archbold's Castle remains today as the most unaltered of the group, though its surroundings were paved in 1986 when the local authority built townhouses nearby.

The Goat Castle, which was converted into a town hall in 1868, belonged to the Cheevers family in the sixteenth century. The name Cheevers, which is of Norman origin, is derived from the word *chêvre*, meaning goat, the same animal being a feature of their coat of arms. During the late nineteenth century, the principal chamber, upstairs, served the Dalkey town commissioners as their council chamber, while a 'modern' hall, added to the back of the castle in the 1890s, has seen much use by the community. The castle is now open to the public as a popular attraction in its own right and is complemented by a small visitor centre, which also gives access to St Begnet's Church.

A busy scene in Castle Street about 1900, as an open-topped tram pauses for the photographer.

An early nineteenth-century engraving of Dalkey shows the two castles surrounded by some cottages and other ruins and, intriguingly, a pair of stocks. The stocks were located at the entrance to the present car park, beside the church, and are a reminder of how law and order were kept in the town. As Dalkey was in Church hands, justice was administered in the archbishop's court, presided over by his seneschal. In the late sixteenth century, Robert Barnewall of Shankill Castle was fined 10s by the court for not having a pair of stocks. Similarly, those accused of certain crimes could seek the refuge of the Church, as happened in the case of a man who stole an anchor in Dalkey and sought sanctuary in the church on Dalkey Island.

Dalkey was granted the right to hold a market in 1482, and the market place may have been located at the wider part of the main street where Convent and Sorrento roads converge.

DALKEY QUARRY

Rocque's map of 1760 graphically illustrates the extremely rocky nature of the whole district of Dalkey. As we have already seen, it was the presence of this rock so conveniently near the surface of the ground that led to many quarries being opened in both Dalkey and Bullock during the eighteenth century.

Granite, as already noted, was much in demand for paving in Dublin and for the construction of the South Bull Wall at the entrance to the Liffey. The Ballast Board, who were

Massive slabs of remaining granite bedrock bear witness to the immense undertaking of creating Dalkey Quarry, where half the hill of Dalkey was blasted away and transported to Kingstown.

charged with improving the port of Dublin, removed large quantities of granite from quarries here.

The history of quarrying in Dalkey culminated in the opening of the massive quarries at Dalkey Hill in 1815, to provide stone for the building of Dún Laoghaire Harbour. Dalkey Quarry, with its cathedral-like cliffs, represents an extraordinary change to the natural landscape, all wrought by human effort. It is almost impossible to imagine what this hill, once part of Dalkey Commons, might have looked like before quarrying began and it was cut away and removed.

The commons covered two large tracts of land including the present quarry area to the south of the town and all of the land that lay between Dalkey Hill and Dalkey Sound. This included much of the Coliemore and Sorrento Road areas. A description by Peter Wilson of Dalkey in 1768 comments on the very rocky nature of the commons but adds that it 'affords most excellent pasture for sheep'.

It is not generally known that there was once a cromlech on Dalkey Commons and that it was destroyed when quarrying began. Weston St John Joyce says it was removed when the Martello towers were being built. In 1780 Gabriel Beranger made a drawing of it and noted that it was called the Cloch Tobair Gailline, meaning 'the cromlech of the well of Gallion'. It consisted of a massive rock supported in the usual way by several smaller boulders.

Captain Toutcher, who in the early years of the nineteenth century had campaigned vigorously for a new harbour at Dún Laoghaire, got permission to open a quarry on part of Dalkey Commons for the sole purpose of constructing what was at first to be called 'an asylum harbour'. This asylum harbour would provide refuge for ships waiting to sail up the Liffey into Dublin. The need for such a harbour was made all the more urgent when two troop ships were wrecked in Dublin Bay in 1807; some of the 380 victims were buried in St Begnet's graveyard in Dalkey village.

The construction of Dún Laoghaire Harbour was seen as a great humanitarian under-taking and was widely supported. At the height of this enormous engineering project, more than 600 men were employed, many of them working in the quarries at Dalkey. Living conditions were poor and, while some managed to build cottages for themselves, others lived like squatters in cabins and tents on the land of the commons.

It has been suggested that many of the numerous cottage-style houses to be found in Dalkey had their origins as quarrymen's cottages. It may well be that, following the closure of the quarries, the former stonemasons and quarrymen were happy to sell their holdings for a good price to the new middle-class residents.

By 1837 Samuel Lewis was able to comment: 'There are also numerous pleasant cottages, commanding fine views of the sea, which are let during the summer to respectable families.' Small, low-roofed cottages abound in and around Sorrento Road and Leslie Avenue, and these may indeed have once been the homes of quarrymen.

By far the most interesting surviving group is to be found at Ardbrugh Road where a picturesque cluster of cottages is located at the entrance to the main quarry, high up overlooking the bay. There were once as many as twenty small cottages here, approached by paths too narrow and twisting for any car to get in. Some of the smallest cottages have since been joined together or rebuilt.

EIGHTEENTH-CENTURY DALKEY

'Dalkey is the last village within the bay of Dublin. It is seven miles from the capital, and stands on the base of a high mountain. Though now a miserable village, it still exhibits proofs of its having been formerly a place of some importance.' These were the comments of a tourist named John James MacGregor, writing about Dalkey in 1821 in his book *The New Picture of Dublin*, and they were repeated by other writers in the eighteenth and early nineteenth centuries. There is considerable evidence to suggest that Dalkey was a prosperous small town in the fifteenth and sixteenth centuries, thriving as a shipping outpost of Dublin, but from that 'golden age' until the nineteenth century the castles were left to decay and the village lay neglected.

Rocque's 1760 map shows Dalkey as a place not much changed since late medieval times – a small village clustered around a single main street, with one 'road' leading to the cove at Sorrento and another to connect Dalkey with the inlet or creek at Bullock. The bay at Sorrento provided some shelter from northerly and westerly winds, while Bullock offered protection from southerly winds. In favourable conditions, ships could anchor in Dalkey Sound and there was always a little inlet at Coliemore which would have served as a convenient landing place. The construction of Coliemore Harbour with its two short piers was begun in 1868 and the work was carried out by a local builder called John Cunningham.

Later maps by John Taylor, 1816, and a chart by Alexander Nimmo for the Commissioners of Irish Fisheries, 1823, agree with Rocque's layout of roads in Dalkey and show no path or road leading from the town directly to Coliemore.

John Rutty, writing in 1772, observed: 'Near Dalkey is a lead mine, where it is said that some hundreds of tons of ore have been raised. I got 42 grains of lead from 90 grains of ore, fluxed with equal parts of salt.'

All the earlier maps also indicate the location of the Dalkey lead mines at Sorrento Point and blocked-up passages and tunnels have been reported in this vicinity, particularly near Sorrento Terrace.

Dalkey village was a quiet place in the eighteenth century. A map of 1765 by Thomas Reading indicates a house and garden and two inns, the Red Crowe and the Sign of the Ship. The former is now known as the Queen's and was previously called the Queen's Royal Hotel. The Queen's Hotel is probably the oldest and most impressive house on Castle Street and though it may once have incorporated earlier structures, its three-storey elevation, squat windows and thick walls suggest a mid-eighteenth-century date. There is a handsome cut-stone doorcase similar to one in Dalkey Lodge. The Queen's is set back from the street and had its own large gardens to the rear. During the nineteenth century, it changed hands frequently and in 1879 was bought by the Dublin Southern District Tramway Company for the purpose of acquiring part of the lands for their tram depot. It was then purchased in 1894 by Jeremiah Ryan for £710 as a going concern, complete with furniture and billiard-room fittings. Things did not go well for Ryan, and when pressed for a cheque by his solicitor only two years later, he wrote: 'trade has been very bad since the roads were broken up.' This was probably a reference to the ongoing work of laying water mains in Dalkey, which was then being connected to the Vartry water supply. The Queen's closed its doors as a pub and restaurant during 2020 but has happily found new owners and is again open.

The Queen's Hotel in Dalkey.

Barnhill Road, which joins Dalkey at its western end, was once the main road to Dublin and very likely takes its name from the presence long ago of a large barn that might have served the tenants and farmers of Dalkey. Barn Hill is a notable house built about 1906 in the Arts and Crafts style.

Dalkey Lodge, on Barnhill Road, is the oldest surviving house in the area. It was described by Peter Wilson in 1768 as follows: 'On the west side of town stands Dalkey Lodge, a neat house belonging to a citizen.' Wilson is best known as the publisher of *Wilson's Almanack*, a comprehensive eighteenth-century directory that was published annually. On a wet day, having nothing better to do, Wilson wrote a short account of Dalkey as he saw it. He describes the excellent view from Dalkey Lodge across Dublin Bay to 'the new light house and adjacent works, the Hill of Howth, skirted in summer with a mixture of delightful spots of corn and other grounds'.

The Lodge is a large house, three storeys in height and five windows wide, with an attractive cut-stone doorcase of mid-eighteenth-century date. There are also a number of later additions to the side and to the back. In Victorian times the house was owned by Thomas Henry, who installed a sundial bearing the inscription 'Dalkey Lodge AD 1869'. A quarry which once adjoined the lodge has been filled in and there is now a small estate of houses here named Old Quarry.

As Barnhill Road was one of the principal roads into Dalkey, where better to locate the business of a farrier? The remains of an old forge can still be seen in the horseshoe-shaped entrance, now blocked up, at the former Statoil filling station on Barnhill Road. The garage behind was once an old schoolhouse and the buildings now appear to be derelict.

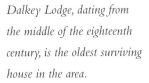

Dalkey Lodge, dating from the middle of the eighteenth century, is the oldest surviving house in the area.

Chapter 9

Nineteenth-century Dalkey

– The Coastline

By the mid-1830s, when Samuel Lewis was compiling his *Topographical Dictionary of Ireland*, Dalkey was beginning to change. The construction of Dún Laoghaire Harbour, which continued from 1815 well into the 1840s, undoubtedly provided much employment in Dalkey Quarry, and boosted the whole economy of the village. Lewis described it as having 'a two penny post' (i.e. its own postal service), a constabulary police station and a coastguard station. He mentioned the Martello towers, the quarry, a national school and about six important houses, among which were the Rev. Hercules MacDonnell's Sorrento, Mr Brabazon's Charleville, Mrs Johnson's Barn Hill, Mr Armstrong's Braganza, Mrs O'Reilly's Shamrock Lodge and Mr Hank's Coliemore.

Within a few years the building of new houses would begin apace. Dalkey was to follow the pattern being set all along the southern shore of Dublin Bay and in the coastal villages of the county. The new middle classes, who had done well in the professions or in business, wanted to live 'rus-in-urbe', that is to say, they wanted country living with all the convenience of being in close proximity to the town and they would travel to the city only when necessary.

The decade of the 1840s was a period of intensive development in Dalkey. One of the first large buildings to appear was the Church of the Assumption, which was constructed in 1840. This was followed by the Loreto Convent in 1842 and St Patrick's Church in 1843. The following year would see the arrival of the experimental Atmospheric Railway in Dalkey, and the first houses of Sorrento Terrace were erected in 1845.

Sorrento Terrace, possibly the most boldly located Victorian Terrace in County Dublin, stands high above the sea, which can be positively Mediterranean on a tranquil summer's day. But when southerly gales battered the coast, the houses needed the storm shutters with which they were once equipped.

The Church of the Assumption was initially a plain, rectangular building with Gothic windows. Transepts and a square tower were added later, and there is a rather unusual fan-vaulted ceiling inside. It was built on a site donated to the parish by the Connolly family, who were bakers in Dalkey.

The Loreto Abbey, or Convent, stands overlooking the sea on lands once owned by Charles Leslie of Carraig-na-Gréine, which we shall discuss shortly. The site, with its open aspect, is certainly a healthy one and can be both inspiring and bleak, especially in winter. The convent and school is an imposing Tudor-style structure, cruciform in plan and built of local granite, with Gothic windows and narrow corner turrets. The date 1842 is carved into a stone over the door, along with the crest of the order and the inscription 'Maria Regina Angelorum' (Mary Queen of Angels). These substantial buildings were further added to in the nineteenth century as the school grew in size.

Other Christian denominations were provided for in Dalkey and in 1861 a Wesleyan chapel, now converted into a private house, was also built. It was greatly supported by the

*The Loreto Abbey Dalkey
(left), built in the Tudor-
Gothic style of the 1840s
by Mother Frances Ball, is
constructed of cut granite like
the neighbouring St Patrick's
Church (above).*

wealthy McComas family who once lived at Cliff Castle. St Patrick's Church stands on a prominent site above Bullock Harbour. Plans for a new Protestant church in Dalkey were first mooted in 1836, and a site was offered near Bullock Castle by Alderman Arthur Perrin. The church was completed by 1843 to the designs of Jacob Owen, and has a cruciform plan with a somewhat squat, square tower. The church is characterised by its beautiful ashlar granite and long, narrow Gothic windows. It was built on a site (leased for 10,000 years from the Earl of Carysfort) lying between an old quarry and the Ballast Office Road. The east window features elaborate tracery which incorporates a Star of David.

Close by, at the entrance gates, stands an attractive granite-built sexton's house, constructed in 1868 to the design of the architect Edward Carson, whose family lived originally in Harcourt Street and later in Dalkey. His namesake and relation became the notable Unionist politician and leader. The Carsons had lived in Dalkey at Mount Alverno. The original designs of the sexton's house show a pointed roof with decorative ironwork finials over the front door, but unfortunately this striking feature has disappeared.

In 1870 Charles Leslie, a wealthy wholesale chemist, made a large donation to the parish for the purpose of building a school and meeting hall. More than a century later these buildings would be the setting of the first non-denominational primary school in Ireland, the Dalkey School Project, which had its origins here in 1978.

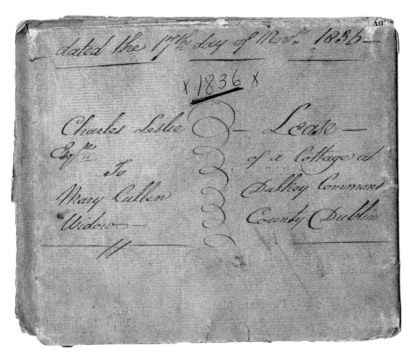

Lease to Mary Cullen, widow, from Charles Leslie for a cottage on Dalkey Common – now Leslie Avenue – dated 1836.

Carraig-na-Gréine, built by Charles Leslie around 1830, is a very striking, if severe, cut-stone house. This Doric-style villa was the height of fashion when it was built. It represented everything that was different from the equally popular Tudor style of the period. This classical idiom, also used for the railway station and yacht clubs in Dún Laoghaire, belonged to the cult of the Greek revival. It stands one storey over a basement, with a central recessed entrance flanked by Doric columns. The tall granite columns are remarkable, as they are cut from single pieces of stone. It was Leslie who constructed the tunnel, now unfortunately blocked up, near the shore at the bottom of his grounds in order to preserve a right-of-way to a well. Leslie had bought up several smallholdings in the area in order to build his house, and had tried to cut off access to the Lady Well, as it was known. The tunnel meant that the public could still visit the well without having to cross his land – and, perhaps more importantly to Leslie, without being seen from the windows of his house! An original lease survives in the O'Flanagan papers in the archives of Dún Laoghaire–Rathdown County Council showing that Leslie rented a cottage on Leslie Avenue for £1 a year to Mary Cullen whose cottage Leslie had acquired some time previously, turning her out, and who, it is said, took legal action regarding access to the well and her own right to live there. Leslie Avenue is one of Dalkey's most charming narrow roads and has some of the smallest surviving cottages in the area, including St Jude's and one called Tiny Cottage.

There was once a fine walled garden and also a collection of unusually attractive coach houses at Carraig-na-Gréine, both of which were recently demolished in order to build sheltered housing for elderly people. The buildings were fronted by a long, symmetrical wall, articulated by granite niches, coigns and string courses. Equally well built is the gate lodge, with its arched windows and pedimented entrance. Like the main house, it is an outstanding example of finely jointed granite masonry. The entrance gates at Leslie Avenue are formed by five tapering granite piers and have an archway of wrought iron.

Among the principal houses built on Harbour Road after 1830 were Beulah, Bartra, Charleville and Glencairn, all situated near St Patrick's Church. Charleville, with its gables and chimneys, is an L-shaped house with cut-stone Tudor-style details. There is a small 'spy tower' built of rubble stone in the corner of the gardens. Nearby stood Glencairn, once called Dalkey House, a large, square structure of Victorian date. It was demolished to make way for a development of red-brick apartments. Beulah is a compact two-storey-over-basement house with prominent overhanging eaves. It was designed in the Regency style and has attractive bow-ended rooms. Standing as it does on a height in nearly three acres of grounds, it surveys all of the coast between Dalkey and Bullock.

A special feature of the larger Dalkey houses with a coastal frontage are the private jetties or boat harbours. Brennan's Folly is so named after Charles Brennan who lived in Beulah at the turn of the century and who may have built the small 'harbour'. There are also substantial harbours and private bathing places attached to Rocklands, Inniscorrig and its neighbour Cliff Castle.

Bartra, built about 1845, is a wide Victorian-style house which stands on a terrace overlooking the sea near Bullock. Originally three windows wide, it was greatly enlarged by Judge John Monroe. It was also the home of the Booth family, who took a great interest in the affairs of Dalkey and put up money to assist the local Urban District Council in the purchase of Dalkey Island from the British War Office. The McCormick family, who operated coal boats out of Kingstown Harbour, were later inhabitants of Bartra. When sold in 1981 it stood on over five acres of lawns and gardens and included the Martello tower, substantial stables and a gate lodge.

The Shangri-La Hotel, which will be remembered by many older residents, consisted of four terraced houses that backed onto the sea. The houses were built in the 1840s and were originally called Henrietta Place. With its three-storey-over-basement houses, Henrietta Place was similar to the many terraces being built in Kingstown at that time, such as Charlemont Terrace on the seafront. They were in the late Georgian style and had typical pillared doorcases and fanlights. Tempe Terrace, on Coliemore Road, is in the same style, with slightly different decorative details, and was built by 1837. The Shangri-La was demolished in 1979 as part of a big development scheme. New apartments were built here, called Pilot View after the plain, villa-type house (built in the 1840s) on the site of which the first phase was erected. A noted resident of Pilot View was author and play-wright Hugh Leonard, who grew up in Dalkey.

Coliemore Lodge, Lota, Elsinore, Inniscorrig, Cliff Castle and Rarc an Ilan form an impressive group of Victorian marine residences which lie between Carraig-na-Gréine

Opposite top: The pedestrian gate to Victoria House is a handsome classical doorcase of cut limestone.

Opposite bottom: The garden gate to Summerfield House on Dalkey Avenue displays attractive ironwork including an arched grille with a shamrock pattern.

and Coliemore Harbour and which in 1834 were the scene of the most bizarre activities. The story revolves around a girl named Etty Scott, daughter of a Scot who had come to Ireland to supervise the granite-loaded trucks that ran from Dalkey Quarry to Kingstown Harbour. Etty, described as a beautiful, romantic girl with fanciful ideas, dreamt that a massive hoard of gold lay buried under 'the long stone', a granite outcrop near Coliemore Road. Somehow she persuaded about thirty-six quarrymen and labourers to devote themselves completely for many weeks to the search for gold. Nothing was found, but years later, some of Etty's followers who had built cabins nearby found financial reward by selling their plots to the builders of the new houses such as Inniscorrig, Lota and Elsinore.

Coliemore Lodge, which was more recently known as the Dalkey Island Hotel, was built sometime after 1844 and at first was called Coliemore Cottage. The site, then called 'the lands of coolamore' was purchased for the substantial sum of £1,100. It stood beside the quaint and tiny harbour, then described as the ladies' bathing place, which in 1837 was sufficiently developed to merit description on the Ordnance Survey map, but still had no piers. Whether the cottage was demolished or enlarged is difficult to say, but the house, which eventually was converted into the hotel, was a large, five-bay, two-storey-over-basement structure. The porch, of which the middle part was original, bore the monogram of the Weldon Moloney family, who once lived here. The house was swept away in 2003 and the site redeveloped for apartments.

F. Milo O'Flanagan, in his article about Old Dalkey (*Dublin Historical Record*, 1941) wrote that Rarc an Ilan was one of the first houses in the area to be given an Irish name, and that the newspapers of the day commented favourably on this new practice. The house was lived in, in 1847, by Robert Cordner, a lace and trimming manufacturer of Parliament Street, Dublin.

Cliff Castle, which has also had a life as a hotel, is a large Victorian house, decked out as an extravagant mock-medieval castle, to the designs of architects McCurdy and Mitchell. The square house

The Dalkey Island Hotel, which offered great views of Dalkey Island and Coliemore, was demolished in 2003 and replaced with apartments.

has three circular corner towers and all the usual Tudor trimmings, but the whole effect with further circular stone-built towers and battlemented terraces, which lead down to a small private harbour among the rocks, is impressive. Cliff Castle was occupied by a Henry Baldwin QC in 1850. It was bought by Timothy and Bride Murphy in 1920. With seventeen bedrooms on hand, Bride decided to open a small hotel: Cliff Castle Hotel became a great success and is said to have been frequented by famous figures such as Arthur Griffith and Oliver St John Gogarty.

Inniscorrig was built in 1847 for Sir Dominic Corrigan, a noted physician. Corrigan, who originally lived at Merrion Square, took a keen interest in Dublin Zoo and built his own aquarium at Inniscorrig. He campaigned for the provision of the Vartry water supply and was critical of the poor-quality drinking water generally available, especially for the poor. He also pointed to the need for an adequate water supply for fire-fighting purposes. A Catholic, and an MP from 1870 to 1874, he was highly successful and well respected. He is buried in St Andrew's Church, Westland Row. Inniscorrig was later the home of J.L. Robinson, the architect of Dún Laoghaire town hall.

Photographs of Inniscorrig taken in about 1870 show a gabled, square, stone-built house with prominent chimneys. Later, the house was almost doubled in size by the addition of a short tower, extra rooms and an enormous conservatory. Corrigan cannot

Below left: Queenstown Castle, with its liberal application of battlements, may have begun its life as Springfield Castle in 1837; it was occupied in 1850 by Robert Smyth, a successful high-class grocer on St Stephen's Green, and had its own small harbour.

Below right: Scotch Rath, later renamed Berwick House, was a large, bow-ended, late-Victorian house which overlooked Coliemore Harbour, and was built of red brick and granite. Over an entrance gate was an inscribed stone brought from Berwick House in Rathfarnham, a retreat house that moved here and led to the change of name. The house was demolished to make way for a block of apartments.

have suffered unduly from modesty (he placed a bust of himself over his hall door, not to mention what appears to be a pun in his choice of name for his house). A visit of King Edward VII to Inniscorrig is commemorated by a crown and a star set in pebbles on either side of the main door. A terrace, protected by a decorative cast-iron railing, looks down on the largest private harbour on the Dalkey coastline. There was once also a small crane and a flagstaff.

Martin Burke, the owner in 1850 of the Shelbourne Hotel on St Stephen's Green, built the nearby Victoria House. It stands overlooking Coliemore Harbour and, like so many houses of the period, began modestly enough but was greatly enlarged in the late nineteenth century by the addition of a new front and a conical capped tower. James Milo Burke, Martin's brother, lived at another Dalkey house called the Khyber Pass and later at Queenstown Castle. He, along with Provost MacDonnell of Sorrento Terrace, became very involved with the Dalkey town commissioners and was instrumental in organising the construction of the new piers at Coliemore Harbour, which were completed by 1869.

Sea bathing was becoming fashionable in the mid-nineteenth century, and Dalkey then had two commercial baths, located on Dalkey Sound: the Queenstown Baths, run by a Mrs McDonnell, and the Clifton Baths run by a Mr Kavanagh. Public bathing places included the Vico, which appears to have been created some time after 1870. It always rivalled the Forty Foot for the excellence of its bathing conditions and is still very popular.

Nerano, high above Coliemore Harbour, is a local landmark because of the large 2.5-metre-high stucco statue of a sailor which stands on a rock in the terraced garden. The sailor, who surveys Dalkey Island, may have come from the MacAnaspie Roman cement and stucco works on Pearse Street, Dublin. The MacAnaspies, who were one of the early residents of Nerano, were noted for their production of stucco eagles, urns

and statues, which were often placed on buildings and in gardens. In any case, by 1863, the statue, which is accompanied by a capstan, an anchor and a seal, was lying on the ground. It was restored by a new owner of Nerano, John Fleming. Nerano and Island View, both of which appear on the 1837 map, are plain houses of the late Georgian type, which have been somewhat altered by later additions. Kilross, which stands above Nerano, is said to have originated as a chapel in the 1830s, when a small oratory was constructed by a Franciscan and locals were permitted to attend mass there. A house was later added to the chapel.

Close by on Beacon Hill are the five houses of the coastguard station, which were built in the 1840s and once incorporated a lookout, a laundry and a well. A report on the coastguard service in 1824 recommended that an eight-person station be established here with a watch and a boathouse, and commented that Killiney Bay is much used by 'pilot boats who smuggle when the opportunity offers'.

SORRENTO TERRACE

The views from Sorrento Terrace and the Vico Road are unparalleled in County Dublin, stretching as they do across Killiney Bay to the wide sweep of Bray Head and the Wicklow Mountains. There is also a marvellous sense of space, with the great expanse of sea and sky that stretches out into the Irish Sea.

Sorrento Terrace, consisting of eight Victorian houses, was probably the most daring

By the 1840s, new houses were springing up amid the rocky terrain of Dalkey, such as Sorrento Terrace, which was already well advanced by 1845.

building project to be carried out in the area. A similar but far more ambitious plan for Killiney Hill, to have been called Queenstown, was proposed by Robert Warren of Killiney Castle in 1840 but it came to nothing. A surviving plan (in a lease of 1845) shows that Sorrento Terrace was intended to run to twenty-two houses. The land was owned and leased out for building by the Rev. Hercules Henry Graves MacDonnell, a barrister, who stipulated that the sum of at least £1,000 had to be expended on each house, which would be designed in accordance with the working plans of architects Frederick Darley and Nathaniel Montgomery. The residents were not permitted to 'alter the proportions, appearance or uniformity of Sorrento Terrace' by 'building, painting or omitting to paint'! The houses were erected by Edward Masterson of George's Street, Kingstown, a local builder of high reputation. The street elevation is handsome, with bracketed doorcases and leaded overlights giving onto a hall which leads to the drawing room overlooking Killiney Bay. As an index of house prices, it is interesting to trace the fortunes of a property in Sorrento Terrace. One house, built for £1,000 in 1845, was sold in 1925 for £650, and later made £450,000 in 1990. In 1998 No. 1 Sorrento Terrace, called Sorrento House, sold for an amazing £5.9 million. In 2006 this property was put on the market with a price tag of €30 million! This house, being the end house, is slightly larger than the others, and was first owned by aforementioned barrister, MacDonnell. It stands at the end

A photograph of Sorrento Terrace c. 1890, showing the street-level balcony that overlooked the steeply sloping gardens, and the Martello tower on Dalkey Island with its ladder in the background. Tucked into the corner of the bay is Sorrento Cottage, which was built by 1837 as a single-storey villa, and was used by the MacDonnells. It was later enlarged by the addition of an extra floor.

of the terrace and its extensive grounds take in the whole of Sorrento Point. During the ownership of Sorrento House by Judge Thomas Overend in the early 1900s, regattas were held here by the Dalkey Amusements Committee. A flagstaff marked the starting line for the Dalkey regatta, while guests were entertained on the lawns of Sorrento House to the pleasant strains of band music.

Sorrento Terrace shared a boat slip and bathing place and it was intended that there should be a common promenade along by the shore. A pleasure garden for the benefit of the residents was planned for Sorrento Hill, now the public park. The Dalkey Amusements Committee was formed by a number of residents in order to arrange events and entertainments in the area and to manage Sorrento Park, which had been donated in 1894 by Dame Blanche MacDonnell and is still open all year round. The remains of a bandstand with its old gas lighting and seats can be seen there.

Most houses built at this time were provided with a coach house and stables, but as there was no space for outbuildings on Sorrento Terrace, some of the houses were given these facilities on Sorrento Road, at some distance away.

A noted resident of Sorrento Terrace was Denis Johnston, broadcaster, playwright and writer, whose novelist daughter Jennifer, now lives in Dún Laoghaire. Another prominent Dalkey resident was Alexander Conan, a master tailor of Trinity Street, Dublin, who was chairman of the Amusements Committee in 1899, and lived beside Sorrento Park in a

Below left: A programme of music organised by the Dalkey Amusements Committee in 1899, to be performed at the bandstand in Sorrento Park.

Below right: The Khyber Pass House (photographed in 1985) was greatly enlarged, probably in the late nineteenth century, by the addition of a whole new front, consisting of two-storey bay windows and an elaborate canopied entrance with a mosaic floor. The entrance was placed at the Dalkey Hill side of the house. The exterior was treated in the Italianate manner with lined rendering and an attractive cornice.

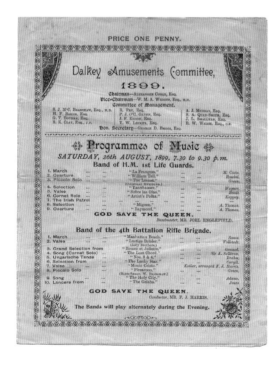

house called Monte Alverno. Conan's initials may be seen on a stone crest on the front of the house, which is dated 1895. A different house called Mount Alverno, built in the 1830s, was one of two properties that Conan amalgamated to create a single house, which he designed himself. The result is a house in the style of a baronial castle, built in granite with wide bay windows, battlements and a small octagonal flag tower. There is also a square folly tower in the corner of the garden.

The imposing Khyber Pass Hotel once stood on a great height over the railway and commanded some of the best views of both Killiney and Dublin Bays. It was demolished in December 1986, having stood derelict for nearly six years. As the fortunes of the hotel declined, blocks of apartments were built in the grounds against a background of considerable local opposition. The house, which had borne the name Khyber Pass since the middle of the nineteenth century, was originally a handsome two-storey-over-basement building with an entrance facing Dalkey. It was built by James Milo Burke, who lived there until about 1880, when he moved to Queenstown Castle, a house overlooking Dalkey Sound. Charles Stewart Parnell lived here for some time after 1859. Major Bryan Cooper, a staunch Unionist, lived for many years at the Khyber Pass. A member of the noted Sligo family of Markree Castle, he was born in Simla in India in 1884 and became a Unionist MP for South County Dublin in 1910. He was one of the few politicians of his background to remain in politics in Ireland after 1920, and he was elected to the Dáil in 1923 as an independent candidate. In 1946 the Coopers sold the house to a builder named M.P. Kennedy, who had developed the lands of Granite Hall in Dún Laoghaire, and he established the Khyber Pass Hotel by converting the old house there. Under the ownership of the Lawlor family, it was later known as the Killiney Heights Hotel and had a notable reputation for good food and jazz music. The hotel went into voluntary liquidation in 1981.

THE VICO ROAD

The Vico Road was originally a private track, inaccessible from Dalkey and closed to the public. As early as 1861 (according to *The Dublin Builder*) there were moves being made to continue this road around to Killiney, and pressure was being applied to Mr Warren, the owner of Killiney Hill, to remove a wall which was built across it. In 1889 the private rights were bought by public subscription and a new road was made, which has allowed the public for over a century to enjoy the outstanding beauty of this area. In 1928 the land between the Vico Road and the sea was put on the market. Local residents saw the opportunity to purchase the Vico fields and prevent further building there in order to preserve the open space and famous views forever. Once again, the people of Dalkey and Killiney responded generously to a public appeal, and the lands were bought for £1,500.

In her appeal to the public on that occasion, local resident and author Katharine Tynan described the Vico Road: 'Cliffs golden with gorse these days, and tremulous with bird-life and bird-song: the bay, sometimes blue as a sapphire, sometimes all a silvery fleece with some mysterious light from overhead: mountains of crystal and chalcedony! – It is God's gift to all of us. Let us hold it sacred!'

The coast near Vico bathing place still bears the name Hawk Cliff, while Polnabro-niagh and Black Castle are the names associated with pools and rocks near Whiterock. Vico and Whiterock were always popular bathing places but the pandemic lockdowns of 2020 and 2021 saw a dramatic rise in the number of year-round swimmers, often leading to traffic chaos as motorists vie for one of the few parking spaces on the Vico Road.

Strawberry Hill was one of the first houses to be built on the Vico Road. It is a single-storey-over-basement Italianate villa with a short tower. The house, possibly designed by Hoskin & Son as part of Warren's grand plan for Killiney Hill, was built around 1850 for a Mr Stevenson, general manager of the Alliance and Dublin Consumers' Gas Company. The spectacular location over the cliffs and railway make it unique and it was used as a small hotel during the 1960s. In 1967 the owners were refused planning permission to demolish the house and erect an eighty-bedroomed hotel! The Minister for Local Government

Below left: A photograph of the 1880s showing the mid-nineteenth-century development of the dramatic Vico Road, winding above the railway and the cliffs. The conspicuous lack of trees and shrubs is evident in this photo taken from the rocks of what would become Sorrento Park.
Below right: *The Vico bathing place, with its many steps, sitting areas and small shelter, offers deep-water swimming at all stages of the tide.*

Top left: An attractive plasterwork panel is a feature on the front of Strawberry Hill.

Top right: The once-familiar Dalkey landmark, Hayes's tower, with its large viewing windows and mock battlements, was demolished in 1986.

overturned the decision and approved the plan. However, the hotel was never built.

The Dublin Builder informs us that in 1861 a pair of houses was completed at Vico for Mr Henry Gonne and are probably the houses which stand below the road and directly above the railway at the Vico bathing place. Designed by Mr Lyons, they 'present gabled cantilevered roofs, with ornamental brackets, large bay windows, commanding magnificent views of the surrounding unsurpassedly beautiful scenery, and fitted throughout with storm shutters, essential during the winter months in this exposed situation'.

San Elmo, on the Vico Road, was built around 1870 by Henry Hayes, a wealthy tanner who had already built a fine house called Stratford in Rathgar. A large house with half-octagonal bows and a semicircular porch, it stands high up overlooking Killiney Bay. In its extensive grounds Hayes built a square viewing tower for his daughter and it is said that a grand piano was housed in the uppermost room. Though not of any great architectural interest, this notable landmark was unfortunately struck by lightning and became dangerous in 1986. As Dún Laoghaire Corporation was unable to assist the owner in repairing Hayes's tower, as it was known, it was demolished. San Elmo is the resting place for the stones of the facade of the original Abbey Theatre, which were rescued in the 1960s by the then City Architect Daithi Hanly. He also salvaged the old ticket office and other objects of ephemera during its demolition.

DALKEY HILL

The name Torca appears as 'Toyca' on the first Ordnance Survey map of the area, published in 1837, and a few cottages are shown in what was otherwise a completely wild part of Dalkey Commons. One of the first detached houses to be built here was Mount Henry, situated at the very end of Torca Road near the famous Cat's Ladder, a

The telegraph tower on Dalkey Hill, photographed in 1906, was used to send messages by semaphore and dates from the early 1800s. It is unfortunate that the tower was shorn of its picturesque fake battlements.

pedestrian right-of-way to Vico. But perhaps it is Bernard Shaw's Torca Cottage that is the best-known house in this quiet area. The cottage may have replaced one of the earlier quarrymen's cabins on the same site, for it is a well-built structure, double-fronted, with a high-ceilinged living room and three bedrooms inside. Shaw lived here from 1866 until 1874, and later wrote: 'I lived on a hill top with the most beautiful view in the world – I had only to open my eyes to see such pictures as no painter could make for me.'

A narrow track runs from Torca Road up above the quarries to the Old Telegraph, the old stone ruin on top of Dalkey Hill, which is generally referred to as a 'castle'. This telegraph tower was built at the time of the Martello towers and was used for signalling or for sending messages by semaphore to ships of the navy and the other various military installations. The tower was built in 1807 and was restored and probably made more picturesque by Robert Warren in the 1850s. As we have already seen, this scenic area around the slopes of Dalkey Hill has long been under pressure from redevelopment, with plans for bungalows in the 1970s along Torca Road to what can only be described as the 'mega-houses' and apartment blocks of the early twenty-first century. The massive scale of all this building is best seen from across the bay on Howth Head, where the dense development of Dalkey, Bullock and Dún Laoghaire can really be appreciated.

Between Dalkey Hill and the town lay the glebe lands, which once belonged to the Church and are now part of Ardeevin Road and Cunningham Road. A number of developments took place on Ardeevin and Knocknacree Roads in the late nineteenth century, including the building of Craiglands House and Ardeevin Terrace on the site of an old quarry. Craiglands, demolished in 1986, was a large bay-windowed Victorian house with an imposing front. It was ornamented with cut-granite details, such as keystones in all windows, and a large arched porch which was approached by a particularly long flight of granite steps.

A noted Dalkey builder named John Cunningham had commenced building houses on this side of the railway, on the old glebe lands, during the 1860s. He built four semi-detached houses, called Cunningham Terrace, and laid out a new road of the same name. Here in the 1890s he erected two outstanding houses, Harvieston and Santa Maria.

Harvieston, a large house built in the Arts and Crafts fashion, was built for the Eason family, who were the owners and founders of the highly successful bookshops and circulating libraries. It has an attractive corner tower with a slated conical roof, while Santa Maria is a red-brick, bay-windowed house with Gothic features. It was once the home of the Jacobs, a prominent Quaker family, of Jacob's Biscuits fame. Both houses command fine views of Dublin Bay.

Lios Mór, Knocknacree Road, is an unusual cut-stone Edwardian house, with a beautiful timber veranda covered by an ornamental tiled roof.

Mount Salus, a name suggestive of the healthy airs which were naturally to be found

Harvieston, with its circular tower and conical roof, veranda and oriel windows, is typical of the early 1900s.

here, was a mid-nineteenth-century development that included a variety of Victorian residences such as Monte Vista, Combre and a pair of semi-detached houses actually called Mount Salus. The pair at Mount Salus were built around 1840 and have many cut-granite features, including porticos, half-octagonal bow windows and a balustrade.

Tudor House was built around 1840 in a commanding position overlooking Dalkey town, and is an imposing five-bay house. It was allegedly built with stones from the demolished Wolverton Castle and has a plain appearance in a Tudor style with a painted, rendered front and three small gables. In the early 1900s Tudor House was used as a school where boys were prepared for entrance exams to 'Public schools and Osborne Naval College'. The fees were twenty guineas per term for boarders, one guinea per term for the laundress, 3s for stationery and 5s for games. Much of the grounds of Tudor House have recently been built upon, as have those of neighbouring St Joseph's, formerly called Bay

View. Bay View is a modest 1830s type of house with an unusual first-floor balcony, while Melrose and Lynton, also close by, are bay-windowed houses of mid-nineteenth-century date.

Kent Terrace, at the bottom of Barnhill Road, is a distinguished row of four Tudor-style terraced houses, which were built by an architect, one Frederick Porter, and his brother, William, whose descendants are still resident in Dalkey. The houses were erected in the late 1830s and have pointed gables, wide Regency-type windows with drip labels and small, Gothic glazed fanlights. Each of the hall doors is studded with iron nails in the medieval manner. A plaque on the last house bears the date 1839, and soon after this we find Frederick Porter resident in No. 1 Kent Terrace. It seems likely that Porter designed this terrace and Tudor House as well.

The Dalkey town commissioners were established in the mid-1860s under the Towns Improvement Act and the first meeting was held in 1863 in the Queen's Hotel. The town hall opened in 1868 in the old castle to which a new hall was added. The commissioners included various notable residents, and had the power to levy rates. Among the many issues that confronted them was that of health, and in the early years of this century there was always the threat of smallpox, which could be fatal. The Dalkey Urban District Council, as it became in the late nineteenth century, endeavoured to provide running water from the Vartry supply and proper sanitation for every dwelling in the district. A windmill had to be erected on 'The Metals' near Ardbrugh Road in about 1860 to pump water up to houses located high on the side of Dalkey Hill. The council prosecuted several landlords and owners of property for not erecting closets, privies or ashpits.

There were many dairies in Dalkey at the turn of the century, and in 1903 the council prosecuted no fewer than five 'dairy men', three of whom were women, for having sold milk which was 'adulterated with ten parts of added water'!

THE RAILWAY

Following the successful completion of the first railway in Ireland in 1834 from Dublin to Kingstown, plans were soon put forward to extend the line as far as Dalkey. Of course, there had been a small railway, with iron tracks, running between Dalkey Quarry and Kingstown Harbour, for transporting granite. Part of this track, known locally as 'The Metals', still exists, but the bulk of it was sold by the Kingstown Harbour Commissioners for the purpose of constructing the Atmospheric Railway.

This experimental railway was designed by Robert Mallet to run on the principle of suction or atmospheric pressure. It was a unique invention and attracted much interest. A fixed engine, attached to a cylindrical pipe, drew the train along by means of a vacuum at speeds of up to 40 mph (60 km/h). Near Barnhill Road there was an engine house, equipped with three Cornish boilers and a tall chimney which was for many years a landmark in Dalkey. Similar projects had been tried with limited success in Paris and London. The service commenced in 1844 and lasted for ten years.

Plans for the railway were not without objectors, as some felt it would be noisy and disruptive, such as Alderman Arthur Perrin who was a neighbour at Castle Park. In Kingstown, the new residents of the seafront terraces requested that the railway be kept out of sight and the company obliged by covering over much of the track in a deep cutting. They provided a terminus at Dalkey between Barnhill and Castle Park Roads.

The old Atmospheric line was eventually widened to two tracks, and the new conventional railway from Kingstown to Bray had become fully operational by 1856. This involved building a new station at Dalkey, extensive tunnelling under Dalkey Commons and excavation of rock along the cliffs at the Vico fields. The station at Dalkey is an attractive single-storey building, with a central open loggia. It retains many of its original features, such as its windows with their elegant Italianate architraves.

A network of horse-drawn tramlines was laid out in Dublin during the 1880s and Dalkey became the terminus for one of these lines. The tram yard, with its stone setts and wide tracks, may still be seen in Castle Street, and some of the tram sheds survive. For many years, the most elaborately decorated and comfortably equipped tram in Ireland lay in the grounds of Wolverton House, where it was once used as a summerhouse and office. This lavishly furnished electric tram was used by the directors of the Dublin United Tramway Company to inspect their lines. It was fitted out in oak with Waterford Glass lamps, velvet-covered seats and a cocktail cabinet, and had windows depicting scenic views of Dublin in coloured glass. Having been almost totally destroyed in 1984 by vandals who set it on fire, it is now being restored by members of the National Transport Museum in Howth.

SOCIETY AND SOCIAL CHANGE

Kingstown had reached a certain stage of maturity by the 1860s. Its institutions and routines were established and settled. Many town services had been implemented, the railway accepted, the hotels respected and the yacht clubs revered. It was an established residential town, and many shops and businesses could look back over thirty years of experience. Above all, the harbour was considered complete and the mail packet service was becoming famous for its reliability and efficiency. In 1860 four new mail packet ships were introduced and they quickly captured the public imagination with their size, speed and elegance. 'Ireland is accused of being devoid of enterprise and industry, but the inhabitants of Kingstown have proved that they possessed them in greater degree than any other town in the United Kingdom,' wrote G.R. Powell. Other observers called Kingstown 'the most popular packet station and the largest and most popular watering place in Ireland ... [with a] steady businesslike look, which speaks well for its future' and 'the wealthiest and most popular township in Ireland'.

Not surprisingly, the year 1860 marked the beginning of another building boom, which was to last for most of the decade. The new 'monster' Royal Marine Hotel was begun, four new and costly churches were built, and two others remodelled and embellished. House development moved inland from the old building line of Tivoli Road and new terraces like Crosthwaite Park, Royal Terrace and Eglinton Park were erected.

TERRACES AND SQUARES: DÚN LAOGHAIRE IN THE 1860S

Once building sites with sea views had been exhausted, terraces built around a central

Above left: The imposing cast-iron gates and railings of the Royal Marine Hotel as they stood originally on Marine Parade, giving direct access from Carlisle Pier to the hotel. The lamps on the top of the gate piers are supported by dolphins. Impressive gate piers in the form of fluted Doric pillars also stand at the Marine Road entrance.

Above right: A fashionable wedding party outside the Royal Marine Hotel in about 1890.

square or park became popular. Two of the more significant, Royal Terrace and Crosthwaite Park, were begun just before 1860. A lease of 1865 for No. 14 Royal Terrace East describes the new house as being situated on part of the lands of Kilahulks – a long-forgotten Gaelic place name. The developer of the first was Francis Nugent, son of successful local grocer and builder named James Nugent, and of the second, John Crosthwaite, a prominent resident and entrepreneur. Royal Terrace consisted of two rows of terraced houses, thirty-two on the west side and sixteen on the east. All were fully occupied by 1864. Two years earlier a survey in *The Dublin Builder* described the terrace as 'a very pretty place, exhibiting all the neatness and regularity of modern street architecture'. The facades of the houses were similar to those of Clarinda Park, but they had only one upper-floor bay window. As in all terraced houses of this period, they were fitted with standard plaster ceiling roses and generously broad cornices. The hall ceilings were often rich and varied. A four-sided square was apparently intended for Royal Terrace, but only the west side was fully completed. The original intention of the square was greatly enhanced in recent years by tree planting and by the construction of terrace-style apartments on the north side. The railed-in square was for many years used as a hockey pitch, but older residents will remember sheep grazing there on occasion.

John Crosthwaite, who lived in Crosthwaite Hall, was involved with various enterprises in the town, including the development of the Victoria Baths and the running of the town commissioners, of which he was frequently elected chairman. Like many well-off Catholics in the town, he subscribed generously to St Michael's Hospital and to St Michael's Church, where there was once a fine Crosthwaite memorial stained-glass window.

The square of Crosthwaite Park, unlike those of Royal Terrace and Clarinda, was formally laid out, planted and enclosed by ornate iron railings and gates. Until recently, there were several stags' heads on the park's gateposts. In 1860 *The Dublin Builder* noted that 'six houses of a very superior class, with handsome oriel windows carried up two storeys in height, and filled with plate glass, are being erected by Mr Crosthwaite'. The west and east sides are each made up of sixteen houses, although they differ from one another in design. They were finished in the mid-1860s. Crosthwaite Park West was one of the most expensive and ambitious terraces in Kingstown, and its grand four-storey elevation is reminiscent of London houses. One unusual feature on Crosthwaite Park East is a pair of doors spanned by a huge bow-shaped pediment. The main drawing room in the houses of Crosthwaite, Clarinda and Royal Terraces was always placed on the first floor where the full width of the house with its bay window could be exploited. Most of the principal rooms in these houses were furnished with handsome white marble mantelpieces.

Among several smaller developments of the 1860s were Eglinton Park (1861) and Carlisle Terrace (1866), both located on or near Tivoli Road, and Willow Bank (1865) off Sloperton. The nine semi-detached houses of Eglinton Park faced southwest over the fields towards the mountains, and they were extremely fortunate in having the open space of Dun Laoghaire golf course before them. This has all changed with the development of apartments on the former golf club, though a good deal of planting of shrubbery has taken place. They were solidly built houses and adopted an elegant but (by then) old-fashioned Georgian frontage. By the year they were finished, there were eight residents, including

Above left: The tall facades of Crosthwaite Park West are generously decorated with broad stucco mouldings, large bracketed architraves over the doors, and horizontal banding on the first floor. The paired doors share exceptionally wide granite steps.

Above right: The houses of Crosthwaite Park East, with their double-height bay windows, are typical of the high Victorian style of the 1860s.

An enamel sign advertising property to rent by the Kingstown firm of Talbot Coall, early 1900s. Talbot Coall, who were successful auctioneers and estate agents, also produced a comprehensive illustrated guide to Kingstown in 1915.

Mr W. O. McCormick, Kingstown's leading coal merchant. In contrast, Carlisle Terrace employed the popular idiom of bay windows and stucco detailing. Willow Bank was a small development of four high-quality semi-detached houses which were let by J.R. Stewart of Gortleitragh to a very 'high-class' tenantry.

House letting in Kingstown was always a thriving business. It was a good investment for the owner, and the tenants enjoyed a degree of luxury and peace conveniently close to the capital. The Parnell family, for instance, rented Granite Hall from the O'Conor Don for about six months in 1860. Most landlords, as in the case of the owner of Sloperton Lodge, were particular about their tenants. A bill for damages sent to what must have been a nightmare tenant of an upper-class Kingstown house in 1871 totalled £22 19s 18½d and ran to four pages! Over sixty items of furnishings were listed as lost or damaged and included such items as: 'one glass globe broken – 1/6d', 'one soap box broken – 1/6d', 'walls a good deal soiled and chipped – £1', 'music stool moulding broken off – 2/6', 'damask table cover missing – 4/-', 'two plain wine coolers missing – 2/-', 'one soup plate missing – 7½', 'steel snuffers broken – 1/-', 'three metal hooks to coach-house missing – 1/6d', chimneys to be swept – 5/-', 'house to be cleaned down – 10/-', and 'gas consumed from 14th July 1870 to 8th March 1871 – £7-0-6d'. No detail escaped the critical eye of the house agent. Among several Kingstown house agents the firm of Talbot, Coall & Son was perhaps best known. From about 1860 they ran a varied business, which included undertaking, auctioneering and furniture dealing from their premises at Nos 18–19 George's Street Upper.

THE ROYAL MARINE HOTEL

By 1860, Kingstown had acquired a reputation as a first-class watering place. It was unreservedly glorified by the official *Handbook of the Kingstown and Bray Railway* as follows:

Thanks to the genius of steam, that modernizing giant and the professional skill of modern Engineers and Architects, the poor fishing village, at the asylum harbour of 'Dunleary', has been metamorphosed into a great highway between this and the sister Kingdom, replete with artificial as well as natural beauty. An important and populous business town with outskirts thickly studded with princely mansions, handsome ecclesiastical, hotel, club, and other buildings, and a noble harbour to boot, with outstretched piers and quays, containing an area of some 250 acres, wherein the stateliest craft afloat may ride, has sprung into existence.

In 1862 a survey in *The Dublin Builder* said of Kingstown that, 'a place of such importance certainly needs hotels and although there are two or three excellent hotels at present open, still one of a larger size, containing accommodation for all parties, with a scale of charges suited to every class, would be most acceptable'.

Such a new establishment was proposed by the Royal Marine Hotel Company, chaired by the great speculator and contractor William Dargan, who had bought out the Royal Hotel in 1863. With £50,000 in capital made up of £5 shares, the new scheme was launched and the architect John McCurdy hired to prepare the designs. This hotel incorporated the original Hayes's Royal Hotel.

The new hotel was designed to the huge scale of contemporary monster hotels then being built in resorts all over Europe and Britain. The enormous hotel in Scarborough was constructed at the same time, which illustrates that Kingstown was keeping pace with the latest fashions elsewhere. Indeed, the Royal Marine Hotel was expressly intended to be 'a first-class hotel resembling in all its arrangements those establishments which have lately sprung up on the sea-coast of England and on the continent'. It was to contain 'concert and assembly rooms, spacious and well-ventilated drawing, coffee and dining rooms, ladies' coffee rooms, billiard and smoking saloons together with numerous suites of private and sleeping apartments ... promenade grounds ornamented with terraced gardens, fountains, statuary' and be 'in direct communication with the Carlisle Pier'.

In 1865 *The Dublin Builder* illustrated McCurdy's hotel and wrote, 'the style is French renaissance, the main body of the structure is covered with a Mansard roof pierced with Lucarne windows, the bows at the ends being surmounted by high pitched French roofs'.

The same volume also noted that the 'central tower and one wing (eastern) have already been erected' and that the hotel 'is a very imposing mass of building'. The western wing, which would have replaced the old Royal Hotel and completed the building, was never finished according to McCurdy's design. Attempts were made, however, to match the old Royal Hotel with the new building by using the same type of mansard roof, dormer windows, and scaled-down 'bows'. The intended scheme was unfinished because the company went into liquidation in about 1867, the same year it bought the International Hotel in Bray, which it mortgaged for £18,000. The company also failed to pay

Cockburn, the contractor to the Royal Marine Hotel, the full £25,000 which was due for the portion already completed.

A Lawrence photograph from the turn of the twentieth century gives a good impression of the hotel as it was when 'completed'. It had an air of ponderous elegance that was reinforced by the large roofs, dormer windows and somewhat lumpy tower – all later crudely shaved off. With the exception of some of the stucco detailing and the porte cochère with its fine iron balcony, which sheltered the arriving coaches, the exterior became a disastrous hotchpotch of old and new. However, when the hotel was refurbished in the 1990s, the original French-style roof and tower were reinstated and much of the exterior Victorian stucco work was repaired, greatly to the owner's credit. Many of the grandiose reception rooms of the interior remain unaltered, the ornately tiled 'Gents' and the dignified double staircase seem to capture the hotel's old-world grace. The hotel remains extremely popular as a venue for weddings and other formal occasions.

The architect McCurdy also rebuilt the Salthill Hotel in 1865. It stood on a natural hill overlooking Old Dunleary village and had been a hotel since the completion of the Dublin and Kingstown Railway. In the rebuilding, the old plain Dunleary House, as it had been called, was fronted by the new hotel which adopted the same 'French Chateau' style as the Royal Marine. It was a handsome brick building with ornate dormer windows, steep

A photograph of the Royal Marine Hotel from the early 1900s shows the hotel in its heyday when it was described as being 'the premier hotel on the coast for comfort, cuisine and position'. It was one of the first hotels to be equipped with electric light, lift and telephones. (This image is reproduced courtesy of the National Library of Ireland [L_IMP_0759].)

roofs and a tower. It was always considered a very fashionable hotel and was run first by the Lovegrove family, then in the 1840s by Marshall, and afterwards by Parry. Early in the twentieth century, it was managed by the proprietors of the Royal Hibernian Hotel, Dublin. The hotel burnt down and was demolished in 1972 and apartments were built on the site.

RED-BRICK DECADES

From about the mid-1860s onwards a new type of machine-produced brick became a popular building material. The new brick was smooth, even and shiny, whereas the older handmade bricks were irregular in texture and form and even varied in colour. The brickwork of Cambridge Terrace on York Road (c. 1865) is an early example. By the 1880s, brick had almost completely superseded the stucco or cement finishes previously used. Banks were among the first establishments in Kingstown to make use of this new medium.

By 1860, Kingstown possessed a branch of the Royal Bank of Ireland as well as a savings bank. The first substantial bank building was erected by the Royal Bank in 1871. This handsome structure is situated in George's Street Upper, facing Northumberland Avenue. It is a solid edifice comprised of a suitably ponderous stone-faced ground floor with three brick storeys above. It was designed by Charles Geoghegan, who was a popular architect, responsible for many of the high-quality modest buildings that characterise Dublin's streets.

The National Bank, which adjoins the Royal Bank in George's Street Upper, was built in 1899. The bank previously occupied premises on Marine Road in the end house of Gresham Terrace. The new bank building was carefully proportioned and the main floor was arcaded with windows similar in shape to those of the town hall. The building gains in grace by being set back from the street, where its paired pilasters and subtle colour contrast between red brick and red sandstone are more clearly visible. The medallion decorations and 'Adamesque' frieze are also well placed.

In 1911 there were four banks in the town, including the Ulster Bank and the Belfast Banking Company. The Ulster Bank, built in c. 1915, stood on the corner of Marine Road and George's Street Upper and was a handsome red-brick building with a peculiar copper-covered mansard roof with roundel windows. It was demolished in 1974 to make way for the present shopping complex and a new bank was incorporated into the new building. Now owned by Allied Irish Banks, the Provincial Bank of No. 1 George's Street Upper was established by about 1922. This building is another well-designed, stone-detailed structure

Many of the prosperous businesses in the town rebuilt their premises and incorporated their initials and date into an emblem at the roofline, such as JR (John Ring), 1904. Some of the red brick was made in the local Kingstown brickworks on Pottery Road while terracotta ornament and shaped bricks were imported from the Welsh town of Ruabon.

of red brick, which was recently and most carefully extended in the same style. In 1933 the Bank of Ireland opened a branch at Nos 1–2 Anglesea Buildings, a block of red-brick shops and once the former premises of a draper's called Lanigan.

Most of George's Street Upper and Lower today presents an endlessly varied upper storey of red-brick facades. The late nineteenth-century trend in favour of brick-faced buildings is the result of a huge scheme of remodelling which altered the entire appearance of George's Street. Many of the facades form gables and are treated in a variety of loosely based Dutch Classical or Queen Anne styles. They bear dates ranging from 1898 to 1910 and employ a variety of decorative tricks and details which could have come straight out of an architectural dictionary. The reason for this brick renovation stems from the expiry of the original ninety-nine-year Kingstown estate leases that had been made with the ground landlords, Longford and de Vesci, in 1804. The new leases were granted on condition that such rebuilding took place, an effort on the part of the landlords to improve the appearance of the town. Many fine old shopfronts and much good stucco and ironwork were lost but almost a kilometre of varied red-brick frontage and skyline was gained. In 1905 the architect Bradbury, who had an office at No. 18 George's Street Upper, designed the premises of the notable plumber and contractor J. Ring. This 15-metre frontage at No. 91 George's Street Lower was planned in conformity with estate requirements and was built of red Ruabon bricks from Wales, with dressings of red terracotta. The owners were 'required by the landlords to build up to the frontage line'. It can be assumed that these conditions, noted by *The Irish Builder* in 1905, were compulsory for all George's Street premises which held such leases.

The fact that the architect Bradbury had a Kingstown office may indicate that he was responsible for much of the red-brick rebuilding of the main street. In 1906 Edward Lee established the Avenue Hotel, incorporating it into his new three-storey drapery store at the foot of Northumberland Avenue. The large red-brick block was partly built on what were the gardens of Anglesea Place. It was begun in 1905 by the builder Thompson to the designs of Kaye-Parry and Ross (who became the architects to the Kingstown estate and were contractors for the Pavilion and Cottage Home). In 1907 Lee further extended his premises to include another six shops with accommodation above. This facade is arranged in groups of windows punctuated by brick pilasters, and the whole building has excellent granite finishings and window surrounds.

Some of the finest red-brick frontages were erected in George's Street Lower. J. McCullagh and Sons took their present premises at Nos 83–84 George's Street Lower in 1871; they rebuilt it in brick with stone finishings in 1901 according to the requirements of the new ground leases. In 1984 Kathleen McCullagh related that the business was founded by her grandfather John, who initially lived with his family over the shop. A one-time town councillor, he attended the Methodist church every Sunday, when he wore a top hat and morning coat, along with his watch and chain, and he sang in the choir. As draper's, they boasted of being in 'constant communication with the leading London and Paris Modistes'. In keeping with a long-standing tradition, the shop closed on Wednesday afternoons, but remained open late on Saturday evenings. Many of the staff also lived on the premises and had their meals there. There was even a billiard room for their use. Like many shops of the early 1900s, its tall windows were fitted with plate glass to button

An 1898 photograph of George's Street Lower showing many Victorian premises which did not modernise with red brick, although the scaffolded site on the right is in the process of being rebuilt. Note the handsome gaslight standard and bicycle on the left. On the right is Brown's tobacconists. Established in about 1869, Browns was an 'importer of Havana cigars, Egyptian cigarettes and fancy tobaccos'. It remained in business up until the 1990s when the building partially collapsed.

display their goods and the double doors of the entrance had long brass handles. Inside there were beautiful mahogany counters, large glazed display cabinets and a system of pneumatic tubes for sending cash and change. The family involvement ceased in the late 1940s when the business was sold to the drapery firm of Nicholls. 'The Arcade', a gabled brick building with cut-stone mullioned windows, was erected for the noted drapers G.B. Morrison. It was occupied by Woolworths in more recent years.

At about the same time, Findlaters rebuilt their old premises, which dated from the 1830s. The elegant new shop was much enlarged and displayed large plate glass windows. The pedimented stone-dressed windows of the upper floor were matched by similar detail on the roofline. The old shop, in Findlater tradition, featured a magnificently ornate two-faced clock on the exterior; this was replaced by a three-faced clock which became a distinctive Dún Laoghaire landmark. Unfortunately, when Penneys took over the premises, this fine clock disappeared. Like its neighbouring Lynch and O'Brien, Findlaters maintained a first-rate delivery service and operated three or four of their own horse-and-trap teams. The former premises of Lynch and O'Brien at Nos 80 and 81 George's Street Lower is one of the town's finest all-brick frontages. The shop was divided in two, one half selling groceries and the other spirits. Lynch and O'Brien, established by 1869, once also owned the Eagle House in Glasthule, and was a very popular Kingstown firm. When the premises was offered for sale in 1901 it was described as having been lately rebuilt at a cost of £3,000

Below left: Findlaters was the leading high-class grocery shop in Kingstown since its establishment in 1834. The premises was rebuilt and extended in the early 1900s and, now serving as Penneys, is the town's most impressive shopfront.

Below right: The premises of Lynch and O'Brien on George's Street Lower is a handsome composition combining a grocery and public house, featuring terracotta brick pediments, brackets and an ornate roofline balustrade.

with a grocery and bar divided by mahogany and ornamental lead-lighted screens. The bar counter had a polished granite slab and there were five 60-gallon casks with nickel-plated taps at each end of the bar. Beneath there was extensive cellarage with facilities for bottling and storing wine, with three large whiskey vats and shelving capable of holding sixty hogsheads of beer. To the rear there were two spacious yards with stabling and a 'first-class supply of spring water'. In 1912 the business was still flourishing under the same name and the grocery sold a wide range of teas and coffees, biscuits, confectionery, pickles and polishes, not to mention every kind of wine, spirit and tobacco. Miss McCullagh of the neighbouring shop recalled the butter being weighed out in pats and the delicious smell of smoked bacon which lingered around the grocery section.

Nos 106–117 George's Street Upper, which were demolished in 1974 to make way for Dún Laoghaire Shopping Centre, incorporated an array of gabled and curved rooflines, with oval and bay windows. Two of these fine shops were occupied by the chemists Suche and Fitzgibbon, and Hayes, Conyingham and Robinson. Others were owned by Galligans, caterers and confectioners, Macfarlanes, and Downeys, a grocery and spirit store. Two more, the Maypole Dairy and the Home and Colonial Stores, were in the 1900s early examples of chain stores. Many still recall that it was outside one of these now-demolished premises, Downey's pub, that the longest-known strike took place between 1939 and 1953! Much of the red-brick conversion in George's Street Upper was unadventurous. For instance, the brickwork of Park House, built as Murdoch's General Mart in about 1910, is not very daring but fits well into the general streetscape. A number of premises feature the open pediment and urn motif, which looks well against the skyline, a consideration that preoccupied the designers of these new shopfronts. It remains a challenge for shopfront designers in Dún Laoghaire to carefully incorporate the upper red-brick facades with new shopfronts below.

Many old firms have completely disappeared from Dún Laoghaire. In the 1840s James Bewley, a grocer, wine and tea merchant, once did business. McDonalds, ironmongers and house furnishers, for years occupied the corner premises on Marine Road and George's Street Lower. The utilitarian frontage of H. Williams supermarket was once graced by the bay-windowed facade of Johnson's London House. Johnson's, like the firm of Hannegan and Shackleton, were among the town's best-known drapers.

Two of the last shops to have been built in the old style (pre-red-brick) were the two branches of Boland's Bakery erected in 1888 in the 'main artery of Kingstown'. They were the retail shops for Boland's newly completed model bakery in Cumberland Street, which had a handsome entrance arch. The Cumberland Street shop with its ornamental ironwork balustrade stood until 2005. Another of the town's early bread shops was the Kingstown Bakery, established in 1860 and run by Robert Heron, 'baker to the Queen and contractor to the Royal Navy'. It seems to have been superseded by Wilson's Bakery and Teashop in the early 1900s. Such shops were elegantly fitted out with mahogany and glass furnishings of high quality.

The Kingstown branch of the Monument Creamery was opened in the early 1900s and is remembered even today as selling miniature breads and 'loose' butter. Johnston, Mooney and O'Brien came to Dún Laoghaire in about 1930. H. Williams and Lipton's stores were, like the Monument, early manifestations of the chain-store idea. Williams and Lipton were established in Dún Laoghaire in about 1901 and traded for about seventy years.

Photography was a booming business as Kingstown's popularity as a resort grew. As early as 1863, Clarendon, a former watch and clock dealer, opened his Photographic Gallery at No. 94 George's Street Lower. Some years later, a photographer named Browne established another shop next door, specialising in stereoscopic views. Both were probably among the earliest-known Irish 'photographic' shops. Cook's Photographers had premises that faced down Marine Road and began trading in about 1902. As well as taking portraits and selling postcards, they also sold souvenirs and fancy goods in what was called a 'bazaar'. Their shop was formerly the handsomely stuccoed premises of the grocer John Sex. Later, Cook's shop featured beautiful curved windows and a long arcade, and was packed with high-quality photographs, portraits and a huge range of postcards. The range of souvenirs and postcards reflected the town's significant role as a tourist resort and there were many views available of the several hotels that could be found on the seafront and

Below left: Small specialist shops, such as J.J. Arthur's watchmakers, once gave employment to carpenters and signwriters.

Below right: Mays, one of the last corner shops in Dún Laoghaire, and Dixons were well-loved newsagents and tobacconists in the town. Their loss is a reflection of society's changing habits – the decline of tobacco smoking and the loss of newspaper sales.

elsewhere. For example, apart from the leading Royal Marine and the Salthill hotels, there was the Hotel Carlisle (later the Carney Arms), Ross's Victoria Hotel, the Lismara Hotel (Haddington Terrace) and the Anglesea Arms Hotel.

Over the years the town council spent a good deal of time and money in maintaining and improving the tourist facilities such as bandstands, seating and deckchairs on the pier, on bathing places including the various baths, and on parks like the East Pier gardens.

Above left: The attractive premises of No. 70 George's Street Lower includes the ornate stucco work of the nineteenth century.

Above right: Thomas Cook was the leading photographer in Edwardian Kingstown, and in the huge curved windows of his new premises at the top of Marine Road he displayed postcards and souvenirs.

CHARITY AND SOCIAL CHANGE

While much of society in Victorian Kingstown lived very comfortably, there were also large numbers of people who struggled to make ends meet. Many charities, which were well supported, were instituted in Kingstown during the second half of the nineteenth century. This was probably an offshoot of the same awakening conscience that led to improvements in working-class housing during the 1890s. For instance, a charity account of the Mariners' Church shows that, between 1876 and 1895, boots were bought for the poor and there was a coal fund. It also supported schooling for poor children, funeral costs, a soup kitchen and provided blankets and stockings in winter. In 1880 it assisted 180 families on an ongoing basis. Fowl were purchased every week for distribution. Frequent small payments were made to individuals in difficulty such as a shipwrecked man, a blind man and a basket woman. In 1886 £27 8s was given to a couple with two daughters to emigrate to Brisbane in Australia.

Three orphanages were founded in Kingstown during this period. It was a favourable environment for charities, with a predominantly well-to-do population from which to solicit funds, but it seems there was always a wide gap between rich and poor.

The town had a reputation for its numerous public houses, taverns, vintners and publicans, and for its frequently drunken seamen and the occurrence of brawling and street fighting, especially on George's Street Lower. Besides the Sailors Reading Room, a temperance hall was founded in 1860 in Sussex Place, but it was short-lived. However, the Kingstown Workmens Club, founded by Professor W.F. Barrett as a temperance club and place where working men would meet to play billiards or read a newspaper, remained open until the 1990s. The club had its first premises at No. 3 Clarence Street. The present solid red-brick building on George's Street Lower, with its granite finishing, was erected by 1915. Its hall has a capacity for 250 people. The former Workmens Club building maintains the scale and proportion of George's Street and blends carefully with the neighbouring Carnegie Library. The large red-brick premises of the Kingstown Men's Christian Institute (now closed down) was erected in 1891 on George's Street Upper. Established in 1888, it provided recreational facilities and indoor sports for its members. Within the building's large bay-window projections are sizeable reading, billiard and assembly rooms, which continued to serve their original purpose throughout the twentieth century. There is also a hall at the back which in 1895 was 'splendidly fitted up with first class gymnastic apparatus'. The institute was the headquarters of a chess club and of the Kingstown Literary and Debating Society. The wealthy McComas family, who were merchant tailors in Dublin and Kingstown in the 1830s, endowed the institute and are remembered by a particularly fine brass plaque in the hall. The chimney stacks, gables and part of the facade are curiously ornamented with red terracotta panels featuring swags. Nearby at the corner of Corrig Avenue once stood the premises of the YMCA, an association with similar aims to those of the Christian institute.

Among the town's first orphanages was the Bird's Nest, which was founded in 1859 by a Mrs Smyly. The Bird's Nest took orphaned children between five and twelve years of age. The girls were 'prepared chiefly for domestic service' and the boys afterwards went to one of the Dublin 'homes'. Known as 'The Institution', it was built in 1861 as a long, narrow building on the slope of York Road. It was formed by symmetrical halves that provided separate accommodation for 180 boys and girls. Although typically institutional in feeling, it is very well built in rough granite with brick window surrounds. It has lately been refurbished as apartments. St Joseph's on Tivoli Road was another large orphanage, built in 1860. It was run by the Daughters of the Heart of Mary, who trained its eighty orphans 'in the habits of industry and order'. Apart from a good stone door surround, St Joseph's was a plain block-shaped building. It was demolished in 1986. The Cottage Home is situated further along Tivoli Road and was established by an endowment from a Miss Barrett in 1879. This Tudor farmhouse-style building was erected in 1886 as a home for orphans under six years of age. The idea of a farm- or cottage-style house was a reaction to the over-severe institutional architecture of the early decades of the nineteenth century. Both the name 'Cottage Home' and the building were part of an attempt to de-formalise and humanise the idea of the orphanage. The Cottage Home was converted into apartments in 2017.

A Magdalene asylum and laundry called St Patrick's Refuge was opened in about 1879, and the building now serves as St Michael's Nursing Home. The asylum was run by the Sisters of Mercy as a home for destitutes and penitents. As already mentioned, this rather grim building was erected with St Michael's Hospital and adjoining convent. The Magdalene Laundries have come under the gravest of criticism since the turn of the twenty-first century for their inhumane treatment of inmates – pregnant girls who were placed in their care, usually by their own families.

During the later nineteenth century, there was 'an establishment for Christian Ladies'

Above: The weathervane of the Cottage Home.
Left: The Cottage Home for Little Children was built in 1886 and was designed by W. Kaye-Parry in the style of an English farmhouse, featuring gables and mock-Tudor timberwork.

at No. 42 Northumberland Avenue, which let furnished rooms to ladies of diminished means at between £7 and £11 per annum. 'The Ladies' House', as it was called, was run by a committee, who particularly undertook to 'study the happiness of the residents'. There were many other organisations which worked for the good of the poor in Kingstown, including the Little Sisters of the Assumption, who have recently left their convent at Tivoli Hall on York Road; the Society of St Vincent de Paul; the Kingstown Labour Yard and Mission Hall, a branch of the Society for the Prevention of Cruelty to Children; the Salvation Army barracks; and Kingstown Penny Dinners. The Mission provided cheap firewood and logs and arranged window cleaning and garden work for old or unemployed men. The Mission Hall occupied the old assembly rooms at the bottom of Corrig Avenue, which neighboured onto the YMCA premises. Kingstown Penny Dinners organised simple meals for the poor from a house on York Road.

From the earliest years of the harbour's construction, slums and shanty dwellings existed in Kingstown. In 1844 a pamphlet published by Charles Haliday described the condition of tenements in Kingstown. Though the town commissioners had been in existence since the 1830s no positive action was taken until 1896 when the first of the artisans' dwellings were proposed and built off Eden Road, in Glasthule. At the same time, similar houses and flats were being erected in Blackrock and Dalkey, but in Kingstown, where they were most needed, the authorities seemed slow to act. In 1903 the Urban District Council sought a government loan of £78,000 (about €7.4 million today) to finance these schemes and an enquiry followed, revealing the still-appalling state of the slums. A row ensued because some of the council wanted the houses designed by their own engineer, while others insisted that an architect be employed.

By 1904/05, sixty-one houses had been built in Dominick Street and there were thirty-eight houses and 191 flats on Cross Avenue. In 1905 fifty-six houses were erected on Barrett Street, off York Road. Though these houses were a great improvement on the cottages and cabins occupied by the poor, they were criticised for their lack of space and generally cramped nature. In 1905 Councillor Mills (after whom Mills Street off Cross Avenue is named) complained that though the houses were well built, they were being offered at a rent of 3s to 3s 6d per week, which was far too expensive for the average labouring man and his family. By 1911, the Kingstown Urban District Council had 500 empty houses in the township because of high rents.

Cross Avenue is composed of a mixture of cement-fronted Victorian-style houses, two-storey brick dwellings and a row of attractive brick cottages. The cottages have two-coloured slated roofs and little pointed timber porches, which give them a rural appearance. The two-storey terraced dwellings that form Desmond Avenue and Dominick Street are well constructed in yellow brick with red-brick detailing and granite window sills. The layout of the whole area of Cross Avenue and Library Road is quite informal and varied.

In 1912 twelve artisans' dwellings were erected on Library Road and a further twenty-six on Mary Street off Northcote Avenue. The Library Road dwellings were part of a prize-winning model scheme that was laid out with spacious gardens and a large playground. The road was planted with trees.

By the 1830s, the west side of Sallynoggin Road was lined with low, small-windowed thatched cottages. The last of these disappeared in the 1980s, along with the original pub called The Thatch. The first artisans' dwellings in Sallynoggin were built on Sarsfield Street in 1904.

Between 1897 and 1936, the Kingstown Urban District Council (Dún Laoghaire Borough Corporation after 1930) erected a total of 1,574 houses. No flats were built after 1914. These houses, which became known as corporation houses, until 1935 were built primarily in the York Road area of Dún Laoghaire. In the 1970s and 1980s, the Corporation concentrated its development beyond the town in the districts of Sallynoggin, Ballybrack and Shanganagh.

The infrequent use of brick in nineteenth-century housebuilding in Kingstown has already been noted and most structures were constructed of rubble stone and afterwards rendered. This also made economic sense as there was a good supply of granite rubble from the various quarries of the district. The occasional brick house had been built on Clarinda Park West and Tivoli Road during the 1850s, using an attractive rough-textured handmade brick. A new type of smooth, slightly polished brick became available in

The brick-built artisans' dwellings on Tivoli Terrace East date from the early twentieth century.

the latter half of the nineteenth century and is first seen at Cambridge Terrace, York Road, which was erected in 1865. The eight houses of Cambridge Terrace were excellently constructed, probably by the builder Cockburn, and exhibit high-quality brick and stonework. Fine workmanship is also evident in the front garden wall, which replaced the traditional iron railings. The houses have prominent chimney stacks and slated roofs interrupted by neat little dormer windows.

During the early years of the twentieth century, several red-brick terraces of semi-detached houses were erected, including Rosmeen Gardens, Leixfort Villas (Corrig Avenue), and De Vesci Gardens (Glenageary Hill). These well-built Edwardian-style houses were the work of a Ballybrack builder named Pemberton. The ten houses of Rosmeen Gardens date to 1905–06 (see p. 228); Leixfort Villas were built shortly afterwards. Both mark a transition between Victorian and modern housebuilding. De Vesci Gardens, begun during the First World War, consists of ten houses fronted in brick and pebble-dash. Many of the houses adopted the names of well-known 1914–18 battles such as St Quentin and Verdun. Elsewhere, similar terraced houses were erected at Breffni Terrace, Sandycove and at Ardeevin Road in Dalkey.

There is yet another interesting type of brick house in Dún Laoghaire. The facades of Nos 8 and 9 Charlemont Avenue and Nos 12 and 13 Tivoli Terrace North are delightfully enlivened by playful brickwork of contrasting colours and varied designs. Pale-coloured bricks form lozenge, quoin and voussoir patterns against the darker red and purple bricks of the facades and chimney stacks. This polychrome brickwork was made fashionable in the late nineteenth century by British architect William Butterfield. Tivoli Terrace North is an unusual Dún Laoghaire street in that it is composed solely of attractive cottage-style houses.

Dunleary House is a good example of the use of yellow brick. It was erected by the coal merchant Wallace in the 1880s at the corner of their coal yard on Cumberland Street, which they had recently taken over from the firm of Alexander Downs. The specially designed house incorporated an office with a separate entrance. It was built of compressed yellow brick with details in brown brick and it has an attractive simplicity.

By the close of the nineteenth century, Kingstown was firmly established as a prosperous town, quite independent from Dublin and equipped with its own improving infrastructure of better housing, transport and other facilities.

Chapter 11

CIVIC DÚN LAOGHAIRE

TOWNSHIP ADMINISTRATION

By the year 1834, Kingstown had sufficiently expanded to prompt its leading residents to form the Kingstown town commissioners. Eighteen notable residents were appointed to supervise 'paving, watching, lighting, regulating and otherwise improving the town of Kingstown'. The 1834 Act which established this administrative body empowered it to undertake street widening and to enforce regulations about the size and location of new buildings. The commissioners also had the power to appoint watchmen, beadles and other officers known as constables. The latter were instructed to preserve and maintain peace and order and were authorised to detain 'all felons, malefactors, disturbers of public peace, disorderly persons, rogues, vagrants, beggars and all such other persons found misbehaving'. The constables were to be provided with 'proper stations, boxes or watchhouses'. In order to make such provision, the commissioners levied a police tax which, for example, in 1854 cost a Longford Terrace homeowner £2 14s.

The first constabulary station was built on Crofton Road in 1834. Some years later a new barracks was established at Cumberland Street; it in turn moved to the old St Clare Convent off George's Street Upper in 1840 where it continued to serve as a Metropolitan Police Station and then as a Garda station until 1992 when it was demolished. The old Garda station, once known as Kingstown Convent, was built in 1822 and contained a

Kingstown Town Council's coat of arms incorporates symbols of industry (the bee skep), royalty (the crown), a fort (the dún) and the Vikings (a ship). These symbols were slightly modified after 1920.

residence, outbuildings and a small Gothic vaulted chapel at first-floor level.

The commissioners were entitled to construct new pavements or footways, although the owners of adjoining property were charged for it. Lamp irons and lamp posts were also to be erected and lit with gas. The town was laid with gas pipes, which had to be located 4 feet (1.2 metres) from any water pipe in order to avoid contamination. At first the gaslight was installed in only the houses of the well-to-do. In 1837 Lewis noted that Kingstown was partly paved and gaslit. But it is probable that these comforts were very sparse and limited to the area around Gresham Terrace and Sussex Parade (Marine Road). It was not until 1863 that a pavement was constructed on the south side of George's Street Lower. The following year the Kingstown Gas Company was formed to supply Kingstown, Monkstown, Dalkey, Killiney and Ballybrack with gas of 'high illuminating power'. Prior to this, gas was apparently supplied from Dublin. The Kingstown gasworks was located in the former Albright and Wilson factory, and a second gasometer was later erected at Mountown. Gradually, gas lighting was extended throughout the town and remained in general use until the 1920s.

The commissioners also took care of rubbish disposal and appointed 'a sufficient number of scavengers or persons for the purpose of cleansing the town'. These men made their rounds every Wednesday and Saturday between 5am and 11am. The scavengers were instructed to 'sound a bell or otherwise give notice to the housekeepers of their approach

A bin lorry collecting waste at Royal Terrace in 1976. All bin collections in Dún Laoghaire were managed by the Corporation up until the 1990s when the service was privatised.

... and collect all dust, dirt, dung and ashes and other filth'. Moreover, 'every person acting as scavenger ... shall cause the words "Scavengers Cart" to be painted in large Roman letters on the front.' Private dumping was prohibited and any slaughterhouse or hog sties were to be removed if deemed a nuisance. A new dustbin collection was inaugurated in 1888.

The town commissioners were empowered to control traffic and place fines of up to 40s on any vehicle found blocking a street or lane. This included 'waggons, carts, sledges, drays, carriage horses, cattle, stage coaches, post chaises or hackney coaches which may stand or ply for hire'. The town's first fire service also lay within the remit of the commissioners who were to provide 'one or more engine or engines for extinguishing fire ... with water buckets, pipes and flexible tubes'. They provided horses and hired firemen on a part-time basis until 1932 when the fire brigade became a full-time service. In 1880 a resolution was passed by the town council to purchase 100 yards of additional hose and more ladders to improve the fire engines. At the time of the Pavilion fire in 1915, the service had two horse-drawn fire engines.

Despite the many improvements made, it is fair to say that the commissioners tended to direct their energies towards the benefit of the middle and upper classes. They were elected by the ratepayers, that is, owners of property with a valuation above £10, and were middle or upper class themselves. Among the commissioners for 1836, for example, were Edward Masterson, the notable Kingstown builder; Bargeny McCulloch, stone contractor; Charles Smyth of The Slopes, the famous St Stephen's Green wine merchant; Thomas M. Gresham, hotelier and developer of Gresham Terrace; G. Duff of Corrig Castle; A. Armstrong, owner of Anglesea Arms Hotel; J. Nugent, builder and eventual developer of Royal Terrace; and J. Turrellini, proprietor of a Kingstown circulating library.

Most of the descriptions of Kingstown from the nineteenth century praise and idealise the new township, while turning a blind eye to the slums around York Road and Glasthule. These slums had begun with the hundreds of labourers who were employed on the harbour works and their families. Many lived in small cabins and shacks in the narrow back streets of the town, which were known as courts. The greatest number of these were to be found off George's Street Lower and at the bottom of York Road. For example, in 1850 there were over seventy such tenements in the ironically named Paradise Row and Paradise Place. There were many dozens of cabins and small cottages at Albert Court, Byrne's Court, Callaghan's Lane and in various courts and lanes off Patrick Street and Mulgrave Street. There were over forty cabins in Sallynoggin, many of which were thatched, and a similar number on 'The Metals' at Perrin's Row, showing the connection between the harbour building works and the rough-and-ready dwellings which were

Below left: Many families lived in one- or two-roomed cottages in the courts and alleys which made up backstreet Kingstown. The cottages seen here in this c. 1930 photo were of a quite decent standard compared to the makeshift hovels described in the nineteenth century but these too were replaced by the new brick houses seen in the background.

Below right: A large sewage tank, seen here on an Ordnance Survey map, was constructed at the back of the West Pier beside the ladies' bathing place in 1877 and marked the beginning of a proper system for the town.

thrown up for the workers and their families. As every aspect of the town developed thereafter, the working population multiplied. Yet no provision in the form of cottages, water supply or sanitation was made for the poor until late in the nineteenth century. The 1843 Ordnance Survey map clearly shows the chaotic and overcrowded development of the George's Street Lower and York Road area of town. Overcrowding contributed to the death toll when cholera struck Kingstown, which it did on several occasions, with the worst outbreaks in 1831–32, 1849, 1861 and 1872. In 1861, 124 inhabitants died.

The conditions of Kingstown's poor provoked Charles Haliday, a merchant and noted humanitarian, to publicise the situation. In 1844 he described Kingstown's tenements, which housed large families in one- or two-room hovels without toilets, light or air. Haliday decried the fact that landlords were not obligated to meet certain standards in the dwellings they let. He also deplored the fact that the railway had cut off free access to the sea for bathing for ordinary people, while the rich such as Lord Cloncurry insisted that the railway company build bridges and private baths for their use. As a result of Haliday's pressure, public baths were eventually built at the back of the West Pier and at Salthill. In 1863 the Ballast Board gave the Kingstown Town Council permission to make a bathing place at the Forty Foot, in front of the battery and in the cove.

Although early town commissioners intended to supply Kingstown with water by means of pipes and public fountains, the situation remained unsatisfactory until 1869

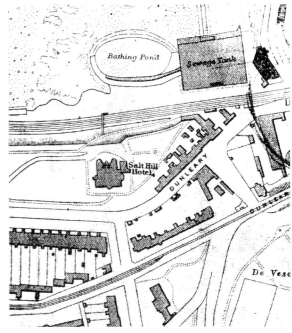

when piped Vartry water was finally made generally available. Prior to this, most houses had relied on a well or pump situated in the back yard. The new Vartry water supply was conducted by pipe from Roundwood and was one of the first real improvements for Kingstown's poorer inhabitants. With piped water people could abandon the old wells, many of which were contaminated.

It is interesting to note that priorities of the early town council did not specifically include the provision of a sewerage system. As late as 1872, it was reported that out of 41,820 feet (over 12.5 kilometres) of streets and road which should have sewers, only 15,000 feet (4.5 kilometres) had sewers that actually worked. In Glasthule the situation was even worse. In that year cholera sheds were erected on the West Pier for fear of an imminent outbreak. It was only under such threat that the town commissioners undertook a sewerage scheme, which included the West Pier Project at a cost of £15,000 (over €1 million today). A 1,000-foot (300-metre) outfall pipe was extended seawards behind the West Pier in 1877 and three years later a Sandycove outfall was proposed. The pollution of Dublin Bay in this manner caused considerable contemporary criticism. In 1872 a sewer was laid in George's Street. Five years later, the Dalkey flagstones that covered it were replaced by iron grit traps and manholes. By 1894, the sewerage system was all joined up to the central tank at West Pier.

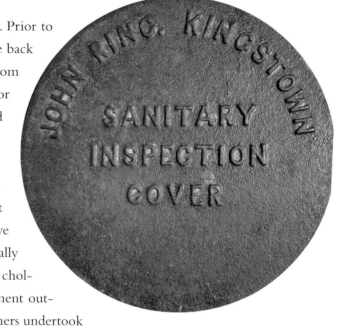

A small cast-iron inspection cover, made by Ring of Kingstown, plumbers, allowed for the cleaning of blocked drains.

The separate townships of Dalkey, Blackrock and Ballybrack were established in the 1860s. In 1899 they became urban district councils, as did Kingstown. (The jurisdiction of the Kingstown Urban District Council extended to Kill Avenue and included Sandycove, Glasthule, Glenageary, Sallynoggin and Monkstown.) In 1930 the four urban district councils amalgamated to form the Borough of Dún Laoghaire. All of Dún Laoghaire's basic services, facilities we accept so automatically, came into being with the original Act of 1834.

PUBLIC BUILDINGS: 1870–1900

Dún Laoghaire's magnificent town hall was one of the last major architectural undertakings of nineteenth-century Kingstown. It is perhaps not surprising that the building most symbolic of any township, the town hall, was not built until the town had reached a certain stage of maturity. Although there had been a petty sessions courthouse and assembly room in Corrig Avenue since 1846, by the 1860s the inhabitants were pressing for a public hall for concerts, lectures, meetings and other functions. In 1864 *The Irish Times*, in noting that the new Royal Marine Hotel was not to contain a large reception or public room after all, commented: 'Kingstown is without any public hall or reception room worthy of a town half of its wealth and population.' The same article described the need for a museum in the town and suggested that one specially devoted to marine specimens be established.

In the following year, John Crosthwaite, notable resident and developer, urged the erection of a town hall and put up £20 in prize money for the best design. The site on which the town hall was eventually built, opposite the railway station in the corner of the Harbour Commissioners' yard, was also available at this time. A temporary town hall was set up at Harrymount near St Michael's Hospital. Ten years later it moved to No. 114 George's Street Lower (originally Kavanagh's Medical Hall, later Perry's Yacht Chandlers, which stood opposite the old Carnegie Library). At the same time plans were finally accepted from the architect J.L. Robinson for a brick building with stone dressings at a cost of £8,000. The commissioners changed their minds, however, and in 1877 decided to erect a town hall and courthouse made of stone. So, after sixteen years

Kingstown's new town hall was opened on 15 July 1880 with great pomp and ceremony and was a fitting emblem of the Victorian town's new status. The Venetian-style building accommodated the council chamber, a courthouse, a public assembly room with a stage, and many offices, and added another tower to the skyline of the town with its public clock and bell.

of 'determining', construction was finally begun in 1878 to Robinson's modified plans. A contract for the construction was made with Michael Meade, the noted Dublin builder.

The town hall was finally erected at the junction of Marine and Crofton Roads at a cost of £16,000. It is a fine building composed of two grand storeys, 15 metres in height, and is surmounted at the north end by a 35-metre tower. The tower, with its familiar clock by Chancellor, is now a local landmark. The main entrance leads to a marble pillared vestibule. From there, a broad stairway leads to a spacious main hall. The council chamber is also a room of noble proportions. The Kingstown coat of arms is depicted in a fine coloured window over the main entrance. On the ground floor were the courtroom, witness and barristers' rooms, and the offices of the town clerk, surveyor, rate collector and sanitary inspector.

The overall appearance of the town hall is that of a Venetian palace, a style originally promoted by Ruskin. The first superb example of this style in Ireland was the Museum Building in Trinity College, which had been erected twenty years earlier to the designs of Deane and Woodward. The Venetian elements in the town hall include the composition of arched windows, the circular pierced balconies and the coloured stonework. The composition focuses on the central windows of the facade. The open stonework of the central balcony and the roofline balustrade (later removed) with its old cornice and high plinth are typical of the Venetian style. The contrasting colours – the red and grey Scottish sandstone used in the arches of the windows and the two-toned roof tiles – is another Venetian characteristic and demonstrates Robinson's love of varying colours in building materials. The entire town hall was gaslit and fitted with what were then ultra-modern pneumatic and electric bells. It was opened on 15 July 1880 'with great pomp and ceremony': a plaque was later erected in the hallway to record the occasion. The quality of the stonework, the roofline ironwork, the polished pine panelling of the interior, the tilework and the unusual circular staircase in the clock tower all point to a building of superlative quality.

The post office adjoining the town hall was also designed by J.L. Robinson. It was built by 1879 and has a simple granite facade of arched windows that contrasts sympathetically with the town hall. The original revolving doorway, a feature which seldom survives, has gone, along with the whole interior of the post office, and only the facade remains as the entrance to the Dún Laoghaire–Rathdown offices. A new post office was built on George's Street Upper on the site of the former courthouse, facing Dunnes Stores. The

Above: The iron staircase balusters of Dún Laoghaire's town hall are pictured with the letters KTC (Kingstown Town Council).

Opposite top: This photograph taken c. 1910 from the Pavilion shows the prime location of the town hall, situated in the middle of the town, opposite the railway station and overlooking the harbour. It also shows the roofline balustrade that was later removed. (This image is reproduced courtesy of the National Library of Ireland [L_ROY_01700].)

TOWN HALL KINGSTOWN, 1700, WL

Far left: A delicate cast-iron spiral staircase gives access to the clock tower of the town hall.

Middle left: The striking entrance vestibule of the town hall with its richly coloured tiled floor.

Left: A furnishing of the original 1880s' council chamber: the chairman's seat with the township coat of arms.

199

Staff pose for the camera in front of Dún Laoghaire post office in 1946.

earliest known postmark from the town dates to 1813 and bears the stamp 'Dunleary Penny Post'. The first recorded post office, however, was situated in George's Street Lower and was under the direction of Joseph Bond in 1833. In 1859 the main post office was located in Sussex Place, and there was a sub-post office on George's Street Lower. A second sub-post office was established at Stoneview on George's Street Upper.

Besides these offices, there were also six pillar boxes in the wider Kingstown area. The green pillar boxes and letter boxes of the town are interesting objects of street furniture, which contribute to the interest of the locality. There are about nine Victorian letter boxes (marked 'V.R.') in the town and many more in Sandycove and Dalkey.

Robinson was Kingstown's predominant architect in the late nineteenth century, and in 1889 he was also the chairman of the Kingstown Town Council. He designed St Michael's Hospital (1874), a new Magdalene asylum (1878), the People's Park (1890) and the spire of St Michael's Church (1892).

Since the earliest days of the harbour construction, an ever-increasing population created the need for a hospital to treat accidents, ill health and disease. In 1831 the Kingstown Dispensary was established and a cholera hospital was set up in Glasthule. The Rathdown dispensary and hospital came into existence in about 1834 and was the forerunner of the now-vanished Monkstown Hospital. By the mid-1830s, Kingstown also had three new 'medical halls', or apothecaries, some of which offered the services of a surgeon. Two

The graceful spire of St Michael's Church was completed in 1896 and is an important landmark on Dún Laoghaire's skyline. No part of the town is more changed than what we see in this view with the loss of Gresham Terrace, the former gardens of the Pavilion and St Michael's Church (of which only the spire of the original remains).
(This image is reproduced courtesy of the National Library of Ireland [L_ROY_00299].)

noted dispensary doctors were Glascott Symes of Gresham Terrace and Foster Newland of Mount Haigh. A Kingstown lying-in hospital was opened in 1842 on the lower part of York Road, but by 1860 it had become the Kingstown Lying-in Institution of No. 57 George's Street Lower. A hospital for the seamen of His Majesty's service was established at No. 1 Sussex Place in 1865. Many of these medical establishments had short-lived existences and, in some cases, the quality of their services was questionable.

During the 1830s, Catherine McAuley, the founder of the Sisters of Mercy, set up a Mercy Convent in Kingstown at Sussex Place House. The Sisters were given a site for a hospital at Harrymount on George's Street Lower by General Sir Michael Galway of Seapoint, and its first stone was laid on 1 October 1874 by Kingstown's notable parish priest, the Rev. Canon McCabe. At its opening two years later, the hospital building was praised for the spacious layout of its wards, their lighting and ventilation, and the decorative simplicity of its facade. The new hospital, which provided forty beds, cost £6,000 (a little shy of half a million euro today) and was erected by Meade and Son. It is sited back from the noise of the main street and consists of three storeys, 14 metres high. The grey Dalkey granite of the facade is soberly entwined with black limestone banding, and cream-and-red brick surrounds on the arched windows. The projecting end bay, which contained the entrance, is gabled and ornamented with a quatrefoil opening and two rather peculiar capitals. It was built so that if and when the hospital needed extending, another five-bay wing could be duplicated on the other side of this central feature. Unfortunately, the necessary addition made in 1938 adopted a conflicting style, which does not match the older work.

Robinson's use of arched openings and coloured building materials bears some resemblance to the style used to such great effect in the town hall. To the rear of the hospital, a projecting four-storey return housed two wards, the kitchens and a lecture theatre. The entire building was fitted with stone staircases, carefully flagged and tiled, and supplied with hot and cold water. In 1878 Robinson was again employed to design a Magdalene asylum, including a convent house, chapel and laundry for the Sisters of Mercy. The asylum, now converted to a nursing home, consisted of a long block executed in stone and brick in an uninspired institutional style, though it was doubtless very practical. The convent was designed in the same idiom as the hospital, making curious use of yellow brick.

The People's Park is located near the seafront on the east side of town. In 1890 Robinson was presented with a golden key with which to perform the official opening ceremony of the park, which he had laid out. The five-acre site had been a Board of Works quarry, and earlier the Glasthule Martello tower had stood there. The quarry was filled in and levelled and gardens were formally laid out around a bandstand and two grand iron fountains from the Sun foundry in Glasgow (see p. 204). The park lodge, incorporating a waiting room, is a handsome red-brick building, and the long iron shelter with its rooftop balcony and seats is a distinctive addition to the park. Elegant iron gates and granite pillars further ornament the park. The idea of a free park for townspeople was first suggested in 1884 when the town commissioners tried to buy Gresham Gardens as a site. It is interesting that the expenditure of public money on a public park came before the clearance of the slums and erection of the first artisans' dwellings in 1896.

The municipal buildings on George's Place were erected in 1899 and comprised a fire station, in which some of the firemen lived, a storehouse for the urban council, a stable for their horses, and a public wash house and baths. The latter was once described as 'a handsome pile of the Corinthian Order'. Its large red-brick building contained a garage entrance and yard behind. The centre of the facade is filled by a gaunt concrete

The ornamental shelter in the People's Park was tastefully converted to its present use as a café and restaurant to the designs of Howley Hayes architects.

portico and it is horizontally ornamented with stone and decorative brick banding and a balustrade. In a strange way its dull grandeur is appropriate to its municipal function, as were the gabled brick-built sheds of the refuse destructor opposite. The destructor was proposed in 1897 and was an avant-garde machine at the time. It was built in 1906 and contained incinerators connected to a tall chimney. It fell into disuse when landfill became the favoured alternative, and was demolished in the 1980s.

Kingstown once carried the curious title of 'the graveyard of schools' due to the rapidity with which various establishments came and went. Throughout the nineteenth century, countless academies, seminaries, boarding and day schools were set up. Many of these schools were dubious and were run by various unqualified ladies or mistresses. 'Academies' seem invariably to have been owned and operated by gentlemen with foreign names. By the mid-1830s, there was already a variety of seminaries and academies in Kingstown. York Road was a particularly favoured locality for schools; by 1838, it included a seminary at Airhill, the Kingstown Boarding and Day School at Wellington Lodge and the Albion House Academy. Tivoli Hall, also on York Road, was in 1860 Herr E.T. Manso's 'Continental Academic Institute'. By 1830, a classical and mathematical school had been established in Northumberland Avenue. It is possible that education as it existed in these early schools was yet another requisite of the fashionable airs towards which Kingstown aspired; it may have been enough to be able

The Tudor-style facade of the Mariners' Church and schools on Adelaide Street combined the church and school entrances with the adjoining rectory (left). The original Gothic-inspired gates and railings are a striking feature.

to say that one's daughter was attending Mrs Hovenden's 'Seminary for Young Ladies' in Rumley Avenue.

With the exception of the Kingstown School at Wellington Lodge, the rest quickly died out. The Kingstown School passed from the first principal, Mr McCaul, to a Mr Stacpoole who kept it going until the 1870s. In the 1880s the school was re-established in the converted Presbyterian church on York Road and was then run by two generations of Devlins. In the 1970s the Rev. M.E. Devlin recalled that the school was one of the earliest to adopt the co-education of boys and girls. In 1911 it was advertised as a 'high class school for boys' which sought to 'train each boy to think for himself' and concluded that many 'pupils have secured appointments in the Indian Civil Service, Home Civil Service, the Church, Medical, Professions and fellowships in Trinity College'. Apart from its academic distinctions, Kingstown School was also well known for its first-class hockey teams. The school was amalgamated in 1968 with Avoca School, Blackrock, and subsequently became Newpark Comprehensive School.

Two other relatively enduring schools were founded in the 1830s: the girls' school at the Mariners' Church and the Kingstown National School. The first evolved into the Mariners' National School, which closed in the early 1970s. The early school building in Adelaide Street was expanded to include extra classrooms, an assembly hall, a new entrance to the Mariners' Church and a rectory. Externally, the building was ornamented in the Tudor style with roofline gable, hood mouldings, small-paned windows and other decorative devices. The central portion incorporating the Tudor arch of the church entrance is carefully composed and is approached through a handsome iron gateway. After a long period of semi-dereliction, it has now been carefully restored and refurbished for a new school. The Kingstown National School was probably established by the aforementioned founder of the order of the Sisters of Mercy, Mother McAuley. The school, which had 152 pupils in 1834, seems eventually to have come into the care of the Dominican nuns who came to Kingstown in 1847. The Dominican St Mary's National School, situated at Echo Lodge adjoining Convent Road, registered over 1,000 pupils in 1911. A private or high school for girls was also run at St Mary's, and its pupils were distinguished by their brown uniforms. The combined primary and secondary schools totalled about 1,000 pupils. Only a primary school now remains.

The Christian Brothers were given a school building by a prosperous Kingstown merchant, Charles Kennedy, in about 1854, and there they established their school, adding a substantial wing onto the back. The Brothers' monastery was accommodated behind the school until 1928 when they bought Fairyland on York Road as a residence. The original school was a wide building with two projecting wings and conformed to the standard national school design of the time. It is shown on the first Ordnance Survey maps of the late 1830s. It was the town's earliest purpose-built school. It was repaired and restored after being condemned in 1962. In 1968, largely due to the efforts of Monsignor Boylan, the Brothers were restored to the old building, but despite all, the school was demolished in 2020 to make way for apartments.

Corrig School, which occupied the former private Corrig House, flourished between 1880 and 1910. It became a well-known boys' school and in 1890 had 300 pupils and eighteen masters. It was noted for its rugby and cricket teams and had playing fields at Eglinton Park, later the lands of the Dun Laoghaire Golf Club. A similar private school operated at Monkstown Park in the early years of the twentieth century.

The Christian Brothers school on Eblana Avenue was demolished in 2020, to be replaced by a block of apartments. The attractive school building, with its symmetrical front, had a Georgian appearance and was erected in the 1830s.

The education of very young children has long been cared for by small private schools as well as orphanages. There was an infant school in Cumberland Street in 1860. St Joseph's on Tivoli Road also maintains a junior school for about 550 children.

Though many of the earlier small schools, and particularly the academies and seminaries, had died out by 1900, they were replaced by a new range of private schools. The Victoria School at Nos 23–24 Clarinda Park East was fairly typical of these. Its first principal was a Miss Hudson, followed by a Miss Moneypenny and finally Miss Knox Darling, during whose time it became a high school and moved to Longford Lodge, where it was renamed Glengara Park School.

In spring 1901 the new technical school held its first classes in temporary premises. The large technical school building on Eblana Avenue was erected between 1904 and 1907. By the 1930s, there were 640 students enrolled there. The building, once used by the College of Art, is a spacious structure with a rather dull cement-faced exterior, which has remained mostly vacant in recent years. Potter's Commercial College was yet another well-known Dún Laoghaire establishment, which for over thirty-five years offered secretarial training classes. It was founded in the 1930s and run by an unusual character and one-time town councillor, Mr T. Potter.

Dún Laoghaire has possessed a surprising number of private borrowing or 'circulating' libraries since the 1830s. The names of Turrellini, Morrow, Kirkwood, Pennell and Davy Stephens, Smith, Barton and Eason were all associated with the borrowing and sale of books. Such circulating libraries were highly popular until the advent of cheap paperbacks in the 1940s. By the 1890s, a public library was located in the town hall. The Carnegie Library, built in 1912 with a very generous donation from Andrew Carnegie, is a handsome neoclassical building of brick and stone. It has remained vacant since the completion of the new Lexicon Library.

The second half of the nineteenth century saw the consolidation of Kingstown as a thriving seaport town, a fashionable place to live, with good shops and other facilities. It was also developing a reputation as a resort for tourists, a place to holiday and from which to explore Dublin and County Wicklow.

The former Carnegie Library in Dún Laoghaire was on George's Street Lower at the corner of Library Road. This well-mannered Edwardian building served the town's inhabitants for over a century. It was named after the Scottish-born philanthropist Andrew Carnegie, who had made his fortune in America and endowed many libraries all over Ireland. The building has been vacant since 2014.

Chapter 12

CULTURE AND AMENITY IN
DÚN LAOGHAIRE

Dún Laoghaire is particularly fortunate, as we have already seen, in possessing a range of high-quality decorative ironwork, especially in railings and gates. If the nineteenth century did not produce an original architectural style, then the mass production of superior ironwork was one of its most distinctive achievements. During the last decades of the nineteenth century, ornamental iron structures such as fountains and bandstands were readily available and appealed greatly to Victorian taste. They were widely advertised in catalogues and were relatively inexpensive. The gates and railings of the People's Park, for example, cost a mere £424 in 1890 and the large park shelter was erected for £666 ls lld. Such outdoor furniture was brightly painted and contributed to the general air of festivity, elegance and leisure in the town.

Scottish foundries, such as MacFarlanes and the Sun, specialised in ironwork, ranging from gates, railings, gas lamp standards and water troughs to monuments and public toilets. The fountains in the People's Park (1895) are good examples of the decorative exuberance which culminated in the magnificent Victoria fountain at the bottom of Marine Road. The stork-topped fountain is covered by a riotously decorated pierced dome, which is supported by eight Moorish arches. Iron drinking cups were once attached by chains to the fountain, whose water supply is no longer maintained. Amongst the realistic detail of birds, griffins, foliage and scrollwork is a profile of Queen Victoria whose crown tops off the monument. The instruction 'Keep The Pavement Dry' is worked into the ironwork arches, but this only became clearly visible in the replica fountain, which has not suffered

The Victoria fountain was manufactured in MacFarlane's foundry in Glasgow in 1901, but was torn down some eighty years later during the height of the Troubles in Northern Ireland as a protest against our colonial past.

any overpainting. Although the fountain was erected (with a twin at Gray Square in the Coombe in Dublin city) as a monument to Queen Victoria's visit in 1900, the same model had been advertised in *The Irish Builder* in 1898. It is sad that such a beautiful monument was destroyed in 1981. The Dún Laoghaire Harbour Company organised for a replica to be made in the Scottish foundry, which still had the moulds in stock, and the replica was unveiled in 2003.

By the early 1890s, there was an elegant bandstand on the East Pier, whose onion-shaped canopy was delicately supported on spiral columns and vine-scroll brackets. This was later replaced by the present fine, but perhaps less handsome, bandstand. During the summer months, bands played from 7.30pm to 9.30pm each evening, excepting Saturdays. They were organised by the Kingstown Amusements Permanent Committee, which was also responsible for erecting the glass shelter on the East Pier. It was built in about 1894 at a cost of £300 and formerly contained fixed timber seats. The shelter was completely refurbished in the 1990s, only to be badly smashed up in an easterly gale some years later and remains roofless. The Kingstown Committee – composed of twenty-one 'local gentlemen' – organised events such as garden fetes, dances and military bands in their 'endeavour to render the neighbourhood as attractive as possible to visitors and residents'. They also helped organise township regattas and firework displays.

A programme of the Kingstown Permanent Amusements Committee, which was active from the 1890s onwards and organised performances of bands on the pier, as well as dances and other entertainments in parks and gardens.

Though the planned Victoria Square never materialised, the gardens of the Royal Marine Hotel and Pavilion were constantly the scene of parties, concerts and balls. The imposing gates of the Royal Marine Hotel, which gave access to the seafront, used to incorporate a turnstile so that admission could be restricted on certain occasions. The high railings have disappeared and the gates were set back when the Pavilion car park was constructed. The ornate gates are supported by scrolled pillars, each topped with a cluster of dolphins and a gaslight. A set of fine fluted Doric pillars made of cast iron flank the hotel's Marine Road entrance and appear to date from the 1830s when the new hotel and Gresham Terrace were just completed. There were once fine fountains, statuary and a bandstand in the hotel gardens (see p. 179). The Kingstown Pavilion was erected in landscaped grounds adjoining the gardens of the hotel and was conceived in the same spirit of entertainment and festivity, which took its cue from the great English seaside pier pavilions such as Brighton or Margate.

In 1900 Kingstown's popularity was still on the increase. Forty years earlier, Wakeman had commented that the town attracted all the 'belles and beaus of the Irish Metropolis'. The opening of the great iron, timber and glass Pavilion in 1903 further popularised Kingstown by drawing even more holidaymakers and day trippers. The opening ceremony was performed by the Earl and Countess of Longford and the Pavilion embarked on a career of concerts, dances, variety shows and firework displays. On a June evening in 1904, for instance, 4,000 people crowded into the gardens, which were illuminated with fairy lamps, to listen to a performance by a Viennese band.

The Pavilion, designed by C. Owen and erected by Parry and Ross, contained a large central hall and stage which was surrounded by corridors and balconies. There was a rooftop garden and four corner 'belvederes'. Apart from the different promenades, it contained a variety of tea rooms, reading rooms and smoking rooms. The Pavilion's overall appearance was light and elegant, and vaguely reminiscent of pagoda or summerhouse architecture.

In August 1906 the Atlantic Fleet of the Royal Navy lay at anchor in Dublin Bay and a special ball was held in its honour. The preparations were extravagant and included the production of fine programmes, elaborate dance cards and the construction of a large covered bridge over Marine Road which connected the Pavilion with the town hall. The ball was attended by officers, nobility and aspiring society people. The following year another ball was held for the return visit of the same fleet.

The Pavilion, reconstructed after the fires of 1915 and 1919. Such seaside places of entertainment were very fashionable in English and European resorts in the early 1900s and were sometimes erected on piers, as at Brighton. Built of glass, wood and iron with whimsical balconies, belvederes and finials, they were not designed to last forever.

The Pavilion was burnt down on 15 November 1915, and one old resident, the Rev. E. Devlin, recalled in 1977 how the crackling of timber and glass could be heard all over the town. It was largely re-erected only to be burnt again in 1919. On this occasion, a horse from the Dublin Fire Brigade dropped dead on arrival at the fire, probably exhausted after the gallop from the city! Ironically, according to a description prior to its opening in 1903, all interior woodwork of the Pavilion was painted with 'Cyanide Fireproof paint' and nests of fire buckets were placed conveniently all round the building.

A group of ladies with their children on 'the Green' beside the Royal Irish Yacht Club, c. 1900. Kingstown had become a fashionable place for a day out and this well-dressed group are looking out into the harbour, possibly on the occasion of a royal visit.

In the 1920s the Pavilion was converted to a cinema seating 850, and was known as the Pavilion Picture Theatre. It was run by a Mr Gogan, whose wife played the piano accompaniment to the silent pictures. The last portion of the original Pavilion to disappear was the elegant ticket office and entrance which stood at the corner of Marine Road. The entrance gate was originally flanked by two octagonal kiosks with pointed roofs, and it is rumoured that one of these survives as a summer house in a Foxrock garden. The building was gradually deformed into an ungainly concrete structure but provided fond memories to cinemagoers for many years.

It was bought in 1975 by Dún Laoghaire Corporation, who ran it as a theatre and later leased it to the Dublin City Ballet Company. It closed as a venue in 1984 and some years later a plan to build a planetarium on the site was mooted. In 1990 a new plan for a hotel and leisure complex was welcomed by councillors, who agreed to dispose of the site to private interests. The eventual deal in which the developers of the shops, restaurant and apartments had to provide a new theatre at least guaranteed some return for the public loss of open space and park.

Though the Pavilion became a cinema as early as the 1920s, it was not the town's first. The Kingstown Picture House began operation in 1913 at Nos 9–10 George's Street Upper and later became known as The Tatler, or colloquially as The Bug House. The building, which once seated 450 cinemagoers, later housed Burton's Tailors and a restaurant, where its fine coved ceiling may still be seen. A third cinema appeared in 1946 when the Adelphi was opened at 46 George's Street Upper. A feature of all these cinemas was the newsreel film, which allowed the public to see for the first time what is now taken for granted in nightly television news.

The Adelphi, never a particularly attractive building though faced with red brick, was demolished in 1971. The site was vacant for many years, but an apartment block called Adelphi Manor and an office block have since been erected. Some of the rubble from the cinema was used as infill at the National Yacht Club to create a waterfront terrace for yachts.

The small but very popular Gas Company Theatre was another loss to the cultural life of Dún Laoghaire. The present premises was bought by the Gas Company in about 1934 from

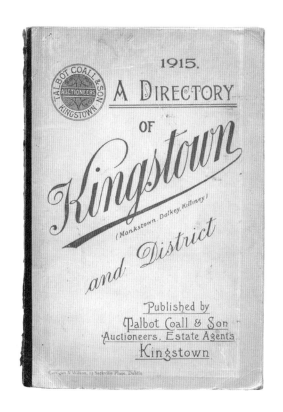

Talbot Coall's Directory of 1915 is a portrait of Kingstown in the early twentieth century and marks the end of an era.

Browetts, who had maintained a notable ironmongery and nursery store on that site.

Another entertainment venue to disappear was the Top Hat Ballroom in Old Dunleary. Having been a dance hall and bingo hall, it became a roller disco before being replaced by a block of apartments. A 'Kingstown Skating Rink' had flourished briefly in the late 1870s, and was revived at the Pavilion by 1910.

Billiards achieved early popularity. The first billiard rooms opened in 1834 in Wellington Street. By 1911, the Kingstown Billiard Saloon had been established at No. 94 George's Street Lower, but now billiards are played in most of Dún Laoghaire's clubs.

Old Dunleary had been noted for its Coffee House since the eighteenth century. The tradition was renewed in the 1890s with the establishment of the Kingstown Coffee Palace at No. 104 George's Street Lower. Similarly, Fullers on Marine Road and The Matassa on George's Street were well known up until the 1970s. Since the 1990s, coffee shops and cafes have abounded on every popular street.

Sundry businesses such as hairdressing also have a long tradition in the town: there was a hairdresser and straw-bonnet maker in Kingstown as early as 1837. Among newspaper vendors, the name of Davy Stephens was famous. He was a familiar figure at the mailboat and by the railway station during the early 1900s, with his thick coat and moustache. Davy Stephens was always pictured with a paper ready in his hand, and was known as 'the King of Irish Newsagents'. Another harbour front personality was Bob Usher, who kept a bookstall near the George IV Obelisk during the 1930s.

The Esplanade, East Pier Gardens and Moran Park were among more recent amenities

Below left: Davy Stephens was a famous newspaper vendor at Kingstown railway station for over fifty years. He had become a noted character of the town by the early 1900s and is mentioned in James Joyce's Ulysses. *He died in 1925.* (This image is reproduced courtesy of the National Library of Ireland [L_ROY_08992].)

Below right: Street bookseller Bob Usher (right), photographed at his stall on Marine Parade in the 1930s.

added to Dún Laoghaire, though Moran Park vanished with the building of the new dlr Lexicon Library. The Esplanade, running from the baths towards Sandycove, was first proposed in 1863 but its construction was not well under way until 1922. It was the subject of a long controversy over whether public funds should be spent on such a scheme when housing and sanitation were still wanting. That seafront scheme was only completely finished in the 1970s and since then controversy has frequently surfaced over various plans for the Public Baths site, a marina, an artificial beach and, most recently, the reservation of half the road for cycling. The East Pier Gardens were begun in the early 1900s and improvements continued to be made between 1914 and 1920. The Scotsman's Bay corner of the pier was landscaped with an abundant use of concrete, which jars somewhat with the fine granite of the rest of the pier but it has always proved to be a popular place for taking the sea air and sunbathing. Locally known as 'Little Greece', due perhaps to its concrete pillars, it featured in Manning Robertson's inspiring book on Dún Laoghaire of 1936. In about 1954 the very attractive Moran Park was laid out on land encompassing the old reservoir of 'Tank Field', which was bought from the OPW for £8,000. The reservoir was surrounded by a stone wall and railings and was overhung with trees. The grounds had served as the garden to the harbour master's house, which was itself once intended to become a small museum. No museum has been established, and it is a matter of shame that such an important and large Irish town has no museum devoted to its own town and county history. The location of the building would lend itself to such a use. Moran Park with its bowling green and pond disappeared with the construction of the Lexicon Library, the latter being the site of a covered car park and water feature.

As early as 1864, a newspaper article suggested that a museum of marine specimens be

Below left: A 1960s postcard showing the small beach that once existed in the corner of the East Pier at the Marine Gardens.

Below right: This unusual painting of Dún Laoghaire, signed by Orby, captures the mood of the 1940s, especially in the clothes of the women, the mailboat and the style of lamps on the pier.

Top left: The first colour tourist leaflets of the late 1940s adopted the optimistic style of the artist's impression.

Top right: The Royal Victoria Baths originated in the 1840s and would eventually become the popular Dún Laoghaire Public Baths, where many a local child first learned to swim.

Left: The attractive frontage of Dún Laoghaire Baths, erected in about 1910, was threatened with demolition as the facility lay closed for years. A major refurbishment programme took place, due for completion in 2022.

established at Kingstown, adding that an aquarium would be of special interest to a town with such a seafaring tradition. The Maritime Institute of Ireland opened the country's first maritime museum in 1959 in the old Sailors Reading Room on St Michael's Wharf. But the new car ferry terminal forced its removal in 1965 and the museum was home-less until the institute was offered the old Mariners' Church in 1974. Here an excellent museum has been established and the building completely renovated over a long period. Though it houses the National Maritime collection and receives some state support, it is essentially run on voluntary effort. There is a good collection of prints, charts and models relating to Dún Laoghaire Harbour and Dublin Bay.

SPORT IN DÚN LAOGHAIRE

Members of Dún Laoghaire girls' hockey team at Tivoli Terrace playing fields in the 1940s.

Today Dún Laoghaire is represented in most sports, but in the early years genteel sports predominated: cricket, tennis, badminton, golf, hockey, cycling and lawn bowling are among Kingstown's older sports. Yachting and bathing have already been discussed, though the great swimming galas which were held annually in the harbour should also be mentioned. The Kingstown Cricket Club was founded in 1848 and played in a field near St Paul's Church, Glenageary. A brief history of Irish cricket states that the club never really got off the ground. The Glenageary and Kingstown Lawn Tennis Club was well established by the 1890s and played on the grounds at Silchester Road, which the present Glenageary Tennis Club continues to use. In 1895 the club's patron was the Right Hon. Viscount de Vesci, and its committee included the old Kingstown names of Crofton and Symes. This club maintained the same sort of exclusive membership as the yacht clubs at that time. Tennis was played at Clarinda Park where in 1890 the annual subscription to the tennis grounds was three guineas while the same for Crosthwaite Park cost only one guinea. There were also tennis courts for the residents of Gresham Terrace Gardens and at De Vesci Gardens, where a club still flourishes. Today, year-round tennis is played at Clarinda Park and floodlighting is provided for night-time playing. From about the middle of the nineteenth century, the town boasted at least three racquet courts. Stewart's of Gortleitragh had a private court and there was another at Corrig School.

Hockey was regularly played at Glengara School and Royal Terrace and there was another pitch at Tivoli Terrace. Dún Laoghaire has several football clubs but they do not have grounds within the boundaries of the 'town'. The Kingstown Golf Club was formed in 1910 and a fine Edwardian ranch-style premises was erected at Eglinton Terrace. The club maintained one of the finest open spaces to the rear of the town until it was tempted out to the green slopes of Cattegollagher in 2007. The eighteen-hole course which extended inland from Eglinton Terrace off Tivoli Road has since been developed with apartments. The variety and abundance of recreational and sporting activities in Dún Laoghaire reflects once again its predominantly residential and resort character.

TRANSPORT

Just like running a car today, the cost of private modes of transport were not insignificant in the days of horse-drawn vehicles. As already noted in the case of stabling horses at the Royal Hotel, the bills quickly mounted up. Fodder such as hay and feedstuffs like oats, along with the provision of straw for bedding, were not cheap. A fascinating notebook of sales from Kilbogget farm in Cabinteely covering a five-year period in the 1880s lists well-known local clients and the tons of hay bought for their horses. The Hones of Yapton in Monkstown were their premier clients and their stables consumed vast quantities of hay, straw, oats and potatoes. Five months' straw, amounting to nearly 10 tons, cost £29. The Hones' various relatives, living in Killiney and at Ashton Park and Heathfield in Monkstown, were also on the books. Other noted customers were John Hamilton Reid of Holmston in Glenageary, John Clarke of Adelaide House in Kingstown and Thomas Pim of Glenageary House. Before the existence of the railway, a mail coach carried passengers between the Hibernian Hotel on Dawson Street in Dublin city centre to the packet boat at Dunleary. Throughout the nineteenth century the journey could be made by hiring a carriage from any one of a number of the fixed hazards. A 'hazard' was a stand for cabs, hackneys or carriages, whose modern equivalent would be a taxi rank. The regulations regarding the use of a hazard were rigidly laid down and published by the police in the 1850s. For instance, at the Kingstown jetty, only four carriages were permitted to wait at the railway and these were 'to proceed to the jetty, along the chains, outside, on the arrival of each packet, and if not employed to return to the hazard-horses facing East Pier'. In a list of over fifteen hazards for

Below left: In an age before motorised traffic took over, horse-drawn transport was vital. Here a car waits at the gates of the Royal Marine Hotel, c. 1910.

Below right: This cast-iron water trough for horses, which once stood at the junction of York Road and Mountown, disappeared in the 1980s.

A cabman waits for a fare in front of the railway station, c. 1910. In the background, we see the Victoria fountain and the Pavilion, along with a set of horse-drawn fire ladders belonging to the town council.

Kingstown, the exact number, location and positioning of the carriages was stipulated. The main Kingstown stand was located at James Place, now Cross Avenue. Here twenty carriages were 'to range close by the curbstone [*sic*]' between Paradise Row (Convent Road) and Tivoli Terrace East. One of the last hazards was situated on Marine Road, where the name of Keegan is still remembered as a noted cab owner. A small shelter was erected on Marine Road opposite the post office for the benefit of cabmen, or jarveys as they were known. The Edwardian-style shelter, demolished in 1997, bore a bronze plaque to the memory of Dr R. O'Donovan by whose efforts it was put up in 1912. Most of the once-commonplace horse troughs have disappeared from Dún Laoghaire, although one still survives in Killiney.

The transition from horse-drawn to petrol-driven transport was a long one, and some car proprietors such as P.J. O'Connor of Patrick Street maintained both private broughams, victorias, cabs and motor cars. Most wealthy families had their own carriage and coachman. Some maintained two carriages, open and closed, for summer and winter respectively. Old Dún Laoghaire residents still remember the impeccably kept carriages of such local gentry as Mrs Crosthwaite and the Hamilton Reids who used to pace up Glenageary Hill, sometimes with one or two urchins hanging on the back. Most of the town's large houses and some of the earlier terraces, such as Gresham Terrace, were equipped with coach houses and a dwelling above for the groom or stablehand. Later terraces, such as Clarinda Park, Royal Terrace and Crosthwaite, did not generally have coach houses. Their stables and back entrances were usually approached by lanes, which are still an important aspect of the town's personality. Many a Dún Laoghaire child will remember the fascination of the muddy lanes that ran behind the terraces, where old cars were dumped and household rubbish was once collected.

Some of the lanes behind George's Street, such as Lee's Lane and those stretching across to Convent Road, are still partially paved with old stone setts and could be greatly enhanced by the restoration of this feature. For example, the complete repaving of Temple

An open victoria, probably a private carriage, collecting a fashionable couple from the railway station, c. 1900.

An electric tram on George's Street Upper, early 1920s.

Bar in Dublin city centre in the 1980s instantly transformed the character of that area.

The first horse-drawn omnibuses seem to have run from Dublin to Kingstown in 1861. Horse-drawn tramlines were laid down between Dublin and Blackrock and between Kingstown and Dalkey in 1879 but there was a gap in the line between Blackrock and Kingstown. This gap in the route remained until the Blackrock and Kingstown Tramways Company was formed in 1883. In 1896 the Dublin-to-Kingstown tram route was reopened by the Dublin United Tramway Company as the first fully electrified tramway in Dublin. The journey to Dublin cost 3d (about €1.20 today), which was extremely reasonable even then. The trams remained highly successful until the early 1920s when the first buses began to compete. The service from Dublin was known as the premier route, and by the late 1920s several bus companies were operating around Dún Laoghaire. In 1936 Manning Robertson wrote of the new problem which the buses had brought with them: the pollution of the air. Nevertheless, in 1937 the Dublin United Tramway Company decided to replace all its trams with buses. However, the Dalkey tram lingered on in service until 1949. An old tram, which lay at rest in a garden behind St Joseph's Orphanage, was manoeuvred out on the back of a truck onto Tivoli Road and was restored during the 1980s.

By 1905, motor cars were being advertised in Dublin newspapers and journals; in 1911 Cooks Marine Garage of Kingstown was renting out motors at three guineas for a sixty-mile (100-kilometre) day run. As early as 1935 there were traffic problems on the seafront and the Corporation had to request the Minister for Local Government to prohibit the parking of motor cars on Marine Parade between the station and Dún Laoghaire Baths.

In the 1940s car ownership became more commonplace, and accordingly motor garages and filling stations were set up. In 1941 Dún Laoghaire possessed three garages: White and Delahunty of Marine Road (the successor to Cooks), Kennedy's of Cross Avenue and Martin's of Tivoli Road (now Jones Peterson Motors Limited). Back in 1834 the town commissioners had instigated a 40s fine for careless 'parking', and some early photographs show George's Street packed with horse-drawn vehicles. But it was motor traffic that was to pose the biggest threat to peace and order in the town. In 1957 the volume of traffic was sufficient to cause traffic lights to be erected on George's Street at the junctions of York Road, Marine Road and Park Road. Today, car ownership in Ireland is, per capita, among the highest in Europe. Every street and avenue in Dún Laoghaire is lined with long strings of cars by night and day. The issue of traffic and parking continues to present a major challenge and the closure of two-way traffic on most of the seafront roads has worsened the problem. While cycle lanes are welcome, it is questionable whether they need to take up half of a six-metre-wide road.

THE COAL TRADE

Coal had been imported into Dunleary from England and Wales since the eighteenth century, if not before. In 1768 antiquarian John Lodge noted that sea coal, shipped across the Irish Sea, was the principal fuel of the Dunleary–Dalkey area: 'This is imported from Whitehaven, and in the summer season may be purchased at Dunleary for 15/- a ton.'

Nineteenth-century photographs of Ireland show how treeless much of it was — especially around towns, so there was a great dependence on imported coal. In 1847 William Ormbsy McCormick, the son of a Methodist minister in the town, founded the company of W.O. McCormick in Kingstown with offices in Clarence House, close to the Coal Harbour. They supplied coal to ships of the Irish Lights and the Admiralty and had special arrangements (c. 1900) for coaling steam yachts. In 1880 they had a fleet of six colliers of varying sizes, of which the *Dunleary* was the fastest. McCormicks continued as a family business with their small ships and yards until 1966 when they could no longer compete with larger vessels bringing 10,000 tons of coal from the USA into Dublin Port.

In about 1860 McCormicks bought the Kill of the Grange pottery works from the Ffoliot family and produced a range of bricks, tiles and edging for paths, under the name of Kingstown Pottery. They later established the Boghall Brickworks near Bray. The two families intermarried and it was a descendant, Mr de Courcy Ffoliot Darling of Dún Laoghaire, who informed me in 1977 of his family's connection with the local coal and brick trade. The McCormicks were associated with a number of large houses in the district, such as Yapton in Carrickbrennan, Bartra in Dalkey and Somerset on Stradbrook Road.

Coal and fishing had always ranked as old Dunleary's chief commercial activities, but by the 1860s, the coal business had expanded into Kingstown's foremost concern. Among the town's leading coal merchants were McCormick, Armstrong, Tedcastle, and Downs

The Hampton, *photographed in the Coal Harbour in 1890, was built in 1863 and could carry nearly 600 tons of coal. She was later wrecked on the railway embankment at Salthill (see p. 13).*

whose coal yards later became Wallace's. These big coal merchants fed the thousands of fireplaces in Kingstown's new houses. In 1859 twenty tons of coal brought for a big Kingstown house cost £17 3s 8d. A glance at the forest of chimney pots on the rooftops of the houses today is evidence enough that coal was a flourishing and lucrative business. The now-neglected coal-holes of every Victorian house are a reminder of people's dependence on that fuel not only for heating and cooking but also for industry and transport too. The boilers of steamships and steam engines had to be kept stoked and so there was a steady arrival of coal boats into Dún Laoghaire. Even the name Coal Harbour is evocative of that once dirty and busy trade.

In 1855 the traders' wharf was constructed at a cost of £30,000 (about €2 million today), creating the new Outer Coal Harbour as it is still generally called. It springs from the rocks once known as Ducking Point. The Coal Harbour became the focus of commercial activity – mainly fishing boats and colliers. A large boat slip was added (the best public slipway in the harbour) and in 1912 a turntable was installed which allowed large yachts and other vessels to be winched out and stored in the dockyard. In 1863 the traders' wharf was provided with a railway siding for the export of pyrites from the Avoca Mines in County Wicklow. In one bad gale, 800 tons of coal were washed off the wharf into the harbour. A contemporary observer, Mary Hamilton, described a busy and crowded harbour full of 'fleets of brown sailed trawlers and coal boats with unwashed decks and seamen with blackened faces which showed up the whites of their eyeballs whiter still.'

Below left: A recent photo of a trawler lying on the granite-built Coal Harbour slip, about to be scrapped. This is the largest public slip in Dún Laoghaire Harbour and is much used by sail boarders, waterskiers and dinghy sailors.

Below right: The belching clouds of black coal smoke from this 1860s paddle steamer – one of the four provinces ships – illustrate the extent of air pollution during the steam age.

Above left: *The coal ship* Rowanfield, c. *1920s in the Coal Harbour.*

Above right: *The coal yards of Alexander Downs, later Wallaces, with their many sheds and stores in Old Dunleary, pictured in a billhead of about 1880.*

GAS, LIGHT AND TELEPHONE

In the early nineteenth century, gas became the modern source of power for lighting, especially street lighting. There were several privately operated gasworks in Kingstown before the arrival of the Alliance and Dublin Consumers Gas Company in 1866. The Company occupied the site of the present Clearwater Cove apartments, on reclaimed land. The new gasworks in Old Dunleary was bounded on the west by the Hibernian Gas Company, on the south by the coal yards of Edward Armstrong and Sexton, and on the east by a high bank commonly known as the Pig Bank.

'The Kingstown Urban District Council have evidently no belief in Electric Lighting,' wrote *The Irish Builder* in 1903. Controversy had arisen over the fact that the township was empowered to use electric light but had persistently ignored it. For instance, in 1902 a generating station in Kingstown was proposed, yet the following year the council placed an order with the Gas Company for 500 incandescent burners. It seems likely that the Gas Company and coal merchants resisted electricity, viewing it as a business rival. The Royal Marine Hotel had been fitted with electric light powered by its own generator by 1897, but when the Pavilion was under construction in 1903 it was fitted with gaslight (supplied by the Alliance and Dublin Consumers Gas Company rather than the Kingstown Gas Company). Bray had adopted electric light by 1904 and erected a generator powered by a head of water from the River Dargle, but Dún Laoghaire was slow to see the advantages of electricity. Many Dún Laoghaire houses were wired for electricity only in the late 1920s. In 1932 a contract was made with the newly formed Electricity Supply Board for the public lighting of Dún Laoghaire, and all street lights were converted to electricity by 1935.

The National Telephone Company was established in Kingstown as early as 1899, but lasted only about fifteen years. Some of the first people to avail of the service were grocers who could receive orders over the phone and have them delivered by van. If you telephoned '49' Kingstown in 1911, for example, an order could be placed for fresh fish or poultry at the market at No. 108 Patrick Street and it would be delivered the same day. As their telephone number 180 indicates, the Royal Marine Hotel was a later sub-scriber (1913) to the National Telephone Company. An automatic telephone exchange was installed in Patrick Street in 1951.

As the early twentieth century progressed, life was to change dramatically in Dún Laoghaire as elsewhere. The Great War, the Easter Rising of 1916 and the events of 1921–22 were to see the end of old Victorian ways and herald new social norms, new architecture and new modes of transport.

MODERN TIMES

House developments from 1930 onwards made a complete break from the nineteenth-century building traditions, introducing an entirely new set of shapes and proportions which were often at odds with those of the Victorian age. Typical Victorian houses featured vertical windows, high front steps and an inconspicuous roof. Post-1930 houses in Dún Laoghaire are characterised by a semi-detached plan and prominent slated or tiled roofs, metal-framed windows and pebble-dashed walls. Basements and servants' accommodation were both abandoned, and every house was provided with a garage. These architectural alterations reflect two important social changes: the disappearance of domestic service and the advent of the private motor car.

Many houses of this class were built on Tivoli Terrace South and East, Corrig Avenue, Tivoli Road, Rosmeen Gardens, Myrtle Park, Beechwood Park, Silchester Park and Crosthwaite Park West. While the post-1930 houses are quite functional and more easily heated and maintained than a large terraced house, they lack the grace of their Victorian counterparts. The recent trend has been to upgrade these mid-twentieth-century houses with sympathetic extensions, simple new windows and doors and new insulation.

The early modern houses of Crosthwaite Park West were built in 1929–30 and reflect the Arts and Crafts movement in architecture. They are characterised by pebble-dashing, metal window frames and prominent slated roofs. A builder named Kennedy erected two very attractive modern detached houses in Rosmeen Gardens. Both houses, Rosmeen and Moyola, are Romantic in style, featuring projecting bow windows, arched

entrances and balconies, and prominent roofs and chimney stacks, nevertheless employing modern materials such as concrete, brick and iron-framed windows. In 1947 after the Second World War, Royal Terrace East was extended with the addition of thirty-three new houses, which became known as Myrtle Park. These houses have a horizontal elevation and are finished in red rustic brick and pebble-dash with large projecting tiled roofs.

In the late 1970s a large house development took place in the grounds of Holmston House near Myrtle Park. Approximately fifty detached Georgian-inspired houses were completed. The new development, known as Glenageary Woods, are of a straightforward modern type, garnished with various neo-Georgian features such as small-paned windows, brick fronts and columns.

A number of Victorian residential neighbourhoods and characteristic terrace houses in Dún Laoghaire have suffered the intrusion of insensitive apartment and office block schemes. Many parts of the seafront between Monkstown and Sandycove have already been marred by over-large modern buildings, which bear no relationship to the scale, proportions or colour of the existing terraces. Glass and concrete structures such the

Above left: Rosmeen Gardens, off George's Street Upper.
Above right: Cambridge Terrace on York Road.

office block at George's Place or the Bord Iascaigh Mhara building on Crofton Road seem architecturally inappropriate to Dún Laoghaire. Not all modern buildings, however, are out of sympathy with the Victorian nature of the town. The Crofton Court building on Crofton Avenue successfully blends with the Victorian street. Nearby, the Marine Court block, as previously stated, does at least respect the texture and colour of the seafront. The grant of permission by An Bord Pleanála for a thirteen-storey block on Crofton Road, beside Charlemont Terrace, created a real threat to the character of the seafront. There was much criticism of the size and height of the Lexicon Library when it was being built.

In terms of provision of public amenities, the need for greater access to sea bathing could be provided for by a new outdoor seawater pool at either Dún Laoghaire or Blackrock while the erection of a permanent semi-covered street market on George's Street would represent a real public service to the town. Car parking, as already mentioned, is an issue in every town, and many shoppers avoid Dún Laoghaire because of parking difficulties. Simply closing streets to traffic or making access so difficult as to discourage motorists is not an answer either, as not everyone can walk or cycle. However, Dún Laoghaire now has space at the old ferry terminal, which could be adapted for long-term parking to free up the streets for short-term shoppers.

Mature gardens and plentiful trees add greatly to the richness of Dún Laoghaire's environment. The importance of trees and shrubs in a densely populated district cannot be overstated. They form needed breaks in the street, they absorb dust and pollution, abate noise and add generally to the beauty of the town. The standard of garden design and maintenance is very good throughout the whole district, though a major eyesore is the multiplicity of plastic wheelie bins in every garden and beside every railing and gate.

THE SHOPPING ENVIRONMENT

George's Street today presents a wide variety of shopfronts and signs, differing widely in colour and shape. Although the variety is itself quite attractive, too many of Dún Laoghaire's shop facades are disfigured by brash and over-large signs and advertisements. An effective shop sign does not need to be large, nor does it need to be neon-lit. Careful strip lighting, soft lamps or interesting interior lighting can be highly effective. It is also a pity that many shopfronts and name boards are so out of harmony with the fine brickwork just above them. The combination of too many materials and colours often results in poor frontages. In the 1970s and 1980s the widespread use of aluminium was one of the most

*The Last Corner Shop,
at the corner of Clarinda
Park and George's Street
Upper, is notable for its
seemingly chaotic abundance
of newspapers and magazines,
including back issues.*

disfiguring elements on new shopfronts and, like plastic, becomes depressingly dingy with time. Wood, on the other hand, ages with dignity and can be repainted.

Many of the garden-fronted houses of George's Street Upper have been converted into offices for banks and building societies. It has already been mentioned that the chief factors that spoil these houses are the removal of the railings and gardens and the erection of inappropriate business signs. The alteration of the proportions and colour, the addition of a modern sign in a terrace of houses and the loss of the front garden all seriously affect the appearance of the rest of the street.

The now-ageing Dún Laoghaire shopping centre was clearly the town's most radical commercial development, completely altering the appearance and atmosphere of central Dún Laoghaire. The centre was designed as a complete shopping area in itself, and thus turns its back on the rest of the town. The life of the shopping centre exists primarily indoors: from the street (except for George's Street) people are confronted with brick walls unrelieved by anything of human interest. An entire block of buildings between Gresham Terrace and George's Street was demolished in 1974 and the following year, the shopping centre was begun. At the time, such a dramatic change to the town centre

Top left: *The galleried interior of the old Dún Laoghaire shopping centre.*

Top right: *The modern skyline of Dún Laoghaire is the subject of much critical debate and was much altered by the Lexicon building and the Pavilion apartment complex, but both incorporate valuable public facilities in the form of the very popular library and theatre.*

was questioned by many residents and shopowners, who were worried both about the centre's dominating character and the future of small shops in the rest of the town. In general, the centre was not detrimental to trade in the town, since it drew large crowds who shopped outside the centre as well. Unfortunately, since the turn of the twenty-first century, many of the units in the centre have lain vacant. Functionally, the centre has succeeded. It is a warm, dry place to shop. But what of its atmosphere and personality? Most of the public space is artificially lit, and very little advantage was taken of the elevated site and sea views. And although the designers made some effort to conform to the street line in height, the proportions of the centre and choice of brick colour are inappropriate to Dún Laoghaire. The heavy modelling of the facades and lack of street-level detail have yet to be relieved by the once-planned planting of trees on Marine Road. The centre is based on American and European prototypes, and has introduced an international and somewhat impersonal scale and style into the previously modest proportions of the town. The main part of the shopping centre is focused around a court, where three levels of shops are drawn together, each court cleverly linked by service passages and lifts to the basement where goods arrive. The offices above the centre have the benefit of the marvellous views, but the inhabitants who have to look at the centre every day regard it at best as an eyesore. The great numbers who once flocked to the shopping centre certainly proved its popularity but it now seems rather dated. On entering the centre, one is struck by the same inescapable twentieth-century atmosphere – the same as could be found in any similar shopping centre in the world.

RECENT TIMES

Among the many forces which have brought changes in Dún Laoghaire during the last fifty years, the role of the car is probably the most significant. The small area surrounding the entrance to the Royal Marine Hotel demonstrates how the car once completely dominated, and spoilt the environment of central Dún Laoghaire. Over the last number of years Dún Laoghaire–Rathdown County Council have made significant improvements to both the seafront at Marine Parade and to Marine Road, with the creation of new pedestrian areas by covering over part of the railway track between the town hall and the Lexicon, the provision of seating and attractive new paving and planting. The area in front of the town hall is especially elegant with small borders of box hedges and the trees on Marine Road stretching up to Eason's bookshop add greatly to the environment.

The once-attractive public open space of the Pavilion Gardens was traded for a private commercial development on condition that the new building would incorporate a new Pavilion Theatre and a car park. All this happened and many would say it was a successful trade-off as the Pavilion provides an important cultural facility to the town and county.

It is interesting to compare the fortunes of Dún Laoghaire with Blackrock since 1990. The bypass, with its attendant office blocks, has changed Blackrock radically. Though always jammed with cars, the town has created for itself a clearer identity, with a trend towards coffee shops, restaurants and shops selling gifts, furnishings, fabrics and clothes.

The recent disappearance of almost all butchers, bakers and greengrocers reflects how the two huge supermarket-type shopping complexes have completely taken over the trade in foodstuffs. Small personal grocers in Dún Laoghaire, like the now-forgotten Taggarts, Powers or McGoverns, preserved qualities that can never be created or found in supermarkets or shopping centres. The small newsagent and tobacconist is another casualty of changing times. May's, dating from 1909, sold newspapers, cards, magazines, comics, sweets, ice creams and cigarettes in their corner shop at the bottom of Patrick Street. Dixon's, a similar shop, and its neighbour, Sir Thomas Brown's the tobacconist, were very well known. They, along with many other small businesses like butchers and bakers have all vanished.

Commercial Dún Laoghaire has been allowed to spread away from the centre to what were residential locations, such as Monkstown Crescent. This means that the businesses

and shops of the town are straggled out from Monkstown to Glasthule, and that the centre of the town lacks real vitality.

Since 1981, Dún Laoghaire has witnessed the arrival and departure of the Harbour Market, which was located in the former factory site of Albright and Wilson, and now replaced by the Clearwater Cove apartments. By nature, such markets can at times be seedy, but the Harbour Market drew vast numbers of stallholders selling an extraordinary range of goods, both old and new, at reasonable prices. It drew large crowds to Dún Laoghaire on Sundays and was probably one of the best-organised ventures of its type. Dún Laoghaire badly needs the vitality of attractions of various kinds, perhaps in a pedestrianised area like the stone-cobbled back lanes off George's Street or in the new Myrtle Square. The Blackrock market has proved to be a very successful model, particularly for foods and small restaurants. New street paving and the pedestrianisation of part of George's Street Lower could help revive the town centre.

For many years, there were probably more painters, writers, poets, actors and people involved with the arts living and working in the Dún Laoghaire area than in any other single place in Ireland. Now it has become too expensive for such people, who generally get by on a shoestring, as rents and purchase prices are so high. Despite this artistic legacy, there is no permanent art gallery or cinema. The Pavilion provides a fine theatre with an impressive programme of events, including films. There is a small exhibition space in the Lexicon which is run by the county council's Arts Office but, being in

the library, it is seen as an afterthought and not really adequate to meet the needs of a county like Dún Laoghaire–Rathdown. The former ferry terminal might make a better arts centre, which could combine official and voluntary forces and have a far wider remit. Though there is a small and very successful heritage centre in Dalkey, dedicated to aspects of Dalkey itself, there is still no local history museum which might record and examine the wide-ranging interests of the whole county or indeed of Dún Laoghaire town and harbour and its people.

The Lexicon Library is without doubt a great addition to the cultural life of the town and it too makes a huge contribution to the area in terms of events and exhibitions. Though many were shocked by the size of the building and by its severe external appearance, almost everyone is impressed by the interior and enjoys the calm created by the oak-finished floors, stairs, desks and shelving. The library is extremely popular with students and runs a continuous programme of cultural events. There is an excellent section devoted to local history and a purpose-built archive. The town hall, which was smartly refurbished in 1990, has a fine public hall with a stage but it is not generally open to the public. Public gatherings are held in hotel rooms or church halls and the largest meeting place is the Boylan Centre on Sussex Street, which has the quality of a temporary building and is crying out for redevelopment.

In 1981 Dún Laoghaire's College of Art and Design moved out of town to splendid new buildings at Carriglea near Deansgrange, and since then the presence of students has been missing from the town. Other educational closures also included the Nautical College on the West Pier although a sailing/diving and power boat school now occupies the buildings nearby. Two local secondary schools left the immediate area of the town; one, Glengara Park, joined with Rathdown school and the other, Kingstown school, amalgamated with Avoca to become Newpark Comprehensive School. The Dominican Convent and Secondary School, now closed, was demolished to make way for the Bloomfields Shopping Centre. The original Regency house, with its fine Wyatt windows, dating from about 1810 and possibly Dún Laoghaire's oldest-surviving residence, was swept away in 1995. By chance, this impressive building was not listed or protected, while other properties, perhaps of lesser quality, were. Only the small oratory, uniquely decorated by Sister Concepta Lynch in the 1920s, was saved from the bulldozer.

It is perhaps inevitable that the presence of the DART railway system has meant that institutions with land are under pressure to sell to developers. But the decline of religious orders and dramatic changes in society's attitudes have also provoked the sale of many institutional premises in County Dublin, including many monasteries and convents, schools and former nursing homes. Out of the three orphanages once existing in Dún Laoghaire, two buildings survive. St Joseph's on Tivoli Road was demolished in 1990. The closure and demolition of Monkstown Hospital, a small, intimate organisation with thirty beds, was the result of the government's rationalisation of the health service. Other demolitions include the landmark chimneys of the baths and of the refuse destructor (in 1985), which, as already noted, was itself a fine brick structure. However, it must be said that, in general, the listing of buildings for preservation or protection in the Dún Laoghaire area has worked well and the policy actually engenders pride in the built environment.

The existence of the DART with its regular and reliable train service undoubtedly makes Dún Laoghaire a desirable place in which to live. Despite the fluctuations of the property market, the prices of older period houses here remain very high. During the 1980s, townhouse developments, as they were known, were very popular, but these have been largely replaced by the apartment block. Townhouses were squeezed in on almost any site, making many gardens and, in some cases, period houses prey to the bulldozer. More recently, however, it is the less architecturally interesting houses and bungalows of the twentieth century which are being targeted for redevelopment. All over Dún Laoghaire, Glenageary and Dalkey unattractive twentieth-century houses are being gutted and rebuilt in a contemporary idiom, while larger sites and gardens are targeted for apartment blocks.

Two important initiatives in the 1980s contributed significantly to the natural environment of Dún Laoghaire – the government ban on the burning of bituminous coal dramatically improved air quality during winter, and the new sewage works and pipeline

Above: An office building completed in 2021 at Cumberland Street adopts a striking profile to fit an awkward wedge-shaped site.
Left: Marine Road, showing the new apartments, which were erected on the former Pavilion Gardens.

greatly enhanced the water quality of Dublin Bay – but those improvements are already proving inadequate to cope with Dublin's growing population, and sewage spills in wet weather are again a serious problem.

Major changes have taken place at the harbour. Despite the economic difficulties of the 1980s, car and passenger traffic steadily increased at Dún Laoghaire and larger ships were needed. There were problems with the old ferry terminal and there was pressure for a marina in the harbour. A Planning Review Group, chaired by Professor Dermot McAleese, produced an excellent report in 1988 outlining all the issues and laying out all the options for the future. While fully aware of the high amenity and heritage value of Dún Laoghaire Harbour, it recommended the construction of a new ferry terminal and the building of one or two small marinas. The road infrastructure of the Dún Laoghaire hinterland and its residential quality precluded it from ever becoming a major port for freight. Responsibility for this unique asset was transferred from the OPW to the Department of the Marine, which established the Dún Laoghaire Harbour Board in 1990. Throughout the 1990s, the ferry service flourished, with seven sailings a day, 1.2 million passengers, 200,000 cars and 35,000 freight trucks in 1993 alone. A bigger, faster sea cat came into service in 1995 but over the next fifteen years, as air travel became cheaper, the ferries lost out. Stena made their last sailing between Dún Laoghaire and Holyhead in February 2015. Now the harbour has come under the control of Dún Laoghaire–Rathdown County Council. If the careful repairs to the stonework at East Pier bandstand and shelter are anything to go by, it shows a high degree of awareness and respect for this national monument.

The Irish Lights HQ, a dramatic new building of circular form, reflects the many buoys and lighthouses which that body looks after around the Irish Coast.

During the 1970s and 1980s, a variety of proposals were put forward for one or more yachting marinas in the harbour. A lot of schemes were met with suspicion and aroused a good deal of controversy. Many questions were asked, such as: since the harbour belongs to the state, how can the common good best be served? Among the most ambitious, and many would say outlandish, schemes was a plan to infill up to seventy acres of sea between the West Pier and Seapoint. The reclaimed land would be used principally for car parking and for building apartments or houses and there was to be a small boat harbour. The promoters argued that a marina would bring new business and jobs to the town and would make Dún Laoghaire Harbour attractive for visiting yachts to spend more time there. There were also variations, including proposals in 1992 for three smaller marinas with new breakwaters off the West Pier to shelter the west bight and smaller ones at the Coal Harbour and National Yacht club.

Now that the marina is built and has been operational since 2001 it is possible to assess its success and its impact on the harbour generally. No one can dispute the fact that it accommodates many more boats (820 as opposed to 550 that could be kept on swing moorings), or that it is open to anyone to use without having to be a member of a yacht club, provided they are prepared to pay the substantial fees. It is undeniable that the two breakwaters have improved the amount of sheltered water in the harbour and that a wide range of useful facilities are provided, such as water, electricity, showers and toilets. However, all this comes at a significant sacrifice to the historic harbour along with the infill

Mothership by Rachel Joint, on the seafront at Newtownsmith, is a much-admired sculpture based on the idea of a sea urchin.

and loss of sailing space for dinghies, added to the fact that a great number of the boats kept in the marina rarely put to sea.

Several public sculptures have been erected in Dún Laoghaire since the 1980s, all of which add interest to the town. Perhaps the most notable, not least because of the controversy surrounding it when it was about to be put up in the late 1940s, is the large bronze called *Christ The King*, made originally in 1926 by the noted artist Andrew O'Connor, which now stands between the Lexicon and the Pavilion apartments, facing out to sea. After much debate about its style and religious appropriateness, it lay stored in a garden for thirty years until it was finally erected at the bottom of Haigh Terrace, only to be moved again following the completion of the Lexicon Library. The second is an

A delightful Victorian souvenir tray of papier mâché, oil paint and mother of pearl, made in 1850, is based on a print of the town and harbour.

unusual monument to Dublin Bay hobblers, the unofficial pilots who lost their lives at sea, and takes the form of a tower of old lifejackets, created by Fiona Mulholland, and is located on the Marina pier. One of the most beautiful pieces is a large bronze sea urchin, called *Mothership*, by Rachel Joint, which stands on the seafront at Newtownsmith. The most recent addition is a figurative sculpture of Roger Casement, erected in 2021 in front of the refurbished baths.

The inhabitants of Dún Laoghaire are very privileged to have inherited a town and harbour of style and dignity. The coastline is equally special. Manning Robertson, the town planning advisor to Dún Laoghaire Corporation, wrote in an excellent book, *Dun Laoghaire: Its History, Scenery and Development,* in 1936:

> The amenity of Dun Laoghaire both in its natural beauty and proximity to the capital should be jealously guarded as a national possession.
>
> A culture or otherwise of any state is proclaimed in its buildings and their setting. A high standard of culture not only raises the standard of life and appreciation for the inhabitants but it brings incidentally its financial harvest to the trader and the hotel proprietor. Town planning especially in so favoured a locality as Dún Laoghaire must aim at preserving and enhancing those natural beauties which have been handed down to us and which it should be our pride to hand on, not only unsullied, but cherished and improved.

SELECT BIBLIOGRAPHY AND
FURTHER READING

GENERAL

An Act for … Improving the Town of Kingstown (drawn up by Pierce Mahony, Solicitors), 1834.

Archer, J., *A Statistical Survey of County Dublin*, 1801.

Blake, G. & Middleton, T.B., *The Badminton Library of Sports and Pastimes: Yachting*, Vol. 2, 1894.

Ball, F.E., *A History of the County Dublin*, 1902–20.

Blacker, B.H., *Sketches of Irish Churches*, 1860.

Bolton, J., Carey, T., Goodbody, R. & Clabby, G., *The Martello Towers of Dublin*, 2012.

Boylan, H., *White Sails Crowding: A History of The Royal Irish Yacht Club*, 1994.

Brewer, J.N., *The Beauties of Ireland*, 1826.

Brooke, R.S., *Recollections of an Irish Church*, 1877.

Cannon, S. & Cullen, C., *Monkstown*, 2014.

Conlon, T., *Victorian Dún Laoghaire: A Town Divided*, 2016.

Corlett, C., *Antiquities of Old Rathdown*, 1999.

Cromwell, T., *Excursions through Ireland (with engravings by G. Petrie)*, 1820.

Curry, W., *The Picture of Dublin*, 1835.

D'Alton, J., *The History of the County of Dublin*, 1838.

de Courcy Ireland, J., *Lifeboats in Dublin Bay: A Review of the Service from 1803–1997*, 1999.

ERU, *Dublin Bay Water Quality Study*, 1989.

Eyre, J.R., *The Gateway to Ireland*, 1912.

Frazer, J., *Handbook to Ireland*, 1844.

The Freeman's Journal, 3 December 1795.

Gaskin, J.J., *Varieties of Irish History*, 1869.

Girouard, M., 'All that Money Could Buy', *Spirit of the Age*, 1975.

Goodbody, R., *The Metals: From Dalkey to Dún Laoghaire*, 2010.

Griffith, R., *Survey and Valuation of the Barony of Rathdown*, 1849.

Gunning, D., Curtin, N. and Keyes, M.T., *Divine Illumination: The Oratory of the Sacred Heart, Dún Laoghaire*, 2019.

Haliday, C., *Pamphlet on the Sanitary State of Kingstown*, 1844.

Hamilton, M., *Green and Gold*, 1948.

Harden, R., *St John's Monkstown*, 1911.

Hunt's Yachting Magazine, 1853, 1865.

Illustrated London News, 31 July 1880.

The Irish Builder, 1867–1930.

Joyce, Weston St John, *The Neighbourhood of Dublin*, 1912.

The Lady of the House, 1897.

Lewis, S., *Topographical Dictionary of Ireland*, 1837.

Merrigan, Justin *Dun Laoghaire Holyhead 1826–2015: The Rise and Decline of Ireland's Premier Route*, 2016.

Murphy, E., *A Glorious Extravaganza: The History of Monkstown Parish*, 2003.

O'Sullivan, D., *Dublin Bay: A Century of Sailing*, 1984.

O'Sullivan, D., *The National: Chronicles of a Dun Laoghaire Yacht Club*, 2020.

O'Sullivan, J. & Cannon, S. (eds), *The Book of Dunlaoghaire*, 1987.

Pearson, P., *Between the Mountains and the Sea*, 1998.

Pearson, P. & Power, F., *The Forty Foot – a Monument to Sea Bathing*, 1992.

Pearson, P., *A History of the Royal St George Yacht Club*, 1987.

Porter, F., *Post Office Guide and Directory of Kingstown*, 1911.

Powell, G.R., *The Official Railway Handbook to Bray, Kingstown etc.*, 1860.

Robertson, Manning, *Official Guide to Dun Laoghaire*, 1936.

Ronan, Myles, 'Stones from the Dún of Dún Laoghaire.' *Journal of The Royal Society of Antiquaries of Ireland*, Vol. 62, 1932.

Rutty, J., *A Natural History of County Dublin*, 1772.

Sisk, H., *Dublin Bay: The Cradle of Yacht Racing*, 2012.

Stratten & Stratten, *Dublin, Cork and South of Ireland: A Literary, Commercial and Social Review*, 1892.

Talbot Coall, *Guide and Directory to Kingstown*, 1915.

Thackeray, W.M., *An Irish Sketch Book*, 1874.

Thom, A., *Statistics of the British Isles*, 1855.

'Town's Survey', *The Dublin Builder*, No. 5, 1862.

Wakeman, W.F., *Tourists' Guide through Dublin and its Interesting Suburbs*, 1865.

Warburton, Whitelaw and Walsh, *History of the City of Dublin*, 1818.

Wright, G.N., *An Historical Guide to Ancient and Modern Dublin*, 1821.

Young, A., *A Tour of Ireland*, 1779.

THE HARBOUR

Anderson, *Sailing Ships of Ireland*, 1951.

Bligh, W. Capt., *Survey of Dublin Bay*, 1801.

Beam, *The Journal of the Irish Lighthouse Service,* vol. 7, nos 1–2, 1975.

Colvill Papers. 1802–1820 (ms in National Library).

Enoch, V., *Martello Towers of Ireland*, 1974.

Flynn, H.E., *Proposed Ship Canal to Kingstown*, 1834.

Dawson, W., *Plan for Three Harbours: Howth, Dunleary and Holyhead*, 1809.

de Courcy Ireland, J., *A History of Dun Laoghaire Harbour*, 2001.

de Courcy Ireland, J., 'Dunlaoghaire, A Maritime Profile', Programme of Lifeboat Naming Ceremony, 1967.

Dún Laoghaire Harbour Planning Review Group, 1988.

'Gale at Kingstown', *Illustrated London News*, 9 February 1861.

Instructions for Kingstown Harbour Constables, 1863.

Kingstown Harbour Commissioners, Minute Books, 1815–1836 (Public Records Office).

Marmion, A., *The Ancient and Modern History of the Maritime Ports of Ireland*, 1855.

Ó Suilleabháin, D., *Ó Kingstown Go Dún Laoghaire*, 1977.

Parliamentary Papers, 1843, p. 22.

Powell, G.R., *The Gale*, 1861.

Register of Vessels 1838–1884, Kingstown Harbour (Public Records Office).

Rennie, J., *Report on Kingstown Harbour*, 1835 (ms in National Library).

Seaman, A., *Considerations for a Harbour*, 1811.

Smith, C.V., *Dalkey – Society and Economy in a Small Medieval Irish Town*, 1996.

Smyth, D., *Bulloch Harbour: Past and Present*, 1999.

Stretton, C.E., *The History of the Holyhead Mailboat Service*, 1901.

Toutcher, R. Capt., 'Documents relating to the intended harbour … Eastwards of Dunleary', 1807–1826 (ms in National Library).

Yeates, '70 Years of the Irish Mail', *Sea Breezes*, July 1961.

THE RAILWAY

Dublin and Kingstown Railway Company, Proceedings of the Directors, 1842.

The Dublin Penny Journal, 1834–35.

Lyons, G., *The Story of the Dublin and Kingstown Railway*, 2015.

Mallet, R., *Report on the Kingstown and Dalkey Railroad (The Atmospheric Railway)*, 1844.

Mullins, M.B., *Transactions of the Institute of Civil Engineers of Ireland*, Vol. 6, 1863.

Murray, K.A., 'Dun Laoghaire and the Railway', *Journal of Irish Railway Records Society*.

DIRECTORIES

Wilson's Directory, *The Post Office Directory* and *Thom's Directory* are particularly valuable sources for dating and tracing the growth of the town. *The Dublin Builder* 1859–1866 provides interesting contemporary references to the town and harbour.

MAPS, PLANS AND CHARTS

Admiralty Charts, 1857 and 1892.

Burgh, *Survey of Dublin Bay*, 1728.

Duncan, W., *Map of County Dublin*, 1821.

Ordnance Survey, *Map of County Dublin*, 1843.

Taylor, A., *Survey of County Dublin*, 1816.

LOCAL HISTORY

Since 1992 the Blackrock Society have produced an annual journal whose articles cover many topics of local interest and, since 1990, the Dún Laoghaire Historical Society, under the ever-attentive eye of Anna and Colin Scudds, have published their highly informative journal every year.

INDEX

Note: page numbers in **bold** refer to an illustration or caption.